IMAGES
of America

FALLON

ON THE COVER: From Fallon's earliest days, Maine Street has been the social and economic heart of the community. In the center of this vintage photograph, the theater marquee proudly announces "Fallon." On either side are the kinds of businesses that prospered in small towns of this era. The far right side of the photograph reveals the parking pattern the City of Fallon had then adopted. Cars were parked parallel to the meridian as well as in more traditional diagonal slots in front of the businesses. (Courtesy of the Churchill County Museum and Archives.)

IMAGES
of America

FALLON

Michon Mackedon and Valerie J. Serpa

ARCADIA
PUBLISHING

ISBN 978-1-4671-3222-0

Published by Arcadia Publishing
Charleston, South Carolina

Printed in the United States of America

Library of Congress Control Number: 2014933344

For all general information, please contact Arcadia Publishing:
Telephone 843-853-2070
Fax 843-853-0044
E-mail sales@arcadiapublishing.com
For customer service and orders:
Toll-Free 1-888-313-2665

Visit us on the Internet at www.arcadiapublishing.com

To the people of our oasis.

Contents

FOREWORD

Fallon, compiled and edited by Michon Mackedon and Valerie J. Serpa, was created as part of the celebration of the state of Nevada's sesquicentennial. They have used a mix of images and text to provide—for the most part—a chronological history of the town and community as well the surrounding areas.

Focusing on the people who have made and called this place home, their book portrays an original, diverse community, one that includes and embraces longtime residents and newcomers alike, and one that celebrates the value of local cultures while also welcoming ideas from a wider sphere of experience.

Initially populated by adventurous entrepreneurs who worked the land and created homes, businesses, churches, and schools, the community has continued to expand and grow over the past 150 years. Fallon has always been considered a small town, and even with the recent increase of lunch-hour traffic, one can still cross town in less than 10 minutes and join in on conversations that frequently suggest the values of the city's founders—as valid now as they were at our inception.

As the chapters unfold, we see those who chose to make their lives in Fallon. Many recognized the rugged natural beauty of the area, staying to create a vibrant city as the hub of many surrounding farms and ranches. Our community grew quickly to encompass a wide range of activities for its residents from social, athletic, rodeo, service, and 4-H clubs to an active engagement in culture, music, and the arts.

Michon and Valerie's compilation paints a picture of how life in a small town can provide a multitude of opportunities that enable residents to directly interact with and enhance the lives of others, foster a sense of pride and individualism, and recognize and appreciate our unique *place*.

Our celebration of Nevada's sesquicentennial provides an occasion to focus on, appreciate, and recognize what we have and who we are. It is an opportunity to realize just how much we have, in Fallon, to share and celebrate—especially the sense of belonging and small-town values that have been an integral part of the fabric of our community since its inception. It is a time to look back and remember all we have accomplished, but also an occasion to look toward the future, to realize what might be possible in this place we call home, Fallon, truly the oasis of Nevada.

—Mayor Ken Tedford

ACKNOWLEDGMENTS

The publication of any book is a joint venture, or, we should say, a joint adventure. Without a pledge of assistance from the Churchill County Museum and Archives, we would not have begun the adventure of identifying some 200 historical images of the people, structures, and landscape of the Fallon area. The assistance rendered by the museum was beyond any definition of duty. Barbara Hodges, photographic curator, devoted hundreds of hours to locating potentially publishable photographs and helping us to create a visually exciting layout. She also spent many hours processing and scanning images to Arcadia Publishing. We could not have assembled this book without her.

Donna Cossette, acting director of the Churchill County Museum and Archives, and Bunny Corkill, research curator, provided essential historical background and context so we might guide the reader in interpreting the images. Valuable information was also drawn from editions of *In Focus*, a historical journal published by the museum between 1987 and 2008.

Unless otherwise noted, all images appear courtesy of the Churchill County Museum and Archives. We also consulted with the helpful staff at Special Collections, University of Nevada, Reno. Donnelyn Curtis, director, guided us to pertinent collections in her archives from which we drew several key photographs to share with our readers. We drew, as well, from private collections and from archives located at Naval Air Station Fallon.

Finally, we give our praise and heartfelt thanks to Arcadia Publishing. Ginny Rasmussen, acquisitions editor, provided leadership and advice at each stage of the adventure.

INTRODUCTION

Images of America: *Fallon* is Fallon's story, although it is not limited by city boundaries. It is also Churchill County's story and Lahontan Valley's story. It shares common motifs with other stories of the American West. Before white settlement, the region was home to a Native American tribe, the Northern Paiute, or cattail-eaters. The coming of white settlers changed a pattern of life that had been in place for centuries, and the changes came quickly. During the California Gold Rush, beginning in 1849, a few overland travelers remained behind in the Nevada desert, turning a well-needed rest into an opportunity. Opportunity lay in the fact that a portion of the Overland Trail known as the Forty Mile Desert met the Carson River at what soon became known as Ragtown, named for the worn-and-torn clothing washed in the waters of the Carson River after weeks of dusty travel and hung by the river's shores. Ragtown was a natural stop, a place to bathe, rest, and take on water. Around the settlement, farmers began plowing the land; a small number of gold miners, once bound for California, reset their sights on the mountain ranges nearby. Ranchers discovered that cattle would graze on desert plants, and entrepreneurs capitalized on the knowledge that sojourners would pay for food, lodging, and feed for their horses. The new settlers formed small communities: building schools; holding quilting bees, socials, and dances; helping their neighbors sow and reap; establishing political units (counties, townships and cities); and seeing that the law was upheld in local seats of justice.

In 1861, a mere 13 years after the initial Gold Rush, Churchill County became part of the newly formed Nevada Territory. Three years later, on October 31, 1864, Nevada became a Union-allied state, not because of its growing population but because of its growing troves of silver that were badly needed to fund the Union causes. Churchill County became one of 17 counties in the state. In 1908, Fallon, now the county seat, achieved legal status as the City of Fallon with a population of 1,350. From then on, nothing hindered its survival through years of booms and busts, wars and recessions, and floods, fires, and droughts.

Despite the familiar outlines of the western pioneer story, Fallon's history is especially colorful and unique. There has, for example, always been a central artery, Maine Street, named for city founder Warren Williams's home state of Maine. From the outset, Maine Street has been lined with the city's businesses (saloons and gaming houses were restricted to the west side of the street). Since 1903, a white neo-classical, two-story frame courthouse has loomed above the north end of the business center—a landmark now and in the past. Vintage photographic views of Maine Street provide a microcosm of time past and a history of a special place. Bars and cafés have always flourished, but the stables and harness shops gave way to automobile dealerships, parts stores, and insurance agencies. Maine Street became a leg of the Lincoln Highway, a new kind of overland trail. Since 1929, a 50-foot Christmas tree has reigned over the Maine Street scene during the Christmas season, erected right in the middle of the street, challenging cars to swerve around it. Parades traditionally wound their way down Maine Street, beginning in the first decade of the 20th century when the street was paved with dirt and the sidewalks made of wood. But the enthusiasm was there, manifested in lavish decorations, groomed horses and riders, and many pretty smiles.

An exciting and symbiotic mixture of city and country life is also part of Fallon's uniqueness. The city has embraced progress: up-to-date utilities, well-planned annexations and parks, and ambitious cultural and educational undertakings. Yet, within the city limits or just a few steps away, a person can find livestock auction yards, farmers' markets, rodeo grounds, dairy barns, egg stands, freshly plowed fields, and a web of irrigation canals. A defining moment for the region came with the passage of the National Reclamation Act in 1902, creating the Newlands Project. Nearby Lahontan Dam was completed in 1915, and since then, in summer months, the waters released at the dam flow into the Lahontan Valley where alfalfa grows in green waves (the high school team is the Fallon Greenwave). The dam also provides water essential for growing the melons that Fallon is famous for, as well as tomatoes, squash, berries, beets, and a list of produce too long to include. Dairies and vineyards add to the region's agricultural bounty.

Of course, the area has suffered its share of misfortunes as well. A flood in 1907, a fire on Maine Street in 1910, disappointing oil wells in the 1920s, and a series of silver booms turned bust almost took the life out of the business sector. Two world wars robbed the population of many of its most promising men. The Great Depression readjusted the agricultural economy. At the same time, social ties strengthened. In rural irrigation districts, from St. Clair to Old River to Stillwater, club members raised money to support their elementary schools and kept watch over their neighbors. Located in Fallon, Churchill County High School became recognized for its educational programs and its highly competitive sports teams. Even during the rough years, members of the larger community celebrated life together by dancing, playing cards, and launching theater productions, as well as patronizing shops, restaurants, and bars and sponsoring parades and rodeos. Business enterprises have succeeded as well. For example, during the 1940s and 1950s, Fallon was home to four of the largest road construction firms in the state.

Today, Fallon can claim the best small cultural center in Nevada, Oats Park Art Center, as well as a renowned museum. The city's parks are plentiful, beautiful, and well used. The Labor Day parade is attended by thousands from around the state, especially by politicians on horseback. Fallon's rodeo grounds have trained world champions. Since 1942, the Fallon Naval Air Station (NAS) has been a good neighbor; Top Gun pilots are trained there, and the constant influx of squadrons and personnel punctuates and energizes the rhythms of local everyday business. Recreation is plentiful. One can fish at Indian Lakes and Harmon Reservoir; swim, jet ski, and fish at Lahontan Reservoir; ride dune-buggies at Sand Mountain; shoot trap on Rattlesnake Hill; hunt ducks and geese in the Carson Lake Pasture or the Stillwater marshes; race cars (or watch cars race) at Top Gun Racetrack; ride a horse almost anywhere; and, on many weekends, join a ranch rodeo. It is a good place in which to live.

One

Native Americans, Ranchers, Farmers, Miners, and Station Keepers

History records that Asa Kenyon and Catherine Haggerty were the area's first white resident couple, arriving in 1854 and setting up shop at Ragtown on the Carson River. The 1860 Census describes the 38 residents of Churchill County as all living at Ragtown. Around this time, the Army Corps of Topographical Engineers surveyed a new wagon route through the area, from Utah to the Carson River. It was adopted at once by the Pony Express, Union Telegraph, and the Overland Stage Company, and stage stops soon became a common sight throughout the region.

Cyclical flooding on the Carson River encouraged early farmers and ranchers to establish fields of pasture grass. Then, a new landscape feature, the irrigation canal, enabled watering gardens and cultivating fields of hay and grains. The first large farming development in the valley was a rectangular field of 500 acres, located in Stillwater, about 18 miles east of present-day Fallon. Stillwater is, to this day, an active farming district.

In 1879, the population of Churchill County was 196. It rose to 479 in 1880, and by 1890 it had risen to 830. What census figures fail to show is the number of Native Americans living in the county, most of them having abandoned traditional ways of life to live on farms and ranches where basic sustenance might be had in exchange for labor. In the 1870s, a Paiute colony was established on the Kent ranch in Stillwater. In 1888, under the federal Dawes Act of 1888, a reservation of some 5,000 acres was created near Stillwater.

Of the white populations listed, a transient few lived in boom/bust mining camps, while others ran desert stage stops. The majority of people were engaged in agriculture. Farming districts were loosely organized throughout the valley, among them St. Clair, Harmon, Old River, Soda Lake, Lone Tree, Sheckler, Island, Stillwater, Northam, and Wildes.

The farming pioneers of Churchill County suffered through winters of subzero cold and summers of triple-digit heat, enduring floods, droughts, and failed crops. Yet, they ensured the formation of local neighborhood communities replete with dances, spelling bees, sewing circles, traveling plays and lectures, and, always, school.

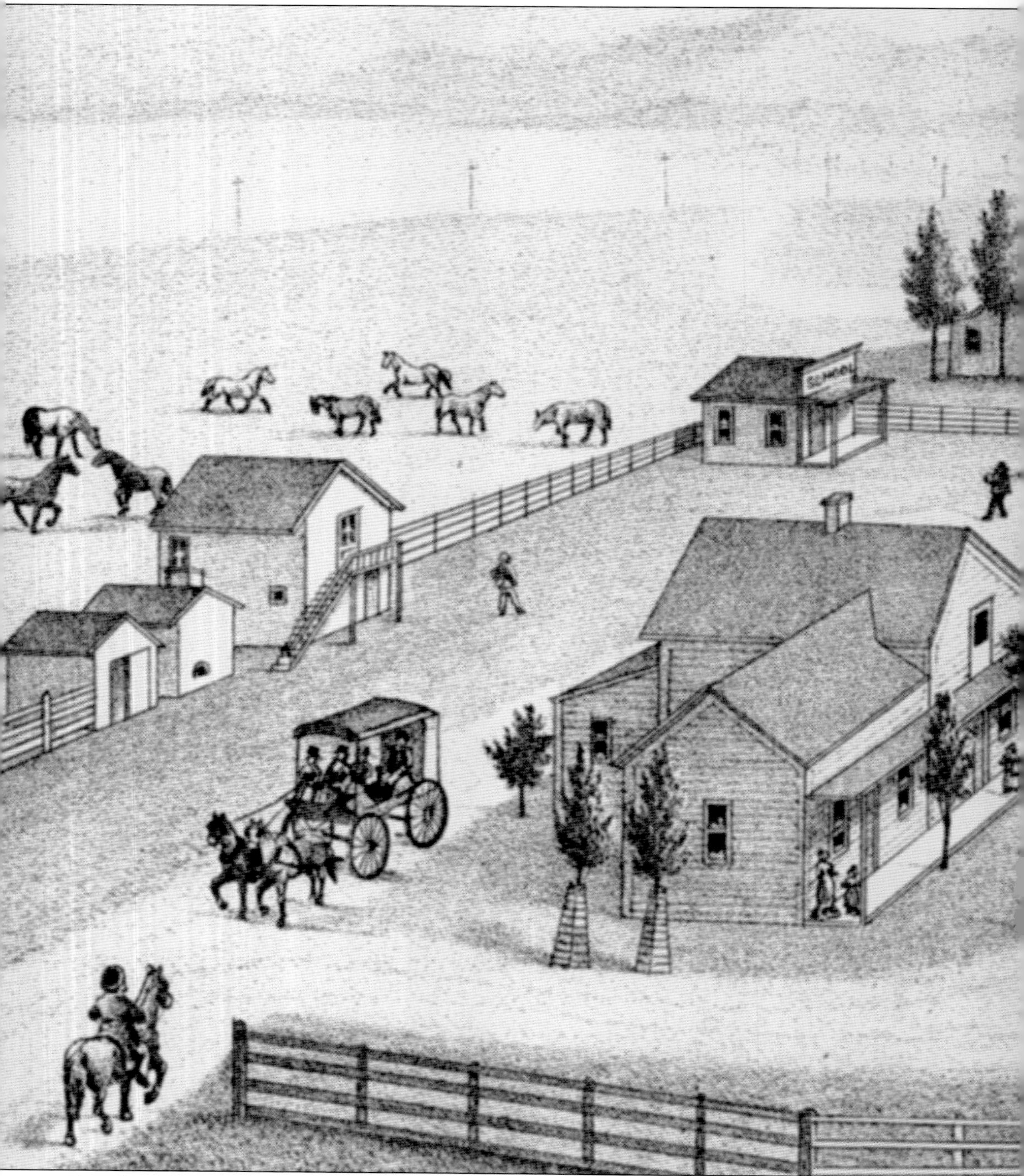

A stylized illustration of Ragtown, the earliest settlement (1854) in Churchill County, was printed in the 1881 Thompson and West *History of Nevada*. The owners of the station, Asa Kenyon and Catherine Haggerty Kenyon, were notorious for charging desperate overland travelers high prices for food, water, ammunition, and livestock feed. Water for livestock cost 12.5¢ per head. Ragtown once contained a graveyard filled with the remains of 200 persons felled by cholera,

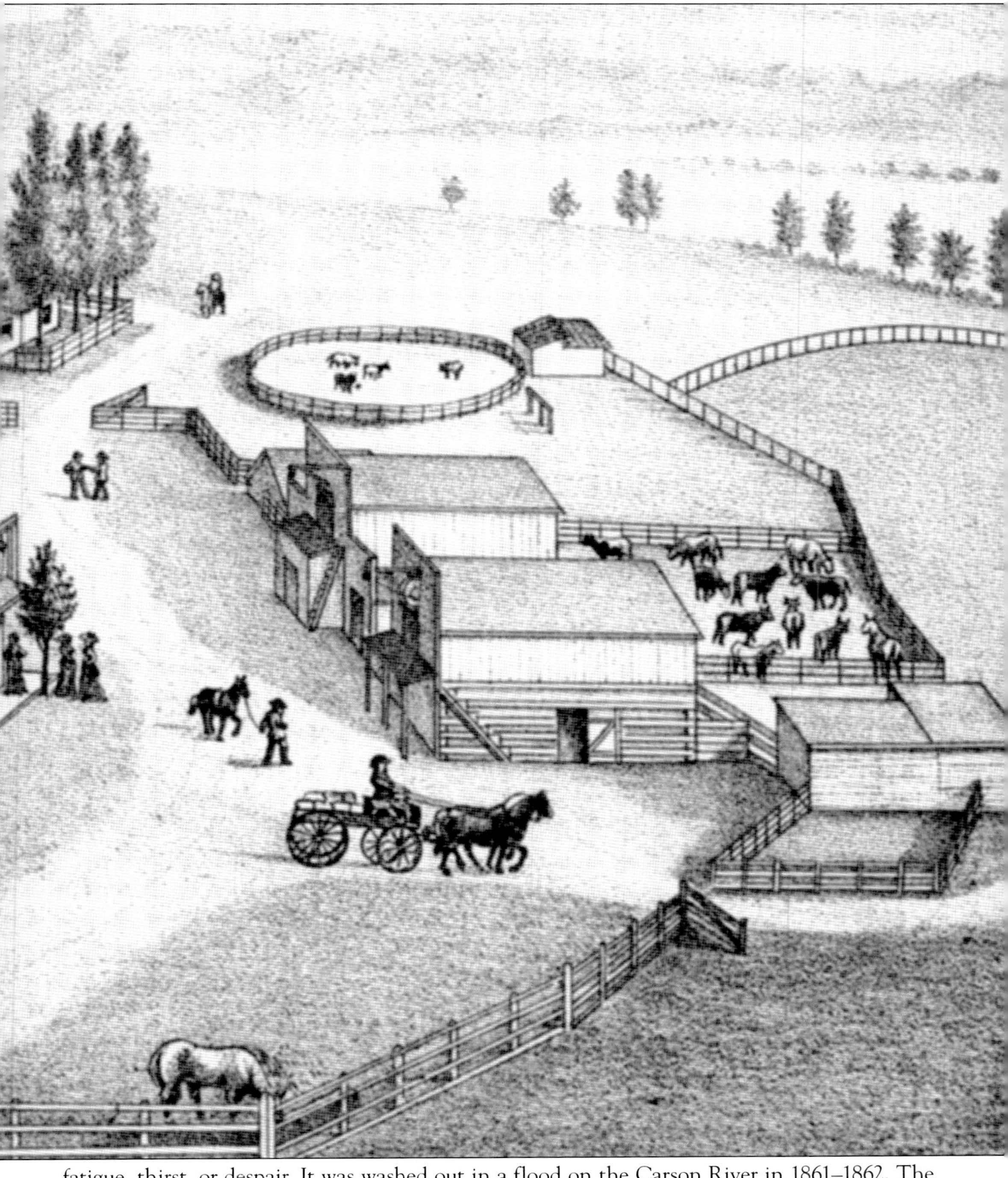

fatigue, thirst, or despair. It was washed out in a flood on the Carson River in 1861–1862. The telegraph poles in the distance indicate that by 1881 Western Union services had reached the Lahontan Valley. Nothing now remains of Ragtown. The closest marker is Leeteville junction, 11 miles west of present-day Fallon.

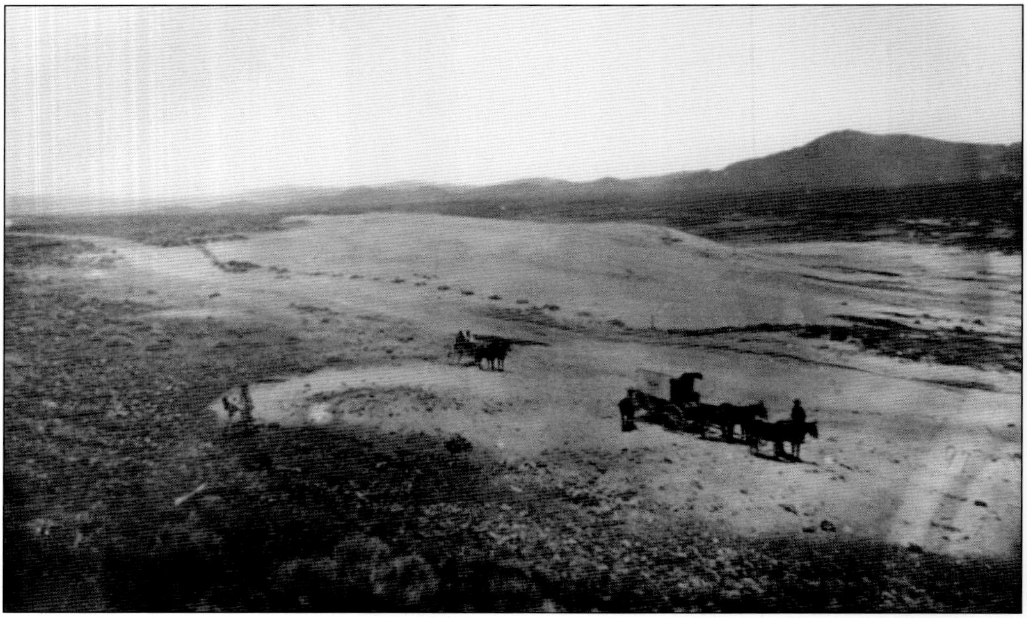

In 1867, Timothy O'Sullivan, an official photographer for the United States Geological Exploration of the Fortieth Parallel (or "King Survey"), documented landmarks in Churchill County. O'Sullivan had worked with the famous Mathew Brady to photograph battlefields of the Civil War. The images taken for the survey are characterized by barren landscapes and curious geological formations, creating a forceful vision of the yet-unsettled American West. Above, Sullivan's developing wagon can be seen in front of an unidentified sand dune on the right, with his camera left of center. Below, an O'Sullivan image shows the photography crew looking out over Big Soda Lake. Beginning in 1867, and lasting into the early 20th century, mining soda from Big Soda Lake and nearby Little Soda Lake was big business.

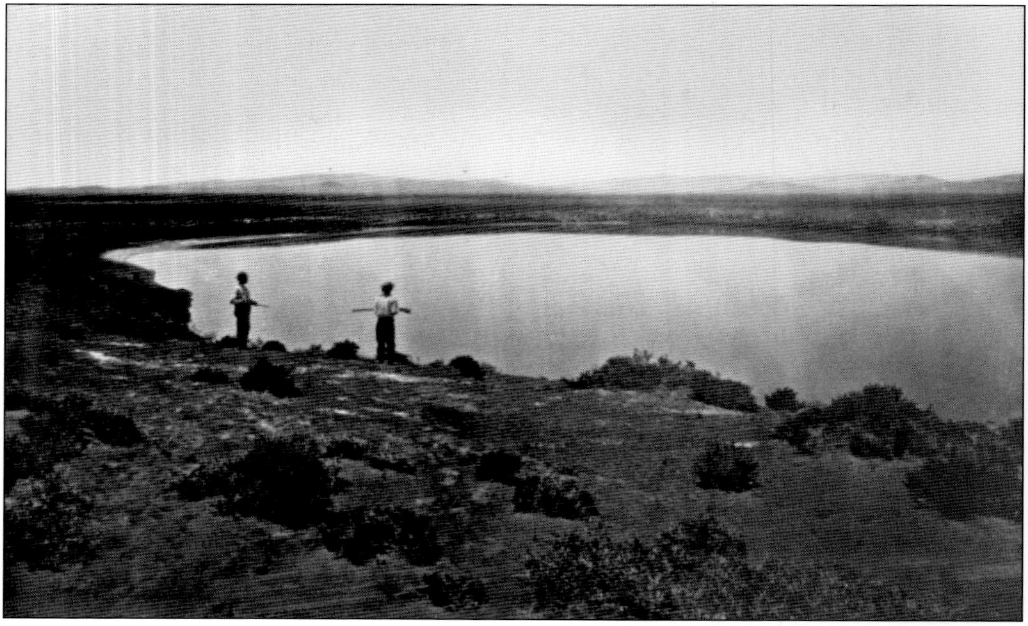

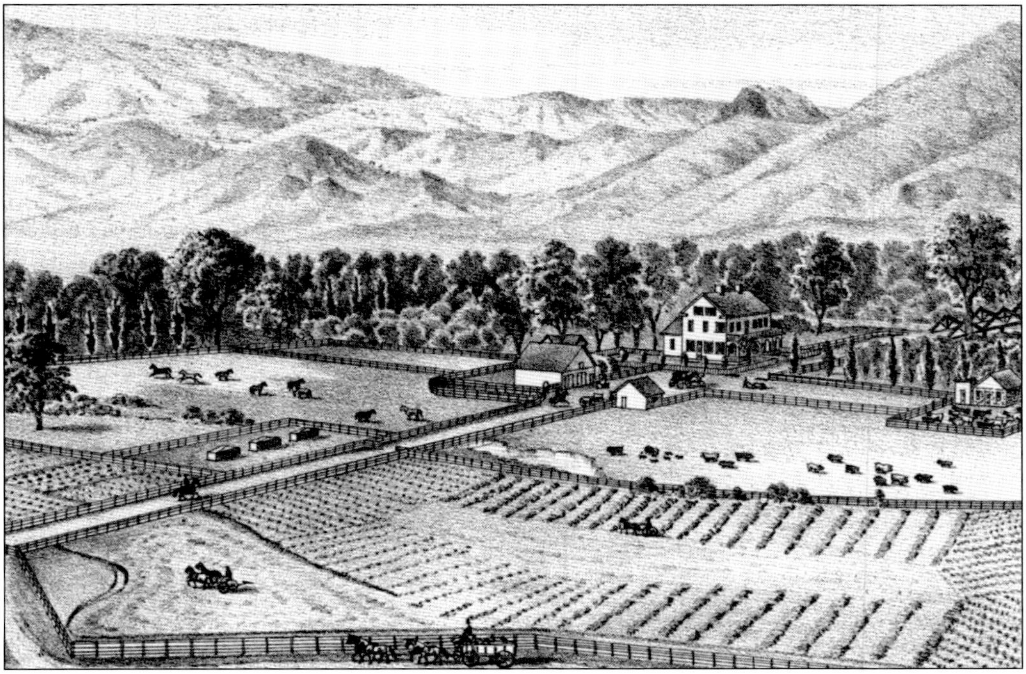

In 1861, Buckland's Station (now Weeks, Nevada) on the upper Carson River was designated as the first Churchill County seat. The county was then part of Nevada Territory. In 1864, a land survey situated Buckland's in Lyon County, and the Churchill county seat was moved to La Plata, a silver mining boomtown east of present-day Fallon. The illustration above was included in the 1881 Thompson and West *History of Nevada*. The photograph below, taken sometime later, reveals the architectural features of the station house/courthouse.

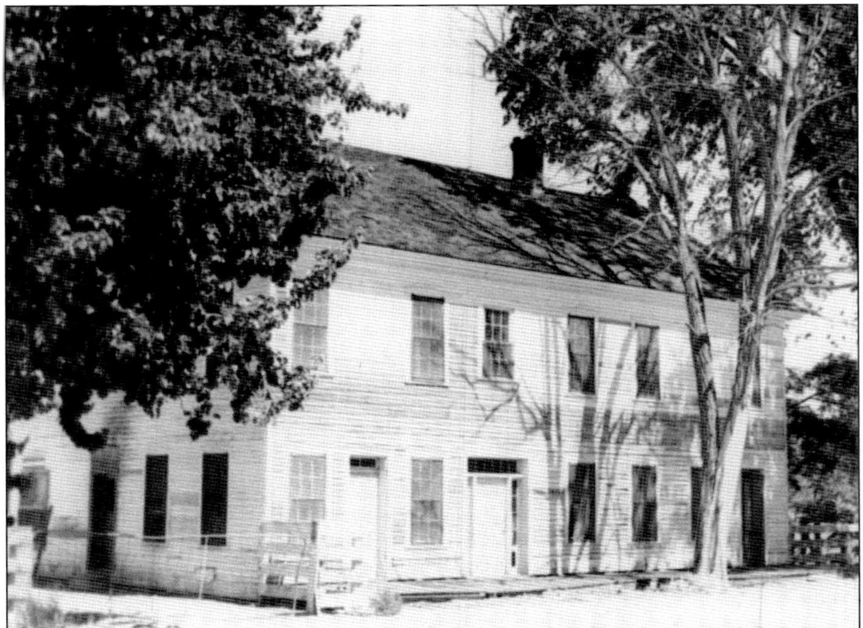

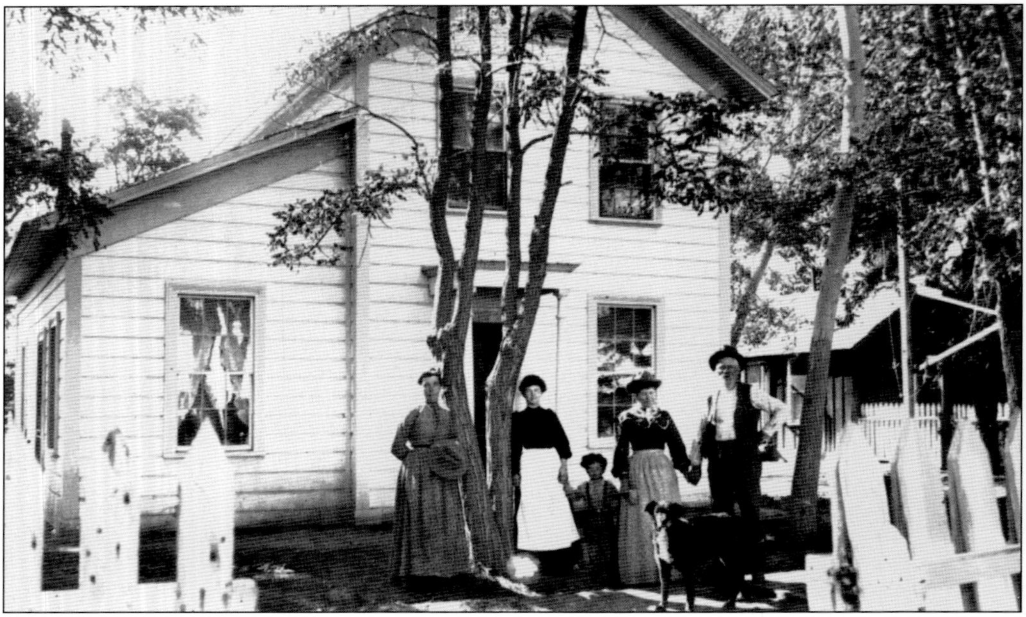

Josiah Jordan Cushman was one of the first ranchers in the valley, arriving in 1861. Cushman acquired 1,700 acres and planted lovely, productive orchards as well as fields of hay and grain. The illustration of the Cushman ranch seen below, taken from the 1881 Thompson and West *History of Nevada*, can be compared to a photograph of the ranch house taken a few years later. Standing in front of the house above are, from left to right, Elizabeth McCulloch Cushman, Dottie Tunney Prime, Pete Cushman, Mary McCulloch Tunney, and Josiah Jordan Cushman. Cushman descendants still live in the valley today.

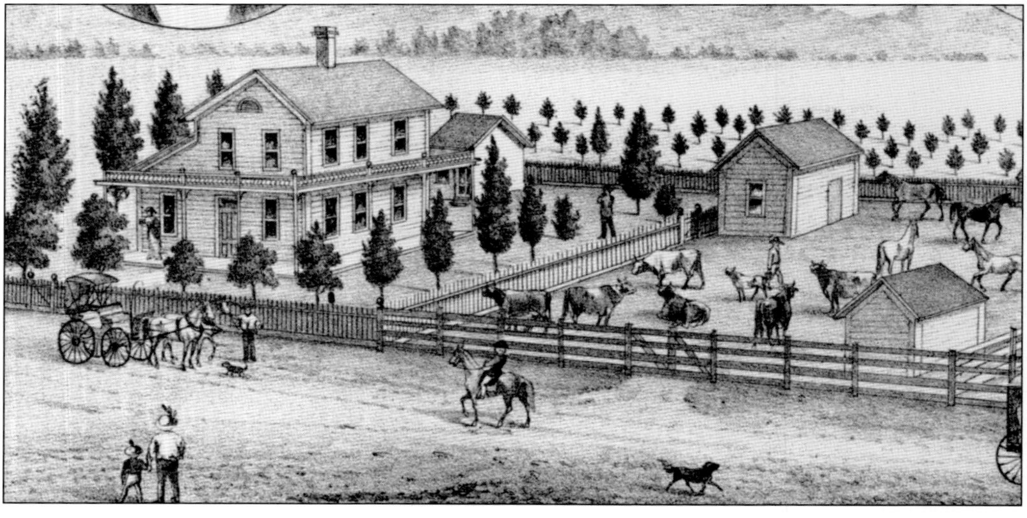

In the 19th century, many productive farms were located in Stillwater, about 15 miles east of present-day Fallon. Ira Kent arrived in 1876 and commenced cultivating land, operating a store, and building a home for his family. Pictured on horseback in front of the Kent home are Myra and Irving Sanford. Their parents owned the Stillwater Hotel.

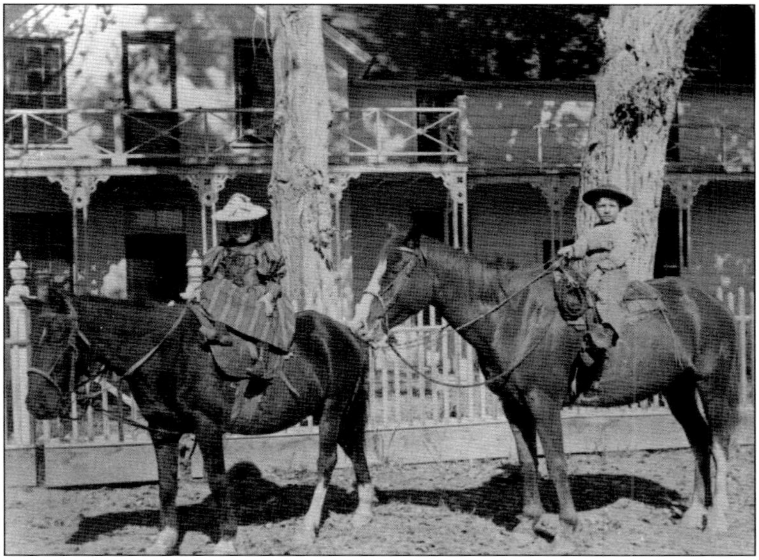

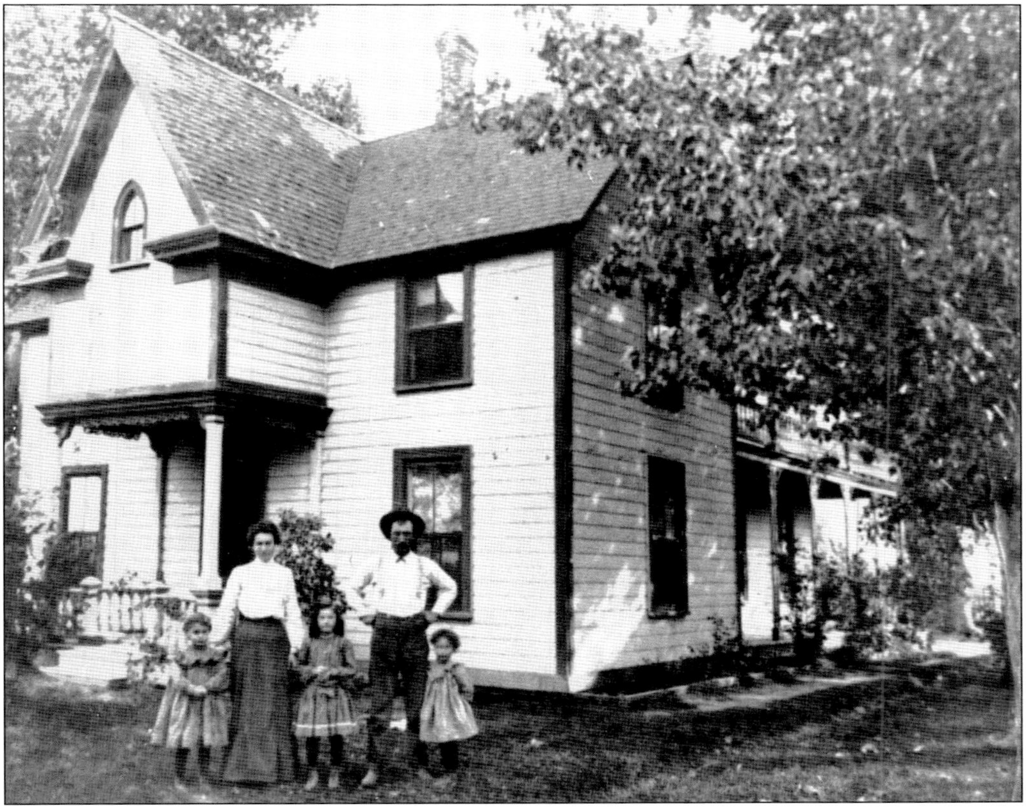

Records indicate that David Wightman was the first white rancher in Lahontan Valley, arriving in 1859 at the age of 21 and eventually acquiring 1,200 acres on the "upper sink," near present-day Pasture Road. In 1865, Wightman married 16-year-old Sarah Jane MacKeachie, the daughter of a neighboring rancher, and built for her (and, eventually, their 13 children) this handsome home.

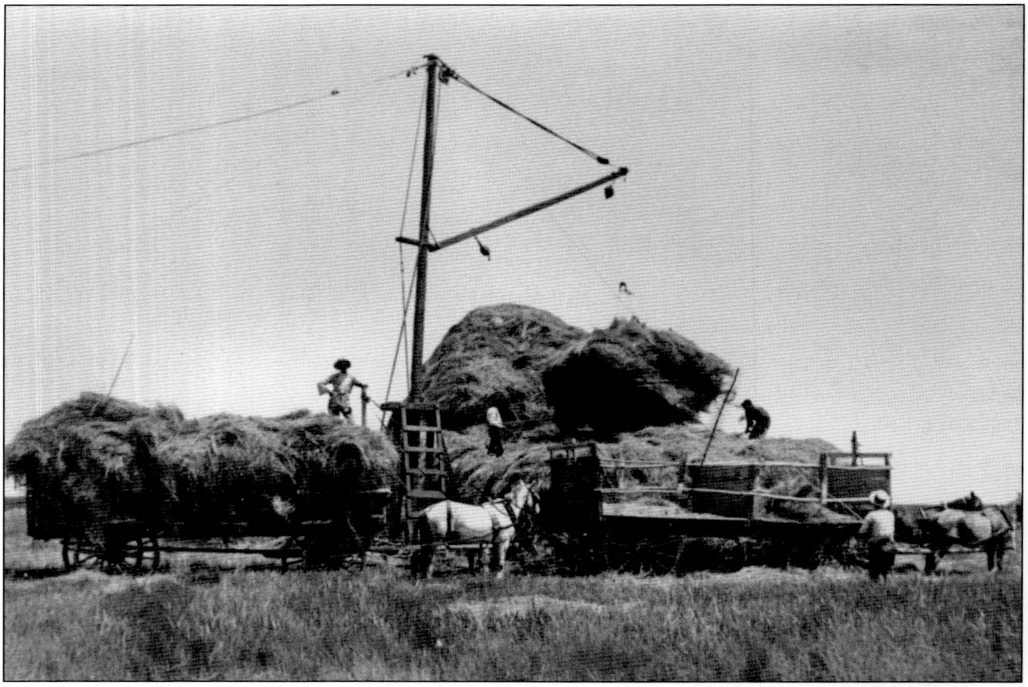

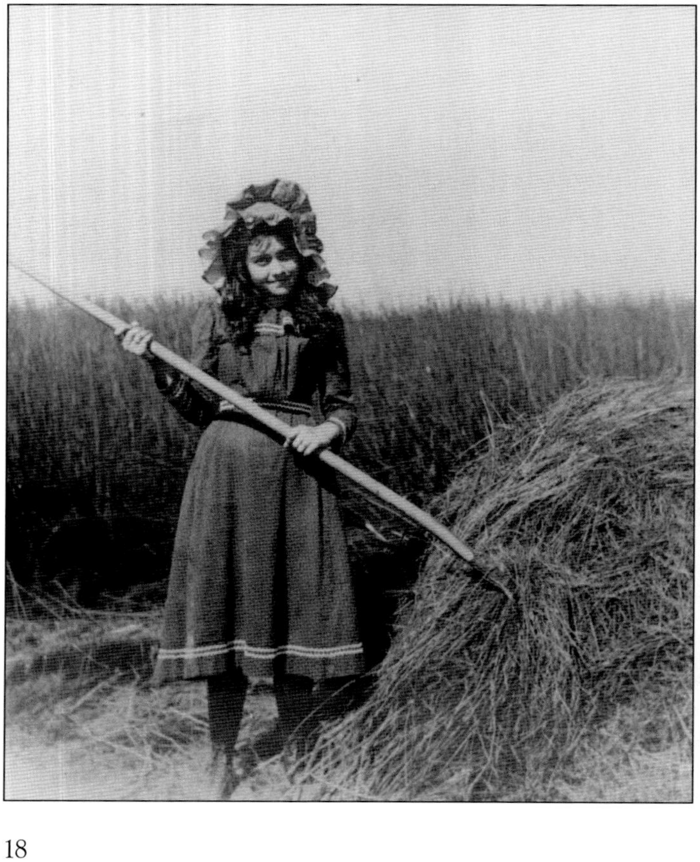

Photographs of early farming show the use of derricks, horse-drawn rakes, and flatbed hay wagons. The work was labor intensive, yet large hay fields and haystacks photographed before 1900 suggest that growing alfalfa was quite successful early on.

A young girl helps with farming chores. The photographer, Mary Freeman (1875–1943), spent the summers of her youth in Stillwater on her father's ranch. Her photographs are a rare contribution to local history, chronicling early Churchill County ranch life, pre–Reclamation Act farming techniques, and, most importantly, views of the Native Americans living and working in Stillwater.

Native Americans were displaced geographically and culturally by the arrival of white settlers. This photograph by Mary Freeman suggests that ancestral lifeways had already blended with the goods and customs of white settlers. The tule dwelling exhibits the traditional form, yet the door is made of wood and the clothing styles are borrowed from the nearby ranchers.

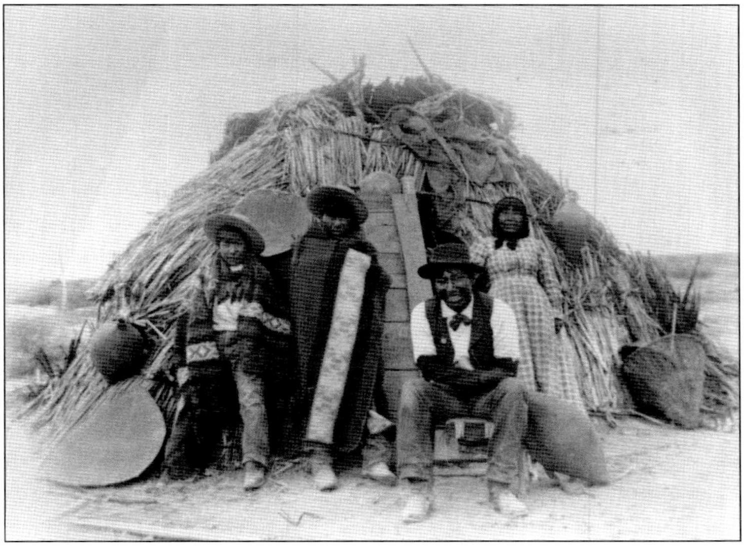

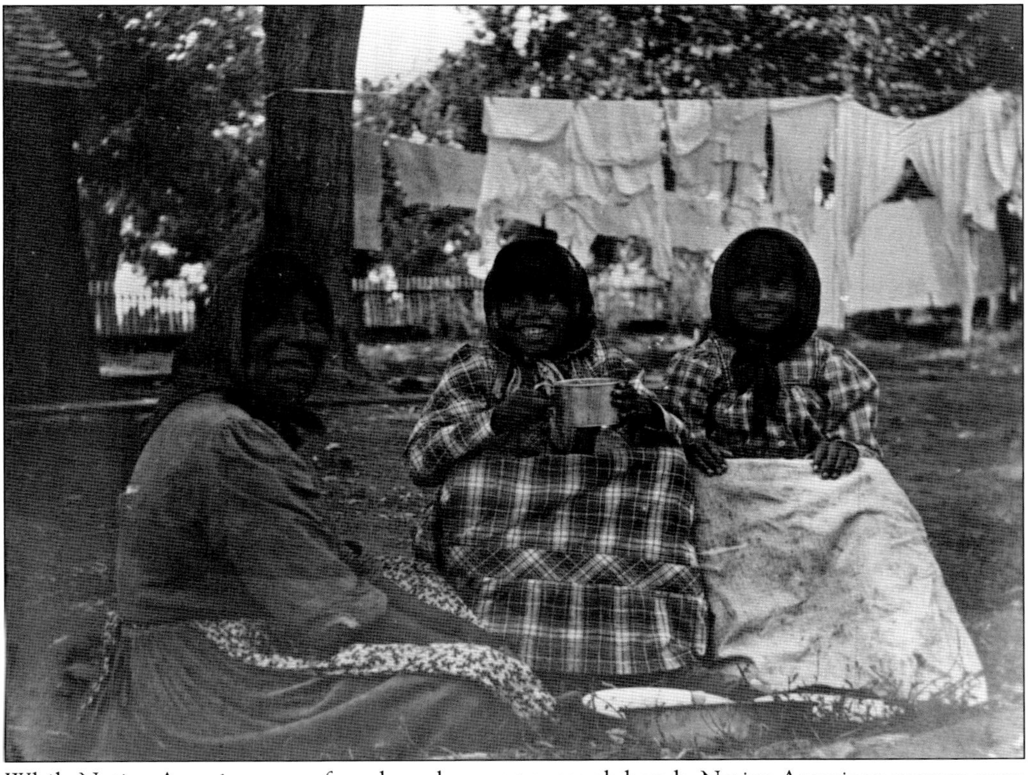

While Native American men found employment as ranch hands, Native American women were employed to wash clothes, cook, and tend children. Photographed by Mary Freeman, most likely on the Freeman Ranch in Stillwater, are, from left to right, Mattie Steve, her daughter Topsie, and Topsie's friend Tootsie Bowser.

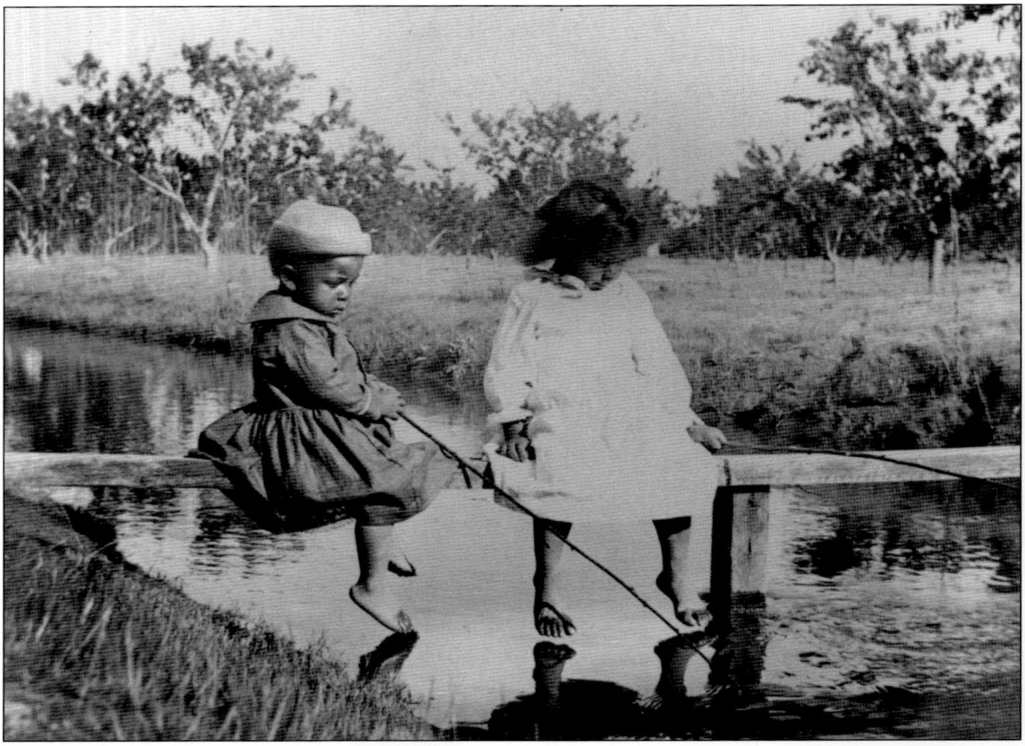

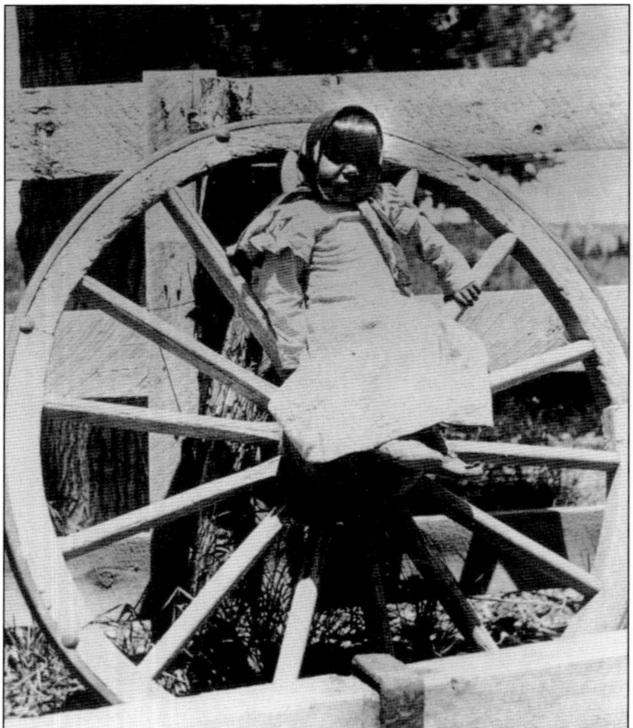

Mary Freeman's camera captured two African American children concentrating on fish beneath the water's surface. Their parents were employed on the Freeman ranch. The irrigation canal was part of a network of ditches dug by horse-drawn equipment to connect the waters of the Stillwater Slough to the Stillwater ranches.

Photographer Mary Freeman was not averse to formally posing her subjects, and she was playful, especially when working with children. This photograph was taken on the Freeman Ranch; the child most likely belonged to a Native American family employed on the ranch.

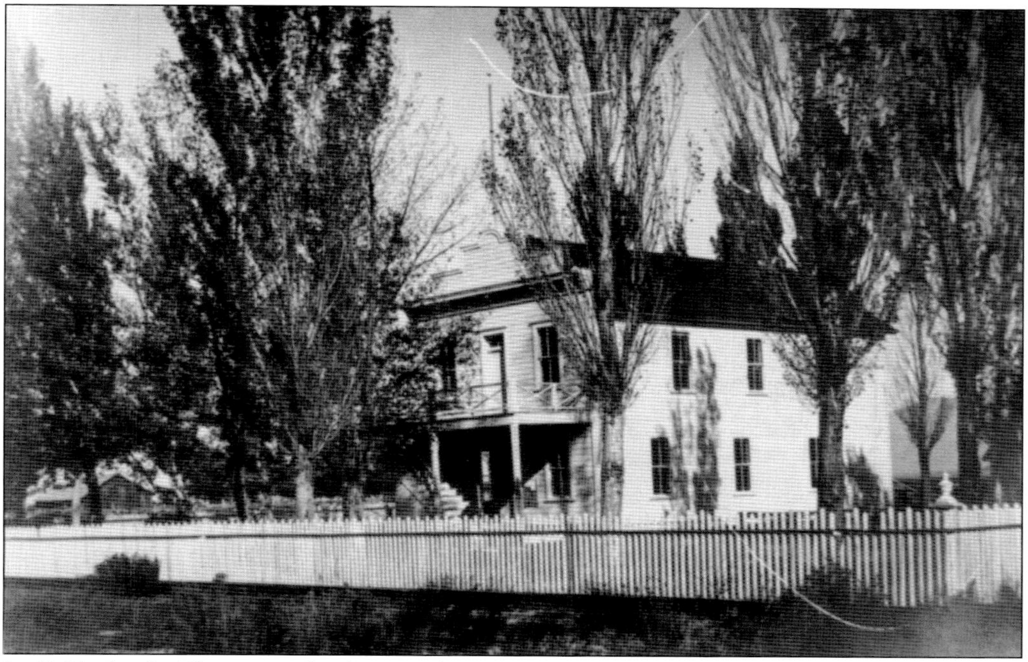

In 1867, after La Plata proved to be more bust than boom, the county seat was moved again, this time to Stillwater. The original courthouse was replaced in 1880 with this $3,000 gem, considered by some to be an unwarranted extravagance. The upper floor was used as a ballroom.

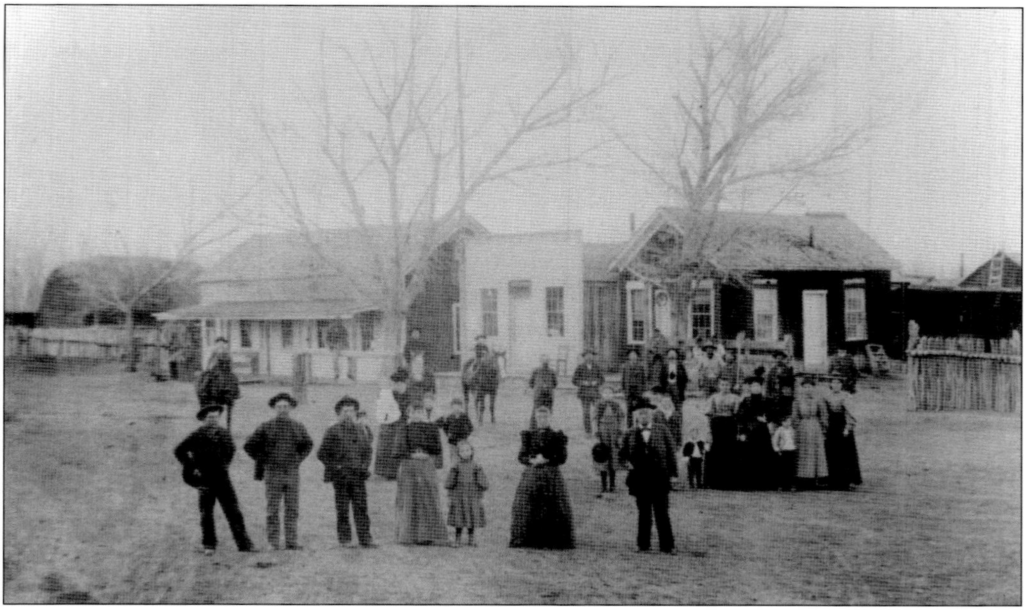

Stillwater's Main Street bustled in 1895. The Sanford's Stillwater Hotel is on the left. From left to right are (first row) Manie Sanford, Elisha Sanford, Will Sanford, Emma Sanford, Myra Sanford, Nancy Sanford, and James Merritt Sanford; (second row) Mrs. Shirley, with baby Jessie, and Charlie Shirley. Also shown are John Higgins, Jim Richards, Mr. and Mrs. Frank Sanford, Mrs. Brannin and "Earl." On horses are, from left to right, Tom Sanford, Fred Williams, and Irving Sanford.

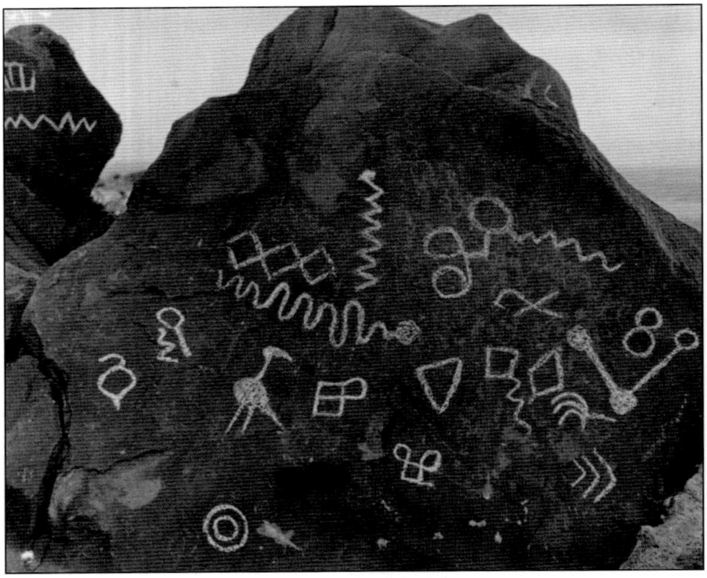

Thousands of petroglyphs were carved in Nevada stone by early Native Americans. Churchill County is home to dozens of petroglyph sites; the most often explored is Grimes Point, east of Stillwater. Anthropologists theorize that petroglyphs record origin stories and mark, among other things, game trails, tribal boundaries, and celestial events. In this photograph, taken on Rattlesnake Hill, near Fallon, the petroglyph lines are chalked over, a practice now frowned upon.

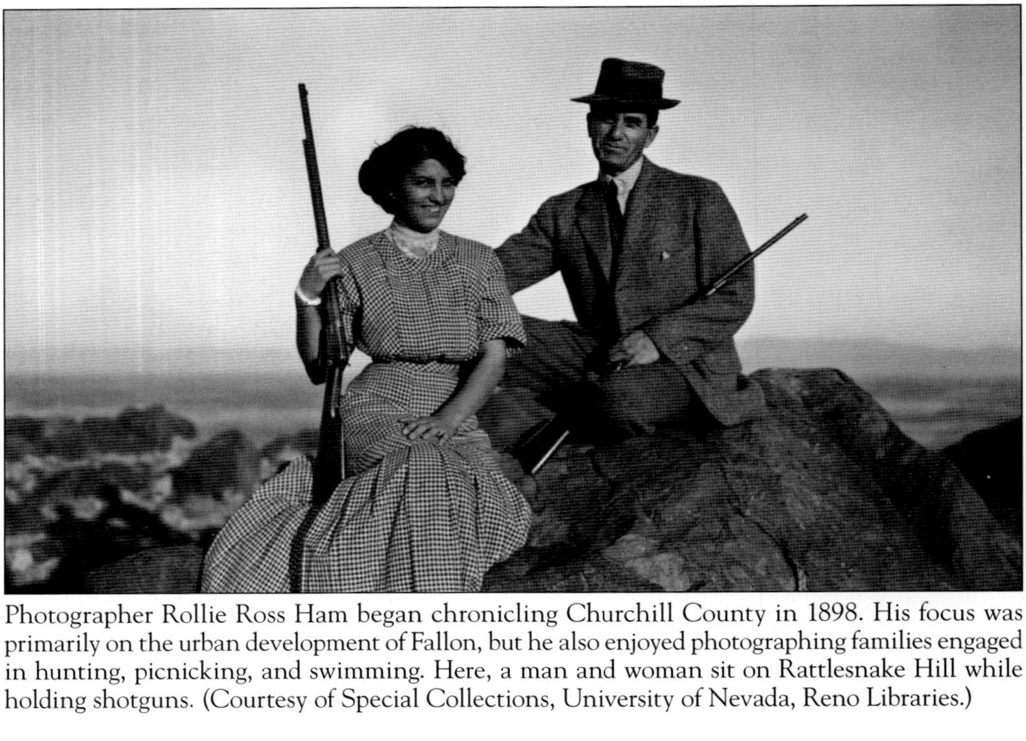

Photographer Rollie Ross Ham began chronicling Churchill County in 1898. His focus was primarily on the urban development of Fallon, but he also enjoyed photographing families engaged in hunting, picnicking, and swimming. Here, a man and woman sit on Rattlesnake Hill while holding shotguns. (Courtesy of Special Collections, University of Nevada, Reno Libraries.)

Rollie Ross Ham captures the moment when a proud predator nets her prey.

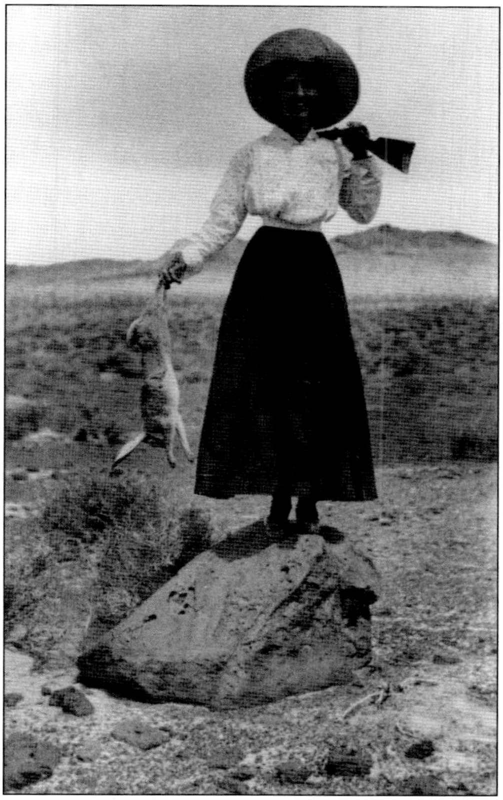

This candid shot of photographer Mary Freeman was snapped by a friend while they were picnicking in the desert. One couple came via buggy and the other on horseback (note the side saddle).

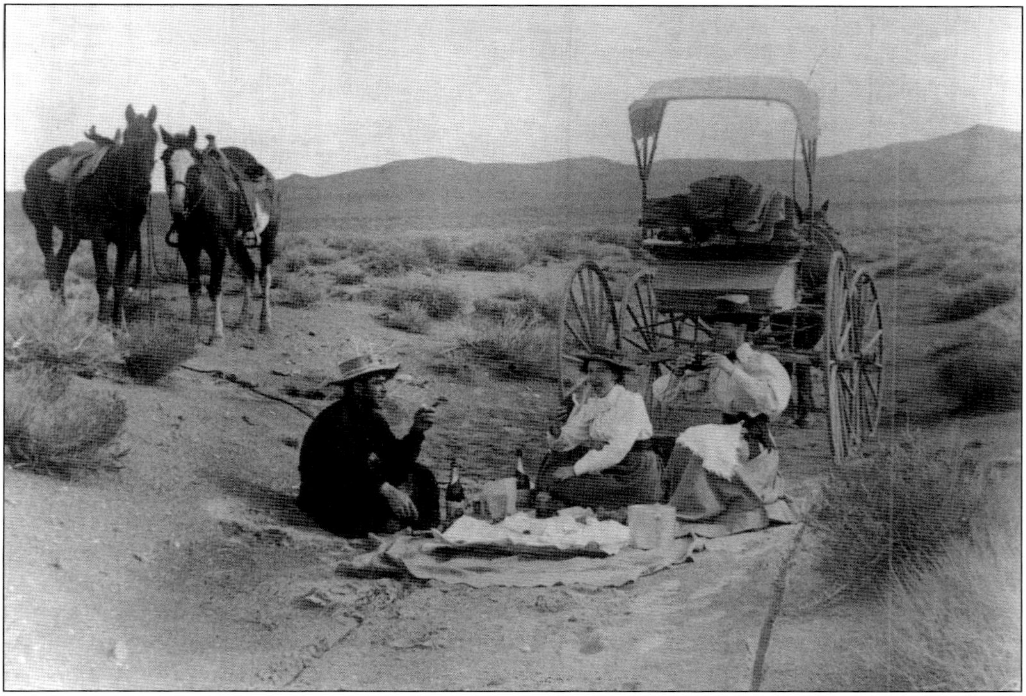

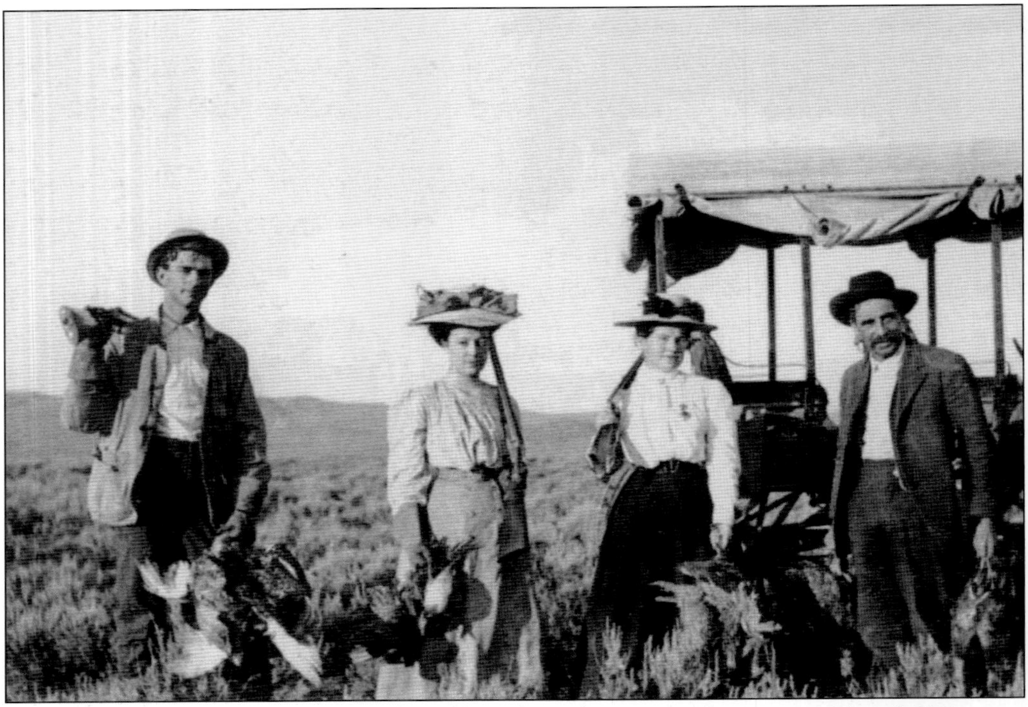

Hunting ducks, geese, pheasants, and quail has always been a popular sport in Churchill County. The Carson Lakes provide tule cover and food for migrating ducks and geese, and the hay fields and undergrowth offer lush cover for pheasant, grouse, and quail. This elegant grouse-hunting party consists of, from left to right, Art and Ada Keddie and Genevieve and George B. Williams.

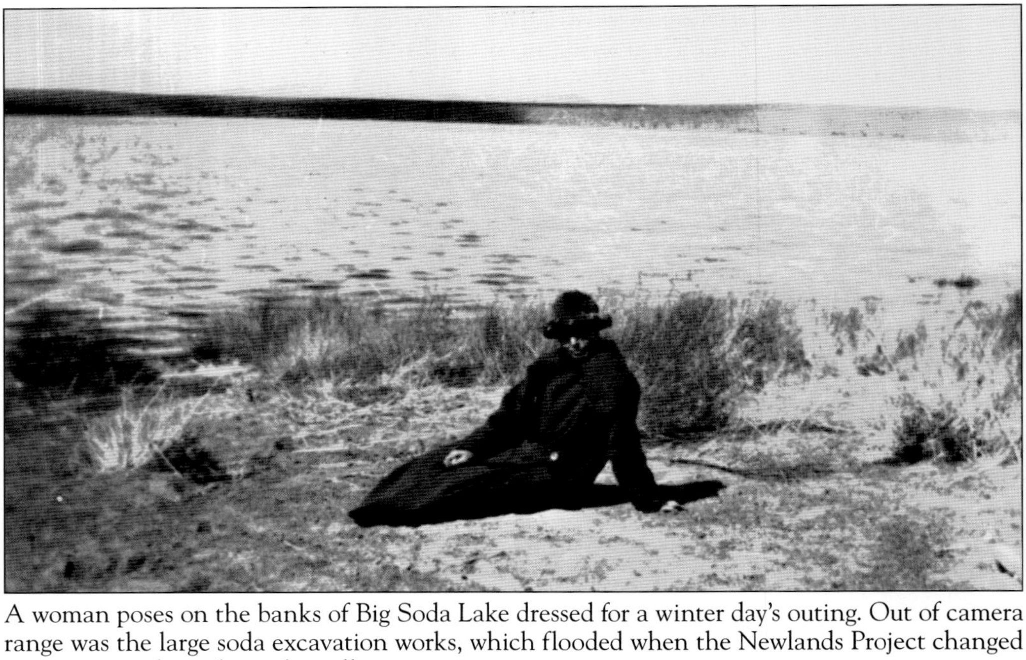

A woman poses on the banks of Big Soda Lake dressed for a winter day's outing. Out of camera range was the large soda excavation works, which flooded when the Newlands Project changed watercourses throughout the valley.

Two

The Birth of a City

As the century turned, from the 19th to the 20th, Fallon began to take shape as a municipality. A post office run by Mike Fallon and a general store run by Jim Richards had been established in the mid-1890s near the crossroads now known as Williams Avenue and Maine Street. The customers were Stillwater ranchers; farmers living along the Carson River in the Island, St. Clair, and Old River Districts; Native Americans; miners chasing dreams of finding silver in the hills of Churchill County; and travelers seeking gold or employment in California. The defining moment for the development of Fallon was the passage of the National Reclamation Act. In 1902, Nevada congressman (later senator) Francis Newlands secured congressional funding to dam the Truckee River (Derby Dam), build the Truckee Canal, and dam the Carson River (Lahontan Dam), allowing for the storage and regulated release of water throughout the valley.

National advertising of the Newlands Project rapidly changed the region's demographics. Construction workers moved into the area and applied for work on the dams and canals. Farmers from around the country heard stories about reclaiming the desert with "cheap" water. Many relocated to the project, and business owners left floundering enterprises elsewhere to sell goods and services to the Newlands Project newcomers. In addition, mines were opened in Churchill County at Wonder, Fairview, and Berlin.

In 1903, Fallon was designated the fourth county seat of Churchill County, replacing Stillwater. A handsome white, shingle-sided courthouse was erected at the crossroads where Mike Fallon's post office had given the town its name. Storefronts appeared south of the new courthouse, up and down Maine Street: a hotel, a general merchandise store, harness and saddle shops, a smithy, a drug store, cafés, and saloons. In 1908, after spirited battles of opposition, the town of Fallon was incorporated as the city of Fallon. The overall picture of the city that emerges from reading the newspapers of the time is one of a community bursting with energy and optimism. A succession of parades, dances, political rallies, school events, and theater productions helped spirits soar even higher.

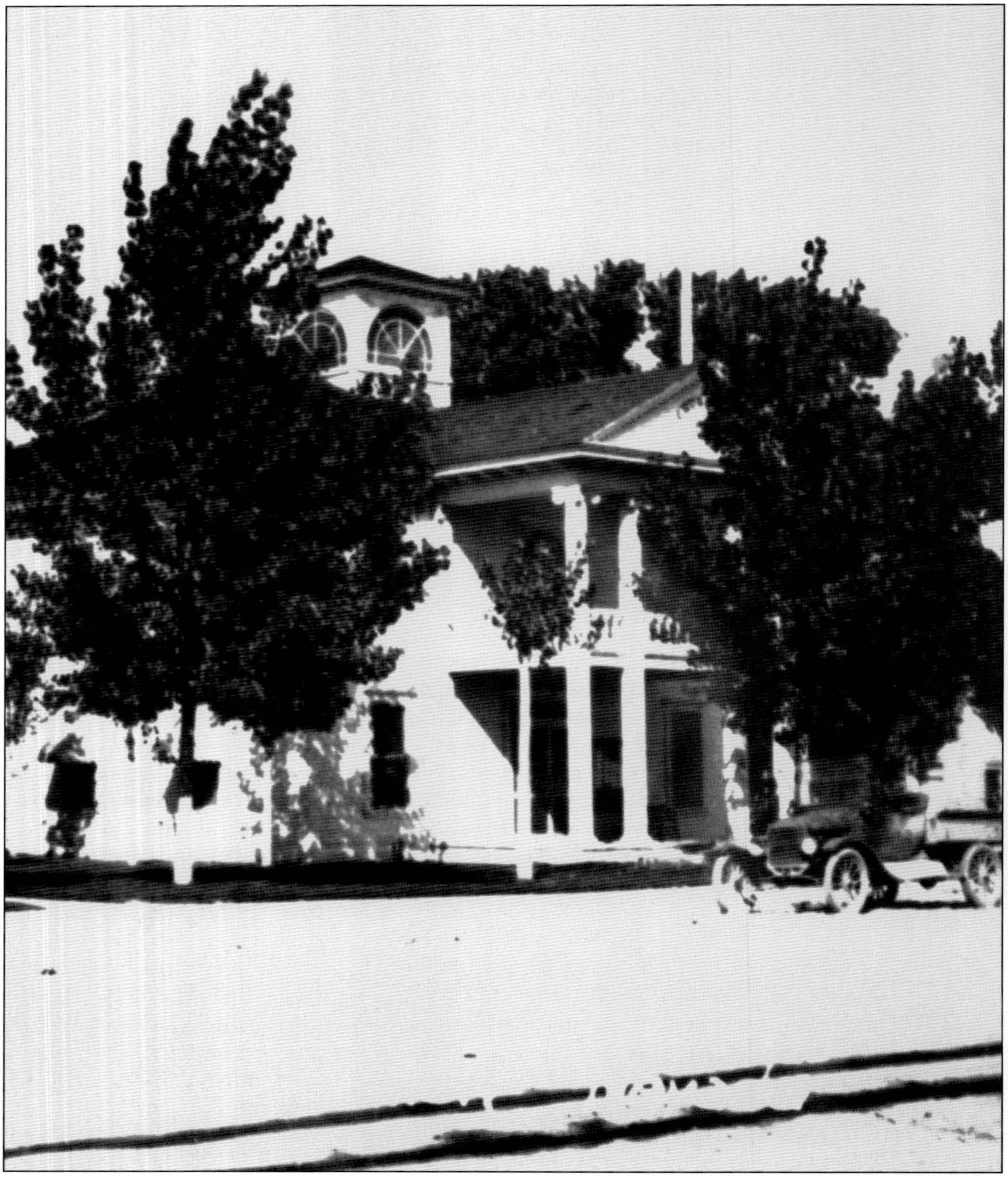

In 1903, the Churchill County seat was moved from Stillwater to Fallon. Arguments were made by prominent rancher Lemuel Allen and other St. Clair and New River settlers that Fallon (at the time merely a crossroads store and post office) was a more central location for conducting legal business than Stillwater. Sen. Warren Williams joined the campaign, favoring a Fallon courthouse after he purchased a ranch near the crossroads. Opposition was voiced by I.H. Kent and other Stillwater ranchers, who lost the battle when Williams sponsored a Nevada statute transferring the county seat to Fallon. The 1904 courthouse, designed by M.B. Myrick, was admired near and far and is seen to this day as a graceful and imposing structure.

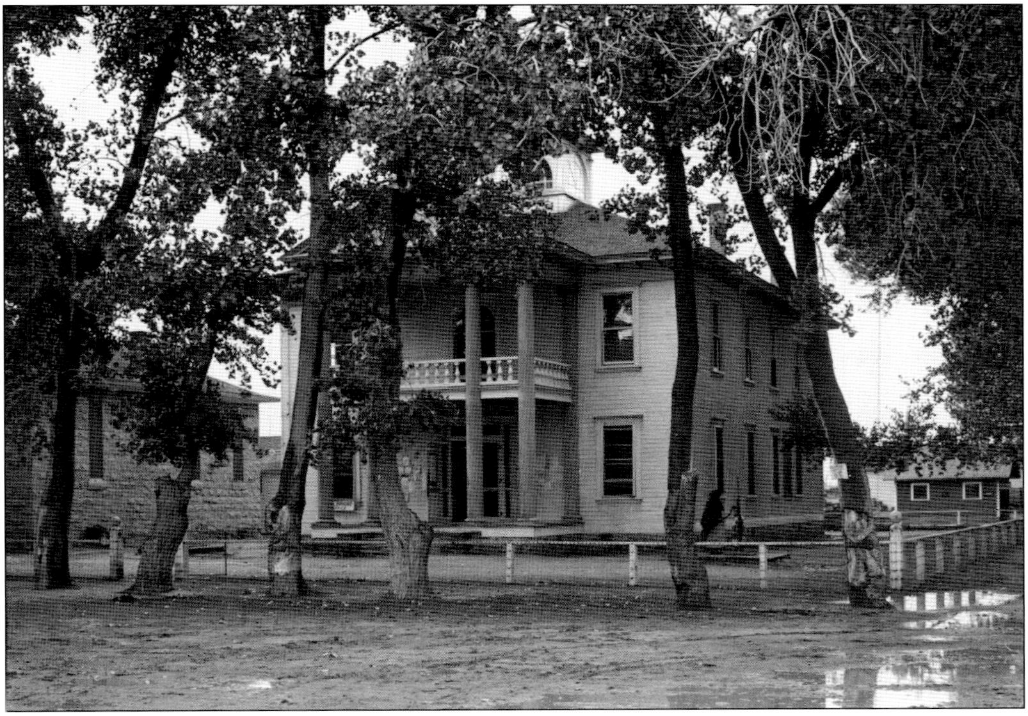

In the image above, the new courthouse wears a mysterious face following rainfall and flooding on the river; or maybe, the face is smug and peaceful. Local folklore has it that residents of Stillwater refused to transfer official documents to the new courthouse. In the wee hours of a morning not recorded in the history books, Fallonites quietly surrounded the Stillwater Courthouse and removed the records. The image below shows an ice wagon parked near the courthouse on a snowy day. Ice was cut in Stillwater and hauled to Fallon businesses and residences for use in iceboxes. (Both courtesy of Special Collections, University of Nevada, Reno Libraries.)

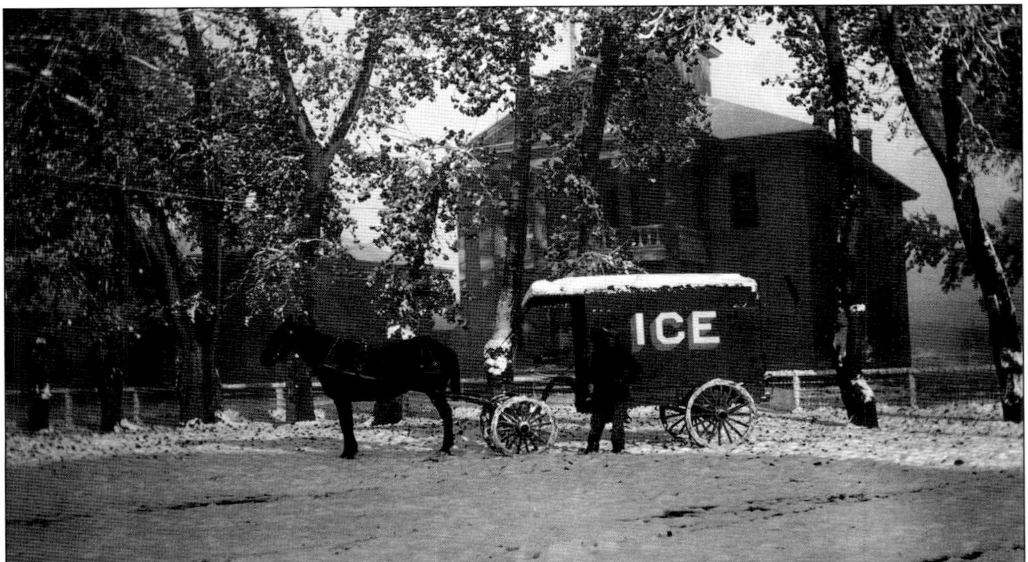

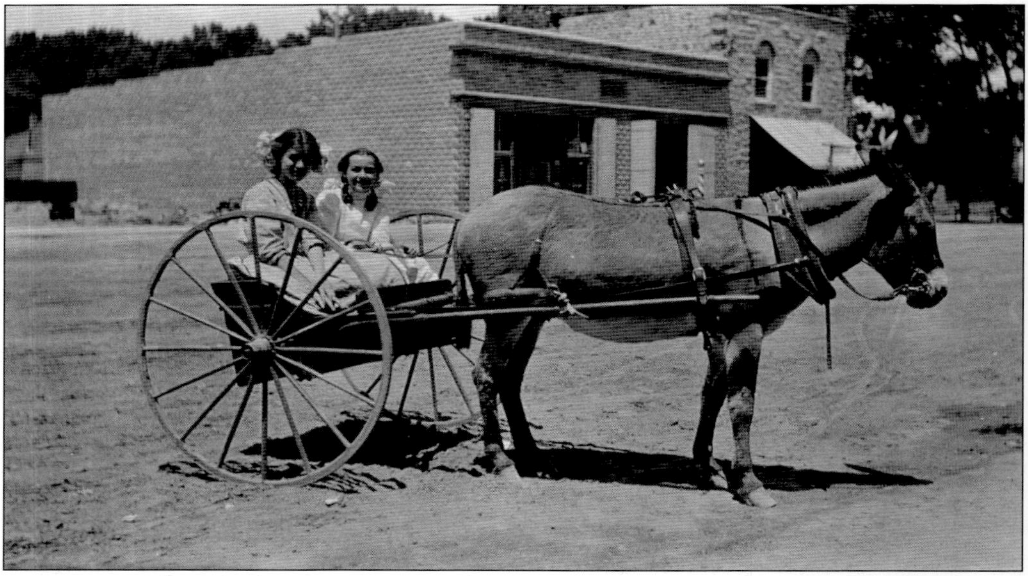

Two young girls embark on a pony-cart adventure down Maine Street. (Courtesy of Special Collections, University of Nevada, Reno Libraries.)

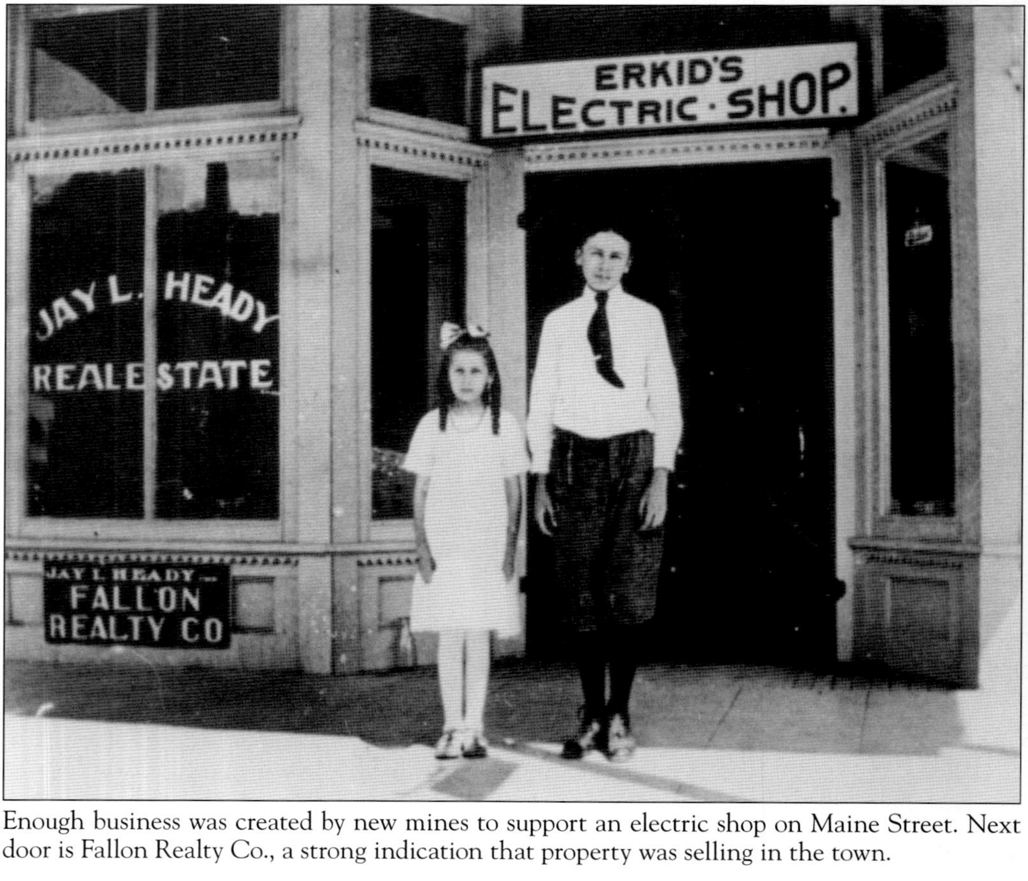

Enough business was created by new mines to support an electric shop on Maine Street. Next door is Fallon Realty Co., a strong indication that property was selling in the town.

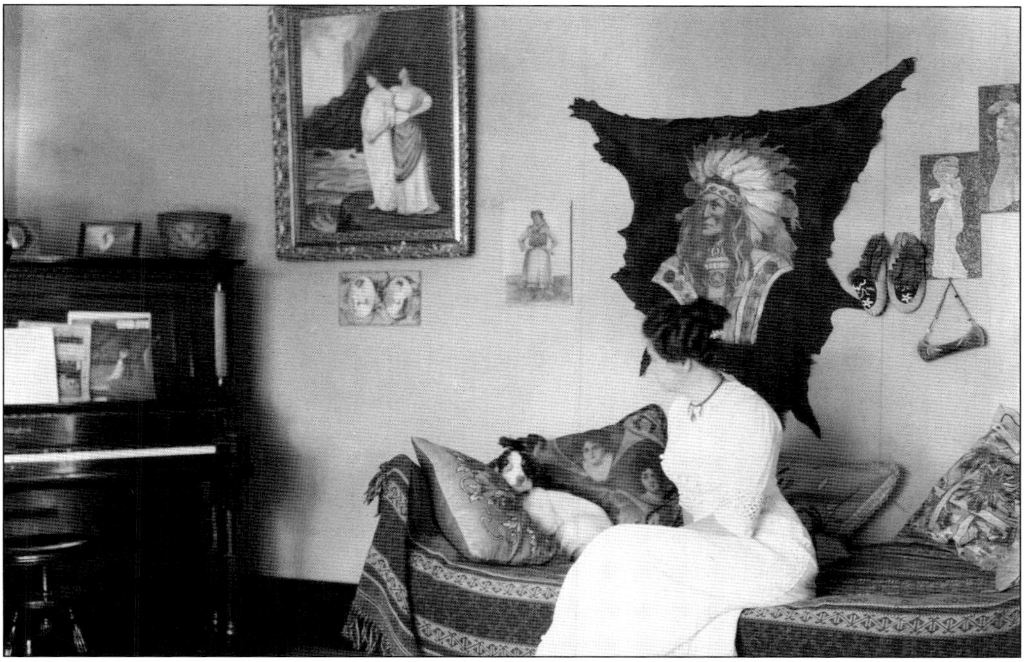

Photographer Rollie Ross Ham recorded interiors of homes and businesses as well as their exterior signs and facades. Here, a woman reposes in her decorated room. (Courtesy of Special Collections, University of Nevada, Reno Libraries.)

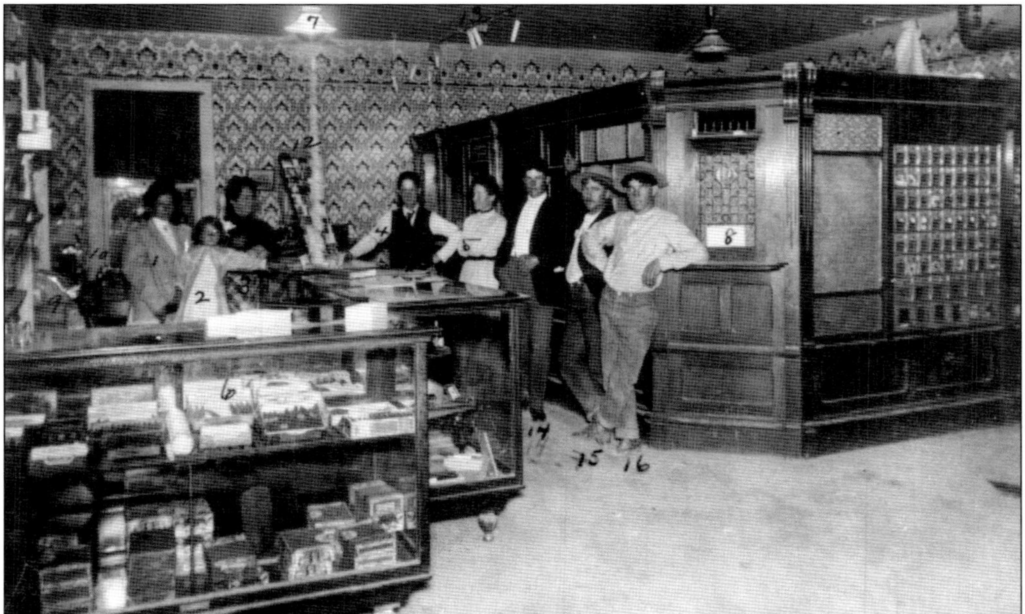

Black and Ferguson sold a colorful variety of objects, including dolls, candles, postcards, toys masks (for masked balls), stationery, and books. The local post office shared the space. Pictured around 1906 are, from left to right, Jessie Mable Woodliff, Jessie Irene Woodliff, Callie Ferguson, Edwin Black, Mary Black, Nate Hardy, Will Danielson, and Irving Sanford Sr.

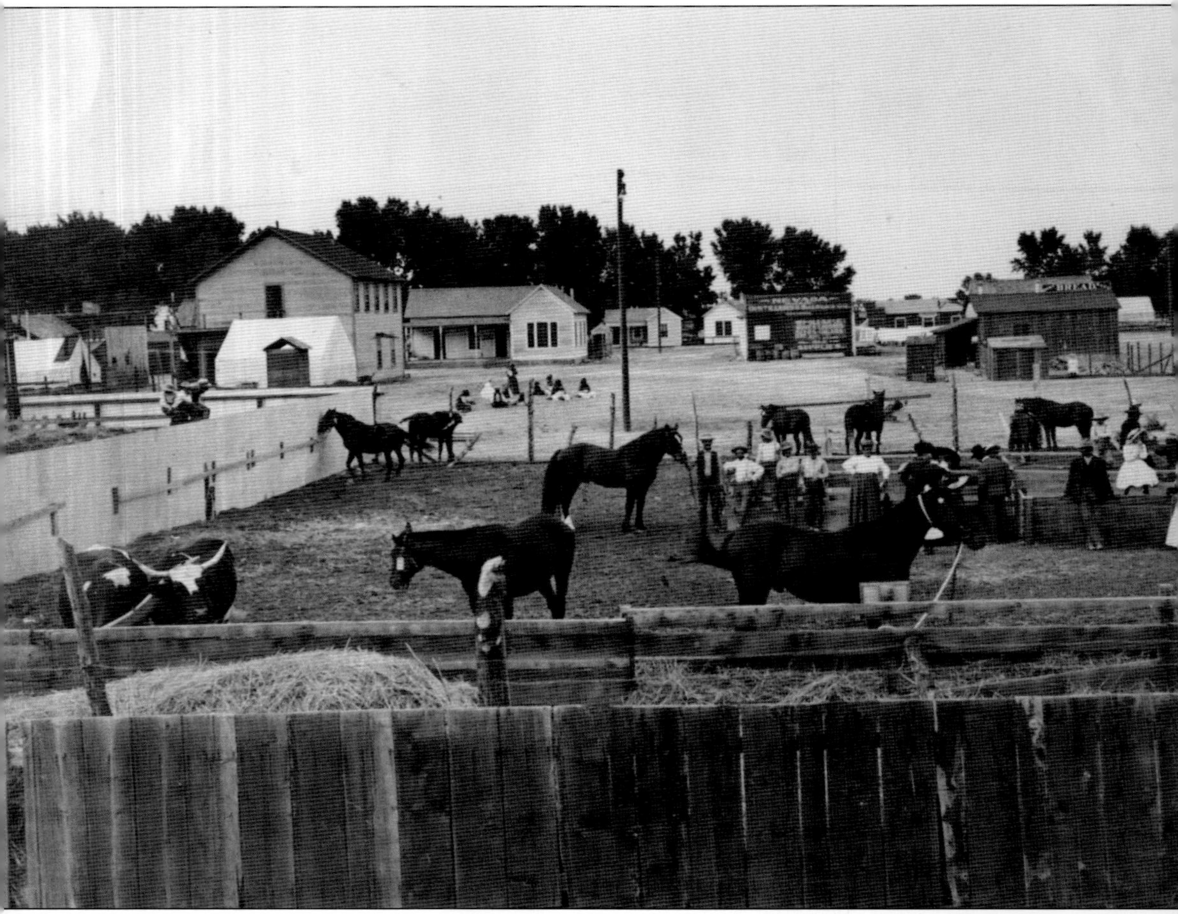

This photograph shows a livestock show or, perhaps, an auction. The women look as if they are dressed to be entertained. East Williams Avenue is to the right; the original Baptist church

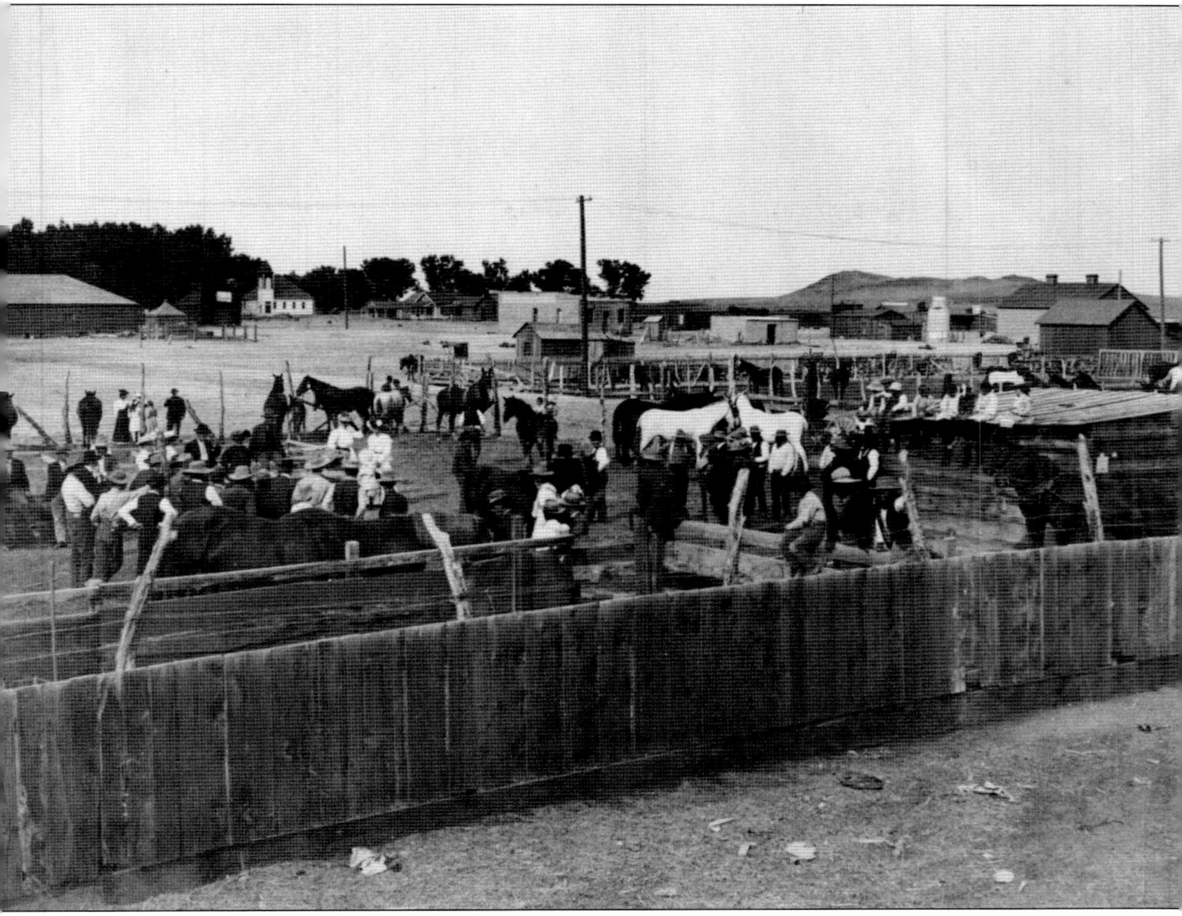

on Broadway Street can be seen. Center Street runs west from the stockyard. The cottonwood trees that once lined North Maine Street and Williams Avenue can be seen toward the top of the image.

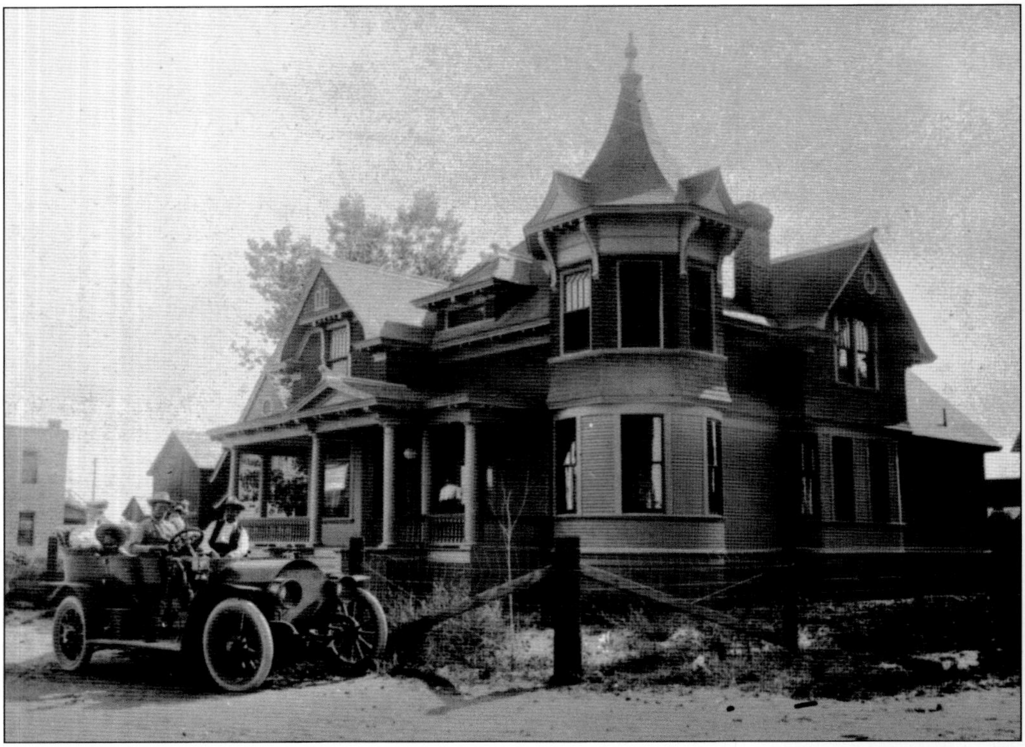

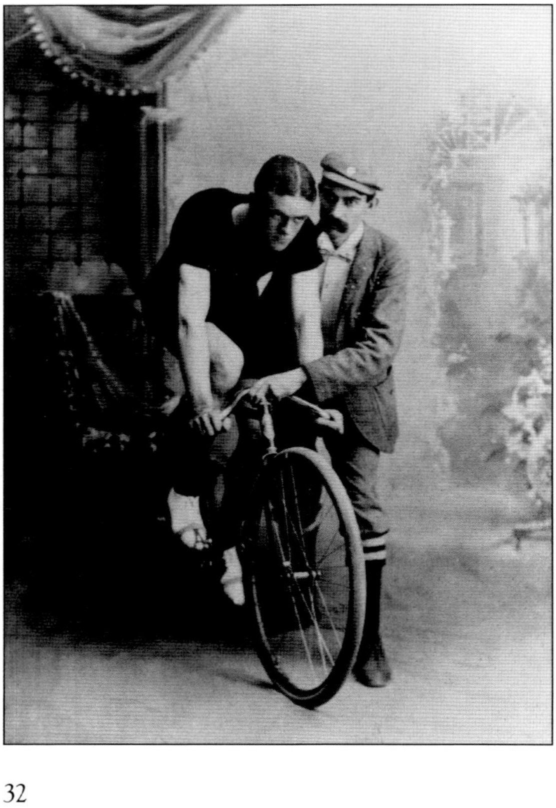

This grand Queen Anne house was built in 1905 by rancher and banker Robert L. Douglass for his new bride, Eleanor Ernst Douglass. The house still stands on the corner of Williams Avenue and South Carson Street and is owned today by the City of Fallon. Douglass installed a revolving platform on the floor of the garage so that his automobiles, after being driven into the garage and rotated, were ready for a quick and safe exit.

Douglass loved fast bicycles and fast cars and gained local fame for racing both. Here, he and his bicycle starter, Ernest J. Maupin, prepare for a race.

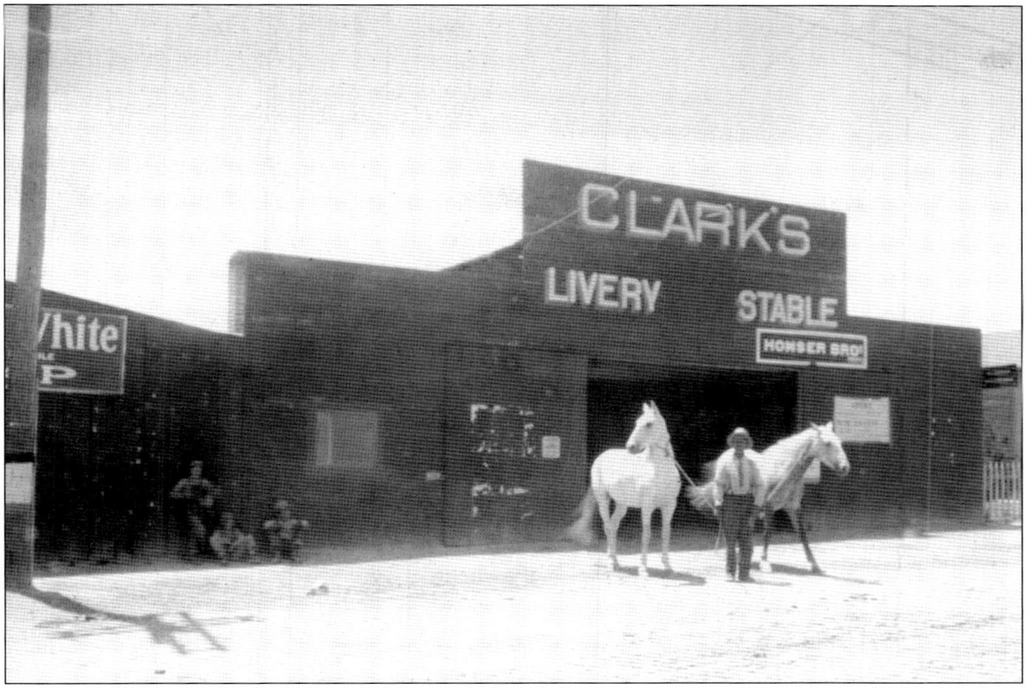

During the first two decades of the 20th century, automobiles shared Fallon streets with horses. Above, Clark's Livery Stable (located on east Center Street) became an important stop for teamsters. Below, teams drove supplies to mines at Fairview, Wonder, Hercules, and other overnight sensations. Horse-drawn wagons also delivered supplies to workmen on the Newlands Project.

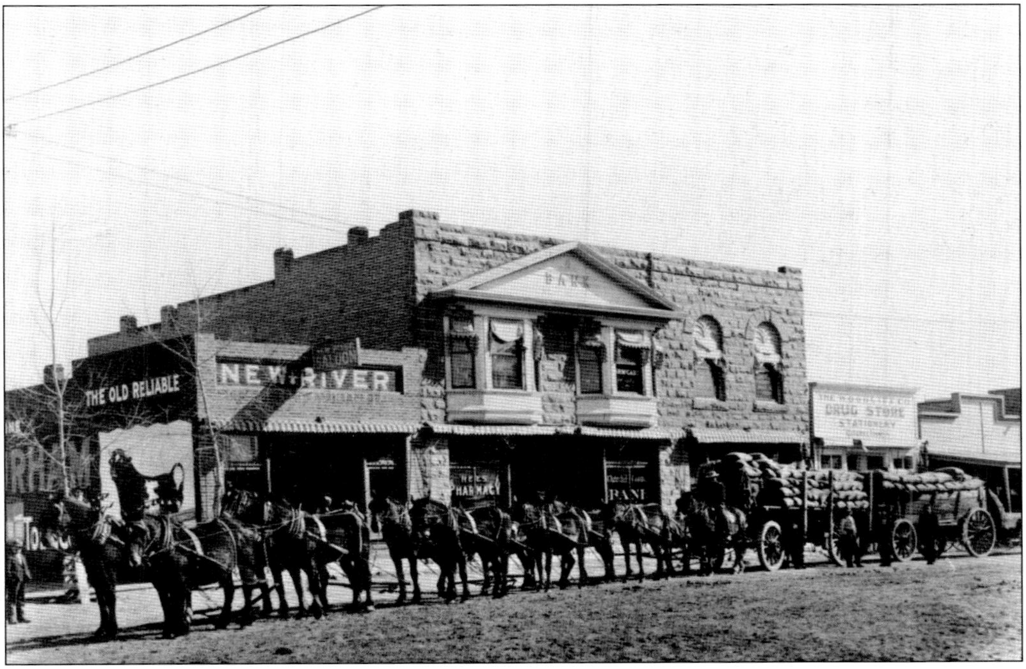

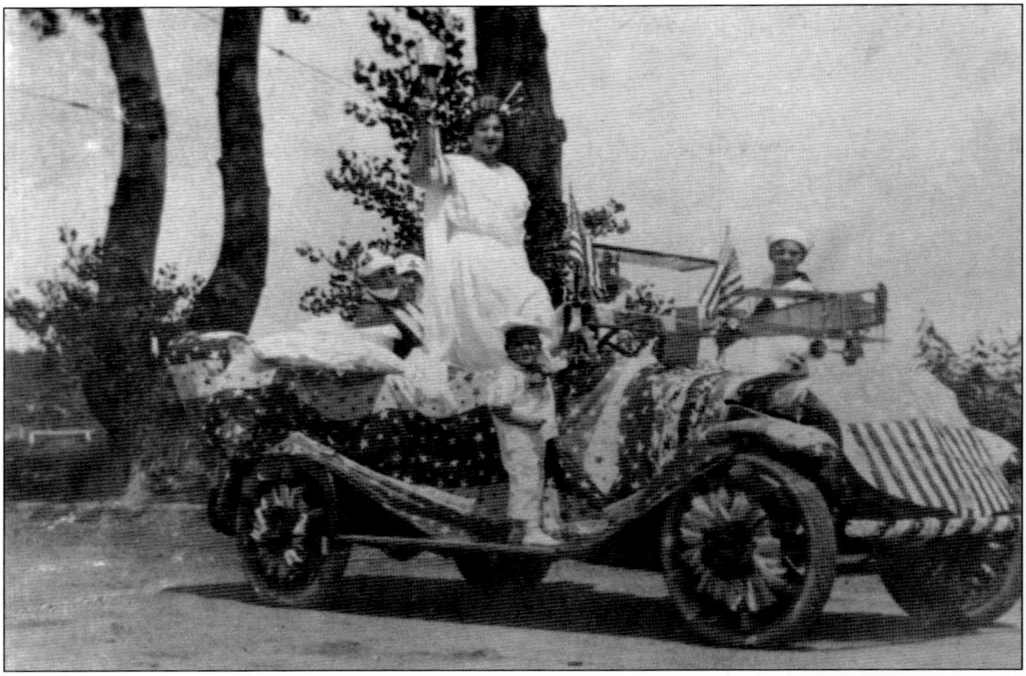

In a show of community esprit de corps, the townsfolk undertook elaborate Fourth of July and Labor Day celebrations. Parades were well-planned affairs replete with decorated floats and mounted entries. Above, the 1906 Fourth of July parade features "Miss Liberty," elected by a penny-a-vote contest. Myra Sanford won the contest with 4,000 votes, beating out Maggie Day with 3,000 votes. Below, a group of mounted Native Americans gathers by the courthouse to join the Fallon parade. (Below, courtesy of Special Collections, University of Nevada, Reno Libraries.)

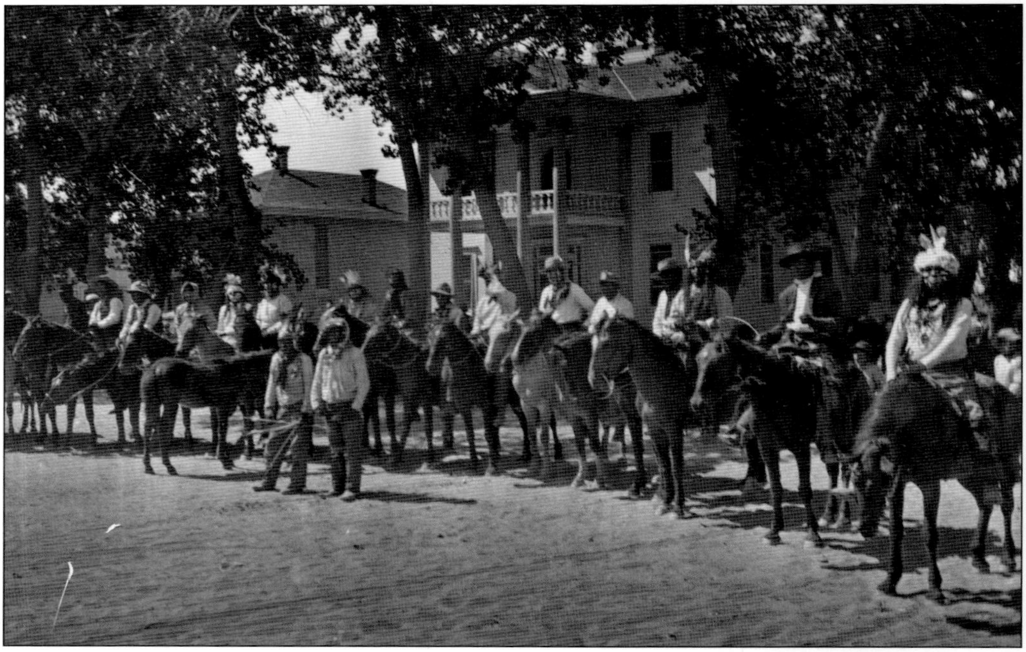

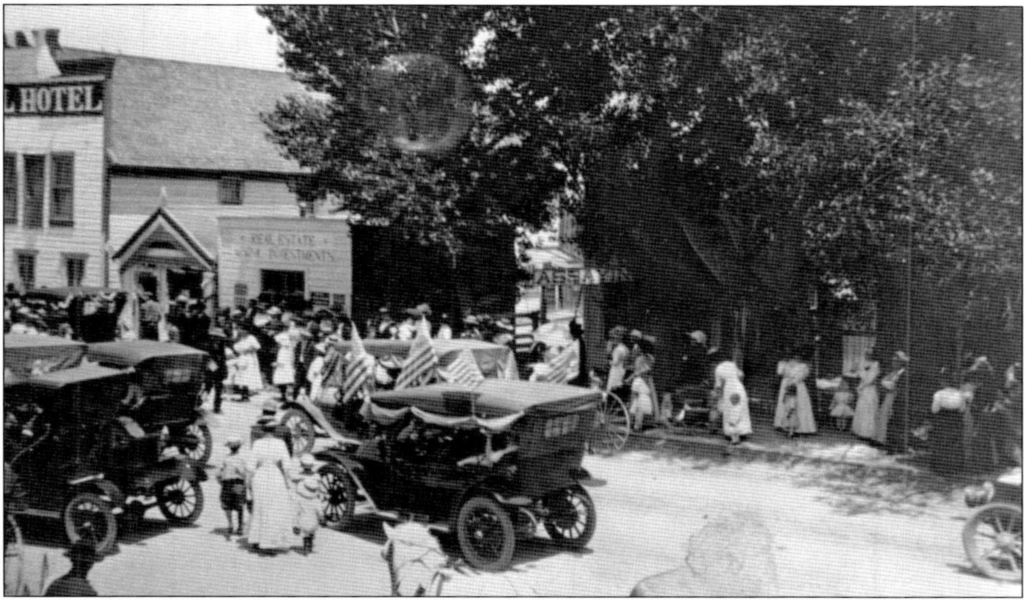

Following the parades, political orations were delivered from the steps of the courthouse, tug-of-war contests (usually between married men and bachelors) took place, and dances lasted until the wee hours of the morning. Sponsors of the parades included the Fallon Commercial Club, organized in 1906 to celebrate community events and promote business.

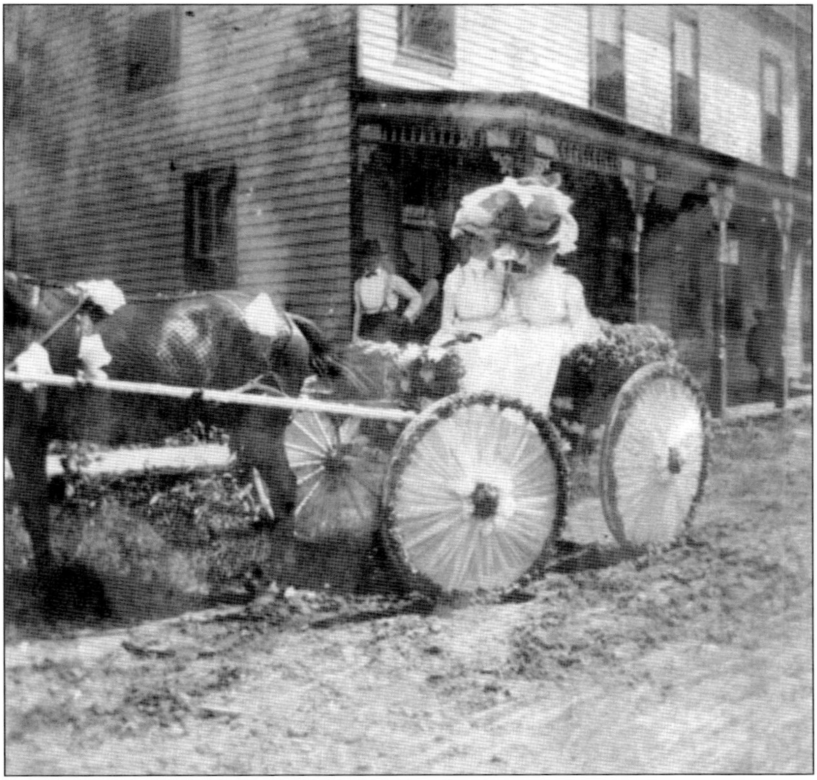

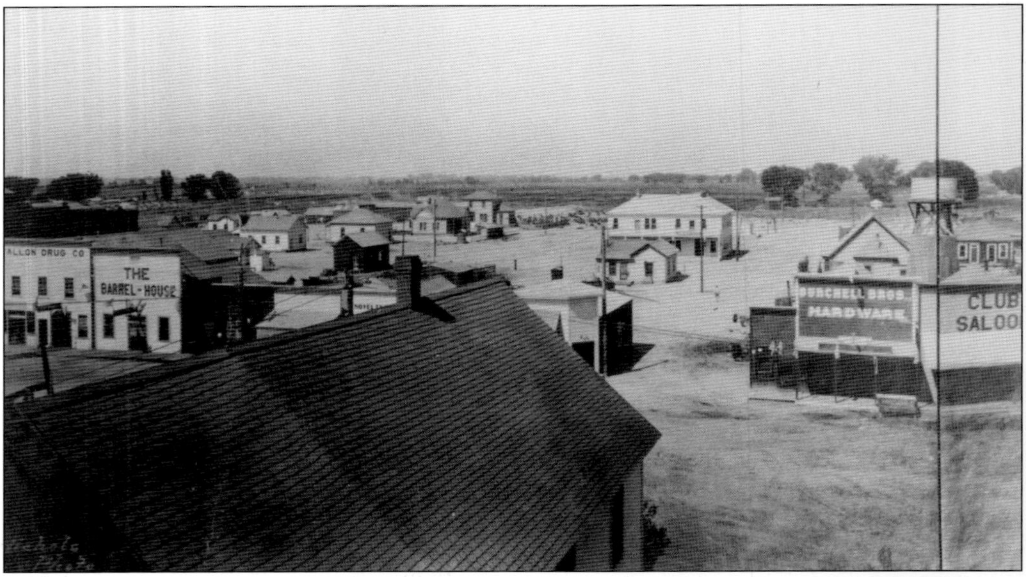

This is a view of the west side of Maine Street to the south of Center Street. The Barrel House advertised, "the best of everything is served over the bar with entrancing music for 'a chaser.' " At the corner of Maine and Center Streets stands Burchell Bros. Hardware. The Mori Ranch can be seen down Center Street to the west.

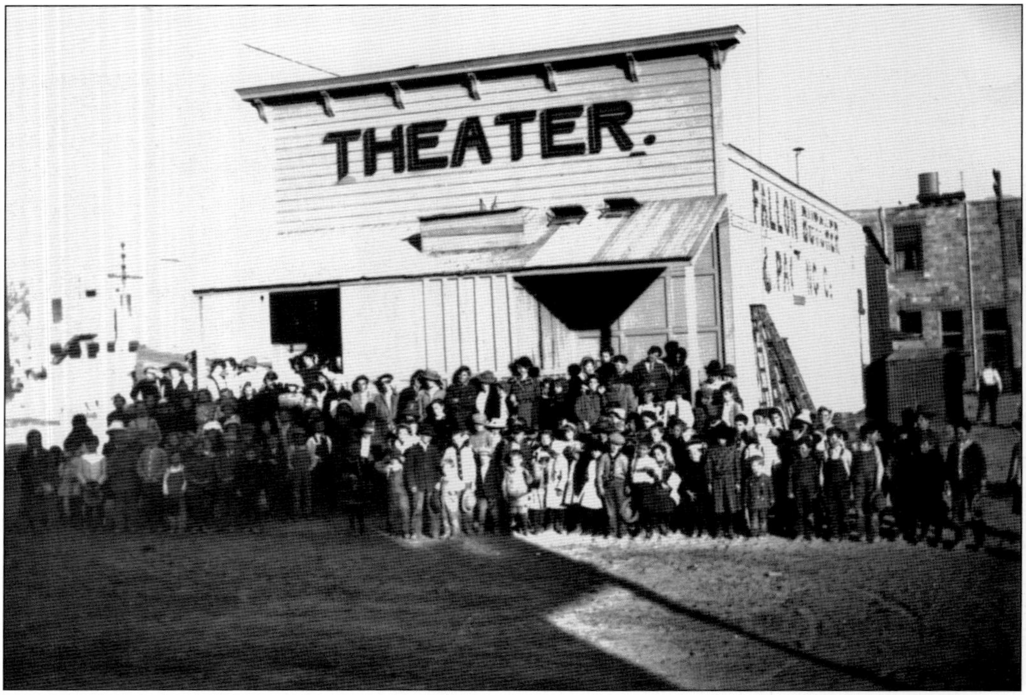

This image provides evidence that Fallon residents have always been interested in the performing arts.

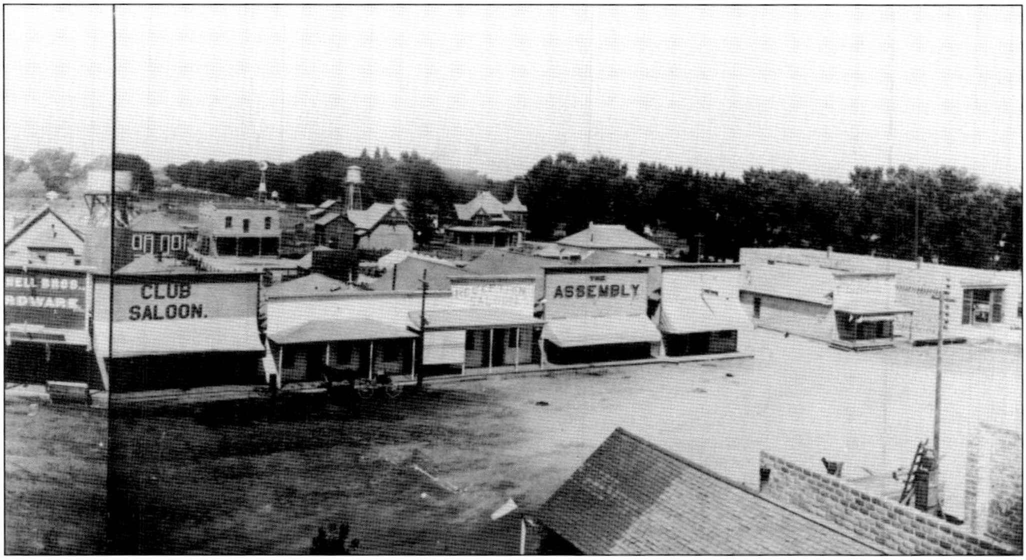

Here is another view of the west side of Maine Street with its popular saloons. The Douglass house is in the background, as are the numerous cottonwood and poplar trees lining Williams Avenue.

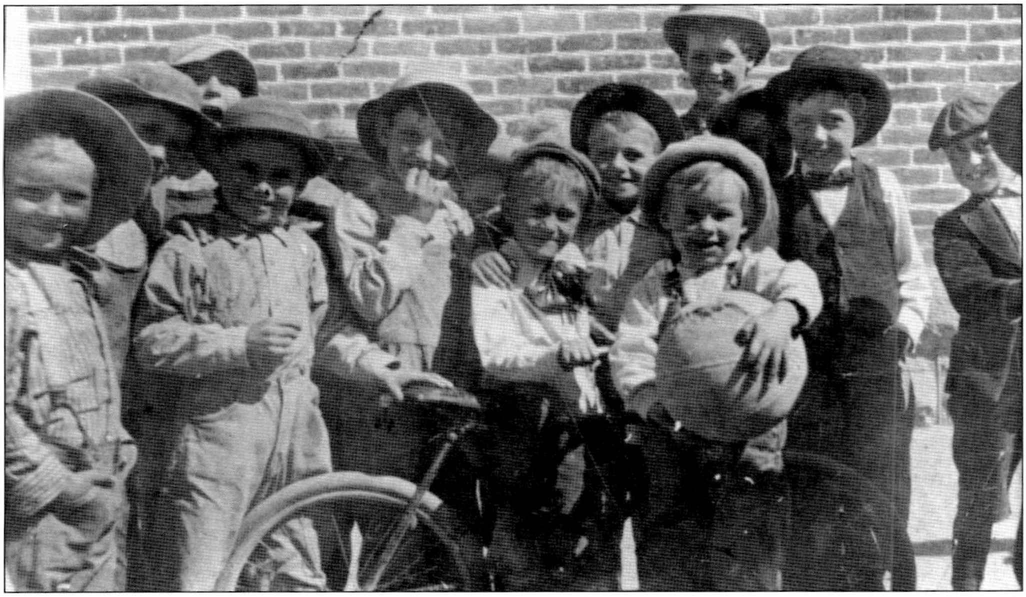
This photograph was taken at the Fallon Grammar School (now Oats Park Arts Center) around 1915. Pictured among the group are Whitney Harmon, Harry Marsh, Everett Maupin, and Bill Dempsey.

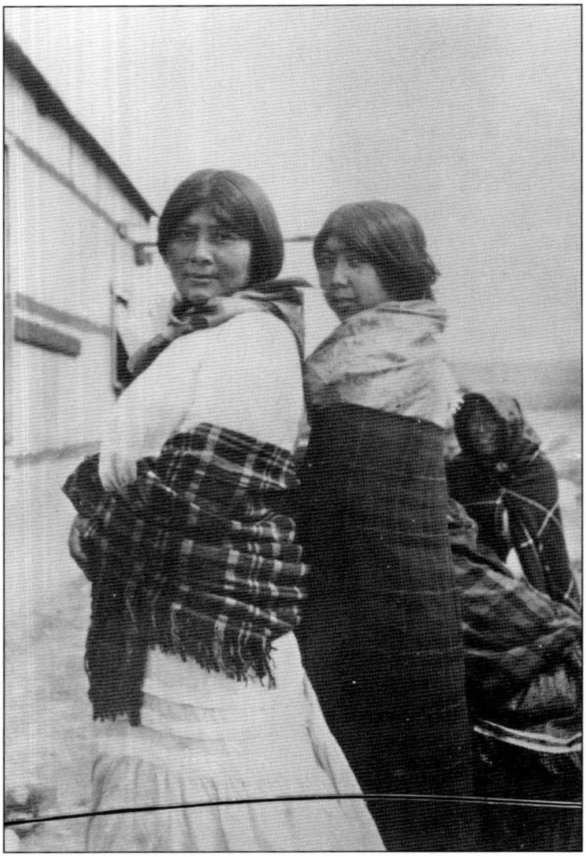

The Fallon Indian Colony was opened by the Bureau of Indian Affairs in 1910. Two Native American women living at the colony look confidently at Rollie Ross Ham's camera. (Courtesy of Special Collections, University of Nevada, Reno Libraries.)

Fallon's first decade brought progress and optimism as well as setbacks, including a destructive flood in 1907 and a fire on Maine Street in 1910. This photograph of Maine Street, taken by photographer Rollie Ross Ham in 1913, is captioned with words indicating that nothing could keep the town down for long. (Courtesy of Special Collections, University of Nevada, Reno Libraries.)

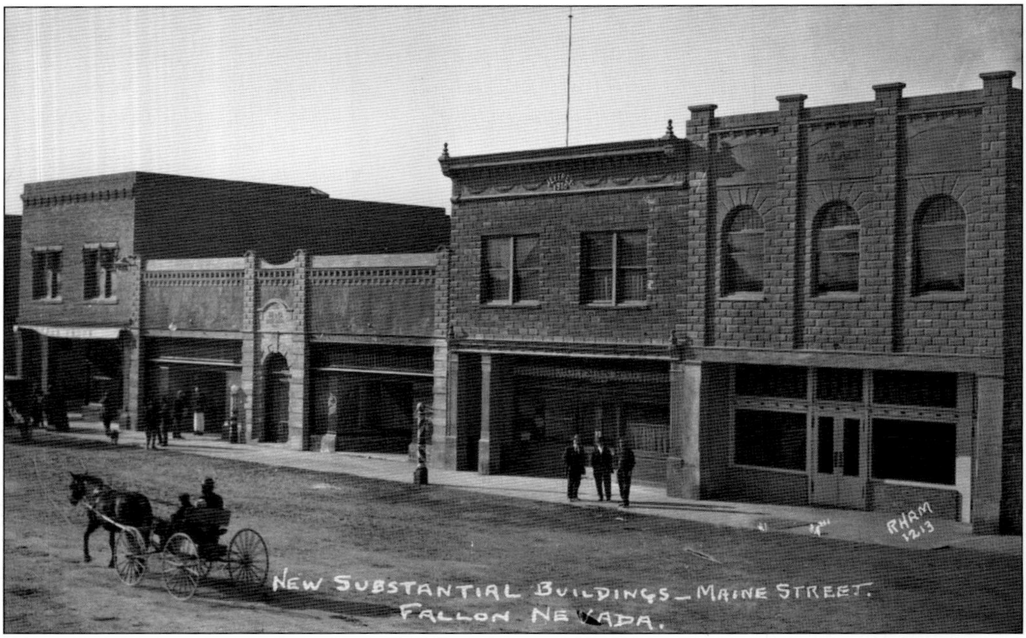

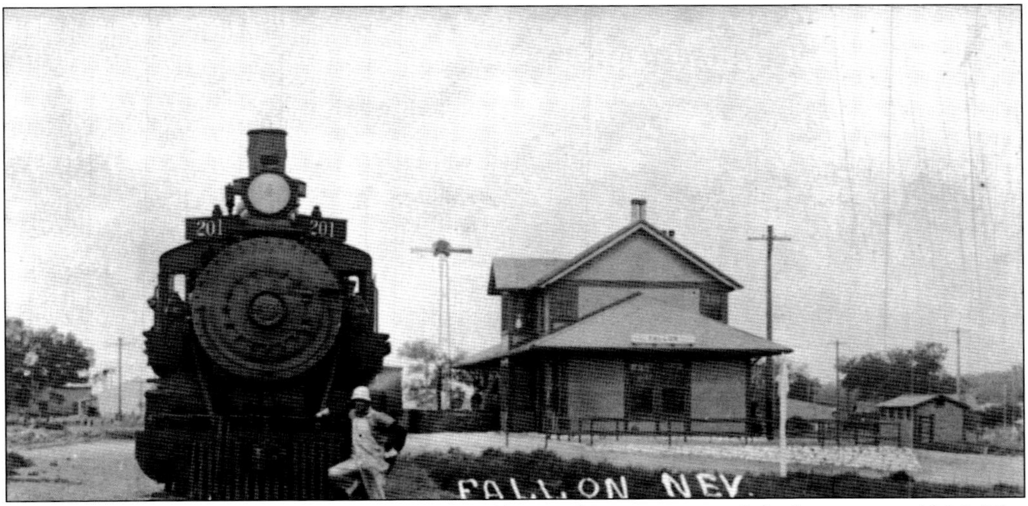

A Central Pacific short line, built between Fallon and Hazen, opened for business in 1906. The rails carried shipments of ore, mining supplies, produce raised on surrounding farms, Fallon turkeys, and freight consigned by local businesses. Passengers, however, had to use the Hazen depot. The large Fallon depot could be seen from all parts of town.

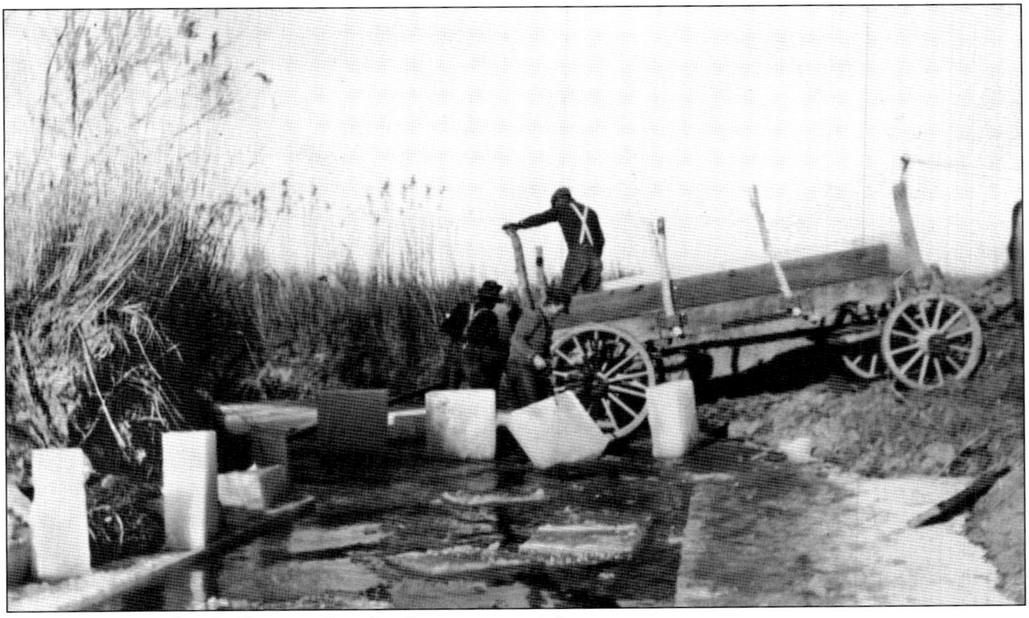

Ice was cut on the Stillwater sloughs for commercial purposes.

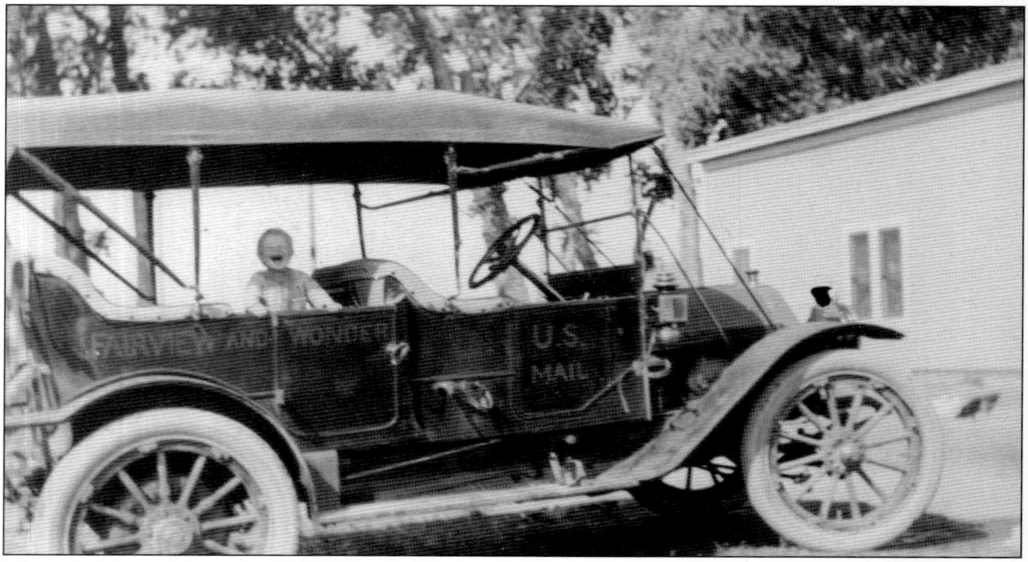

This child must have traveled far and wide, as the US post office vehicle in which he or she rides is labeled Wonder and Fairview, both well over 50 miles from Fallon. Mines at Wonder and Fairview were producing ore during the first decade of the century, with the population at Fairview reaching as high as 1,000 in 1911. Rural mail delivery to such remote locations was a challenge well met.

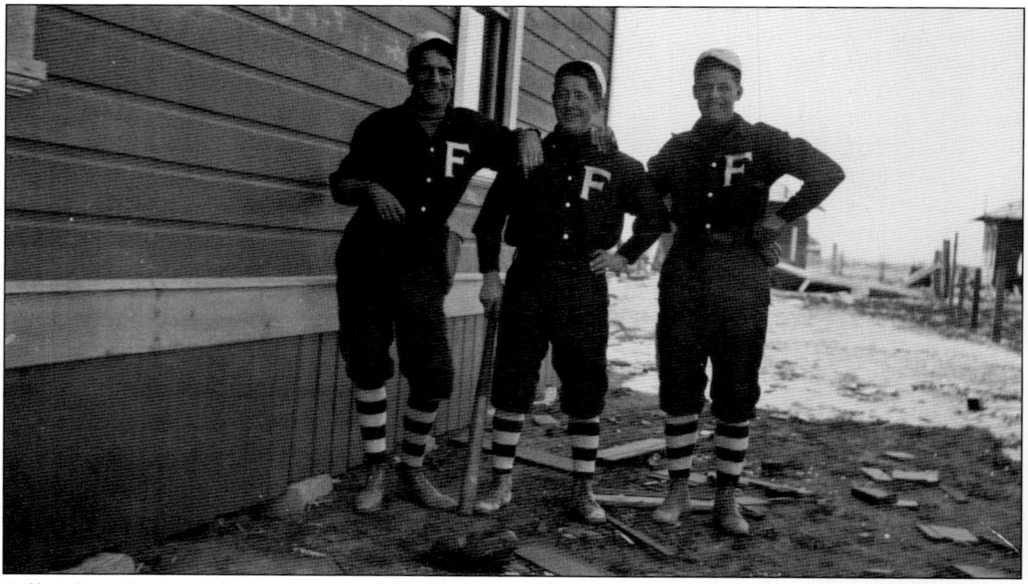

Fallon has always embraced baseball. In 1911, the Fallon city team beat the Sparks team 7-2. That same year, the Fallon team also trounced Lovelock and Reno. (Courtesy of Special Collections University of Nevada, Reno Libraries.)

Three

THE OASIS OF NEVADA

Immediately following the passage of the Newlands Act, work commenced on Derby Dam and the Truckee Canal. Adjacent to the construction sites, small camps and towns sprung up overnight to accommodate an influx of workers. At the Derby site, saloons opened in tents, and daily brawls—even murders—brought notoriety to the Truckee River. The town of Hazen was built close to where the Truckee Canal would eventually transport the waters of the Truckee to mingle with the waters of the Carson. There, more substantial buildings were erected, including the graceful Palace Hotel. Growth in Hazen was further stimulated by advancements in Fallon, as most contractors and residents in Lahontan Valley used the railway station located in Hazen to ship and receive freight.

Adventurers, entrepreneurs, and tillers of the soil, lured by the siren song of land and water, were able to acquire parcels of land in Lahontan Valley as early as 1904. They learned the wisdom of the old saying that tall sagebrush meant fertile soil and the harsh truth that three to five years were required to get good stands of alfalfa. They experienced firsthand the frustration of battling high desert winds and sandy soil. They welcomed assistance when the US Reclamation Service (USRS) opened an "experiment farm" in 1906 to test cultivation methods and seed strains. Results of the experiments were published in the Fallon newspapers. By 1907, a total of 850 farm units had been opened to entry; only 300 farms were occupied. Most of the land was planted in alfalfa, but the USRS also encouraged growing produce and starting up dairies.

Construction on Lahontan Dam began in February 1911, requiring hundreds of men and work animals, plus the most modern equipment the era could provide. Another camp, Lahontan City, served the dam workers and their families during almost four years of construction. Completion of the dam meant that more land could be opened to farming. More farming meant more production, and more production was what the nation needed as it entered the trying years of World War I.

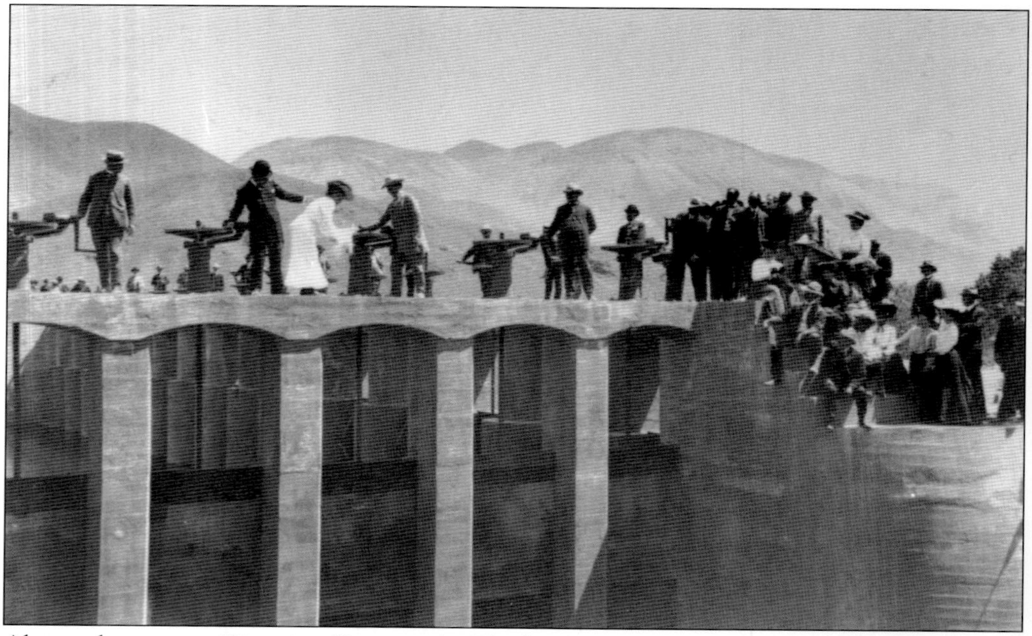

Above, the gates at Diversion Dam on the Truckee River were opened in 1905, sending water down the Truckee Canal to the Carson River. Work on the Newlands Project drew construction crews to Hazen, which was at first a wild and woolly western town. History states that the last lynching in Nevada took place in 1905 in Hazen. The unfortunate victim, named Red Wood, was accused of robbing a train. Hazen also gained status because of its location as a junction on the Central Pacific Railroad. Below, the Palace Hotel in Hazen is seen in its heyday in 1911. The town also sported several saloons and a general store, barbershop, depot, roundhouse, rooming houses, and a tailor shop.

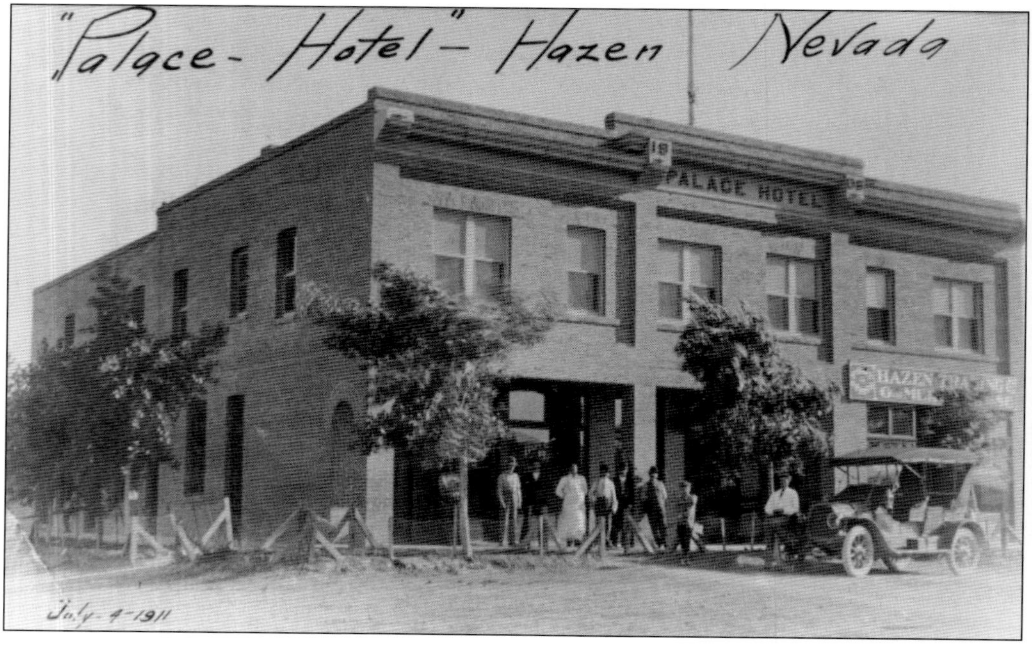

Three young Hazen girls, all dressed up, ride a rail car on the Hazen short line connecting Hazen to Fallon. (Courtesy of the Hazen Preservation Society.)

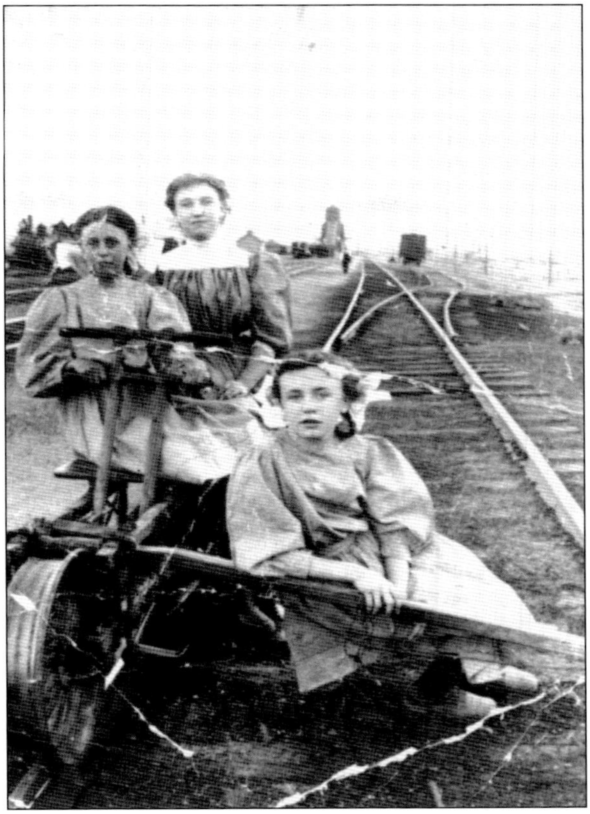

Here is a view of the rail lines at Hazen. This 1910 photograph will no doubt surprise many current area residents who are not aware of how busy Hazen was at the time. The railroad brought in those seeking work on the Newlands Project as well as potential homesteaders from all across the nation.

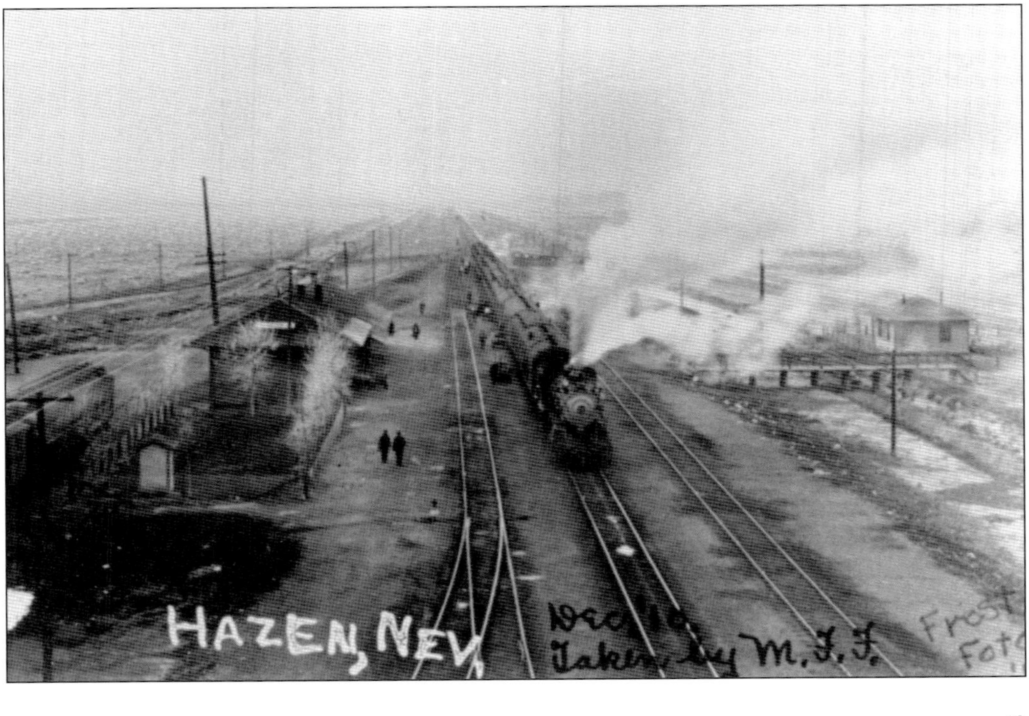

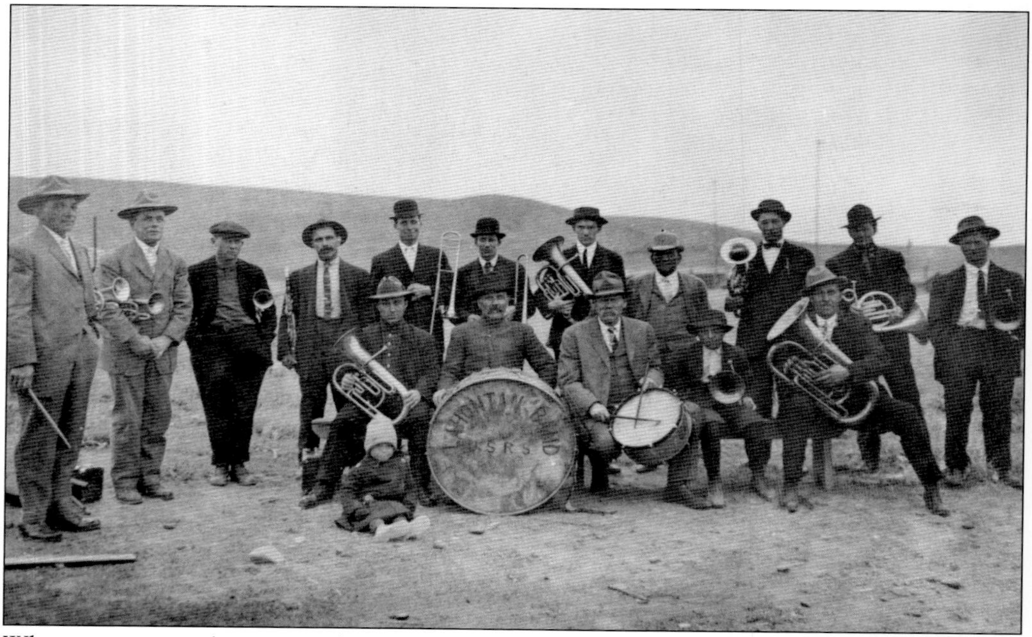

When construction began on Lahontan Dam in 1911, another new town sprang up to accommodate the crews. Named Lahontan City, the town was part tents, part frame housing. Residents exhibited the same enthusiasm as their Fallon neighbors, holding parades and festivals and even forming the Lahontan City Band, shown above, and a baseball team. The dining hall could feed 300 people. Below, a couple living in Lahontan City, Mr. and Mrs. Cooke, explore their surroundings on an Indian motorcycle.

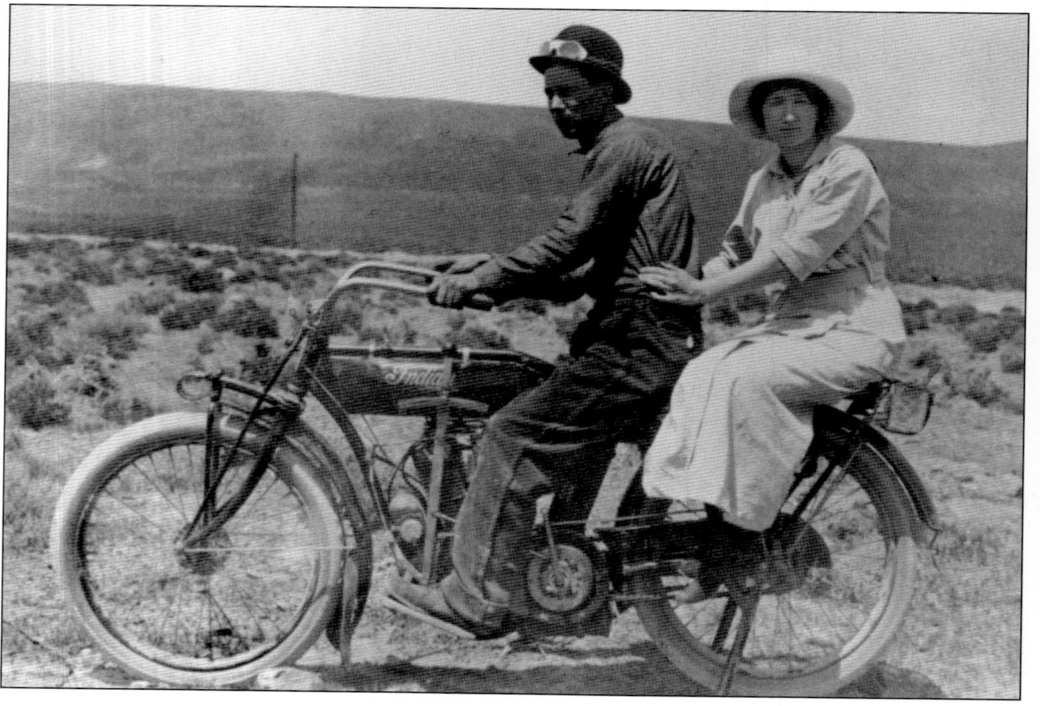

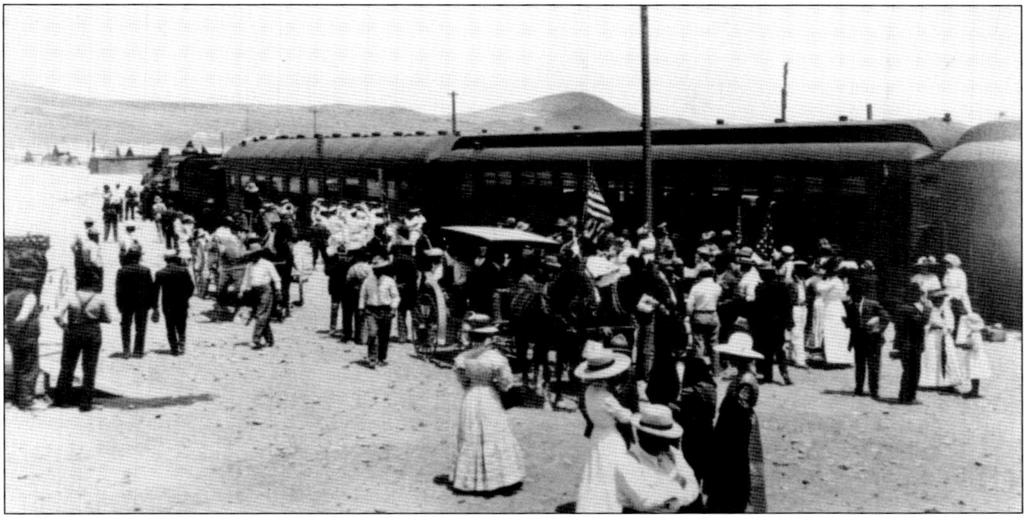

Lahontan City was located adjacent to the rail line, close to where the Truckee Canal now crosses Highway 50. In this photograph, celebrants gather on the Fourth of July with their flags waving, wearing straw hats to shield them from the blazing hot summer sun.

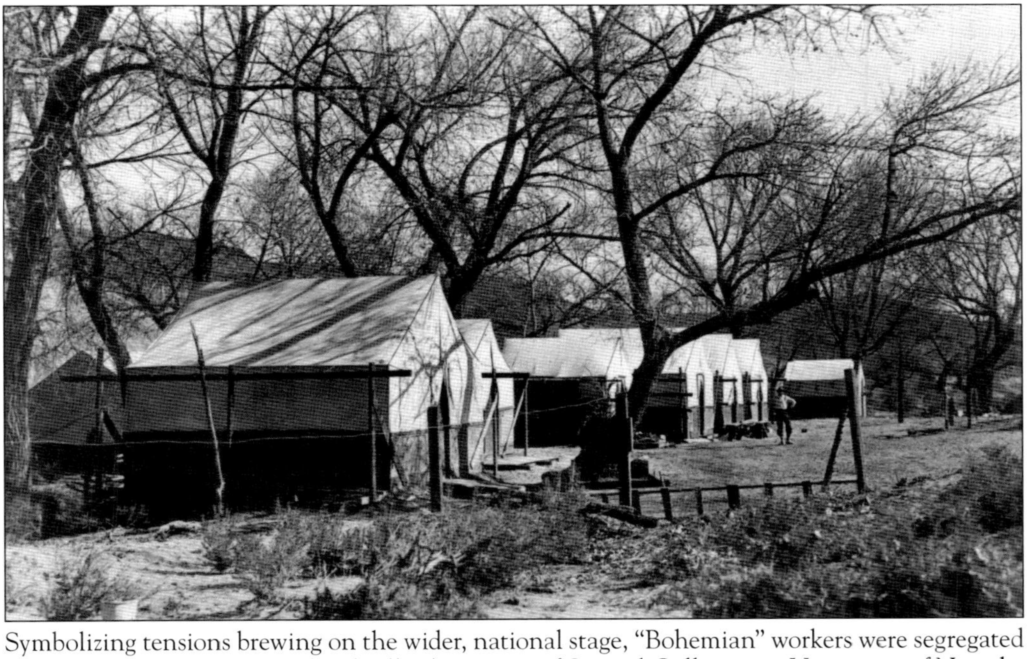

Symbolizing tensions brewing on the wider, national stage, "Bohemian" workers were segregated to a tent camp known as Bohunkville. (Courtesy of Special Collections, University of Nevada, Reno Libraries.)

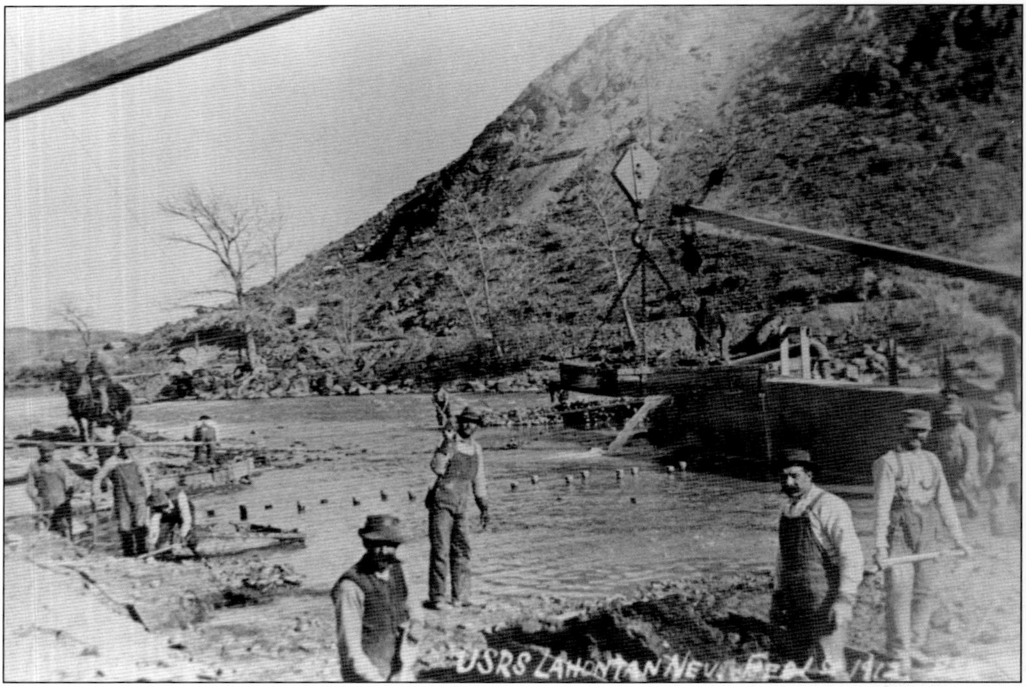

Lahontan Dam was four years in the making, reaching a height of 124 feet and designed to include massive concrete spillways, concrete conduits, and a modern power-generating facility. At the peak of construction, over 800 tons of rock and gravel were moved each day. Seen here around 1912, men, work animals, steam shovels, and trucks form a hive of activity. Wages were about $2.50 per day.

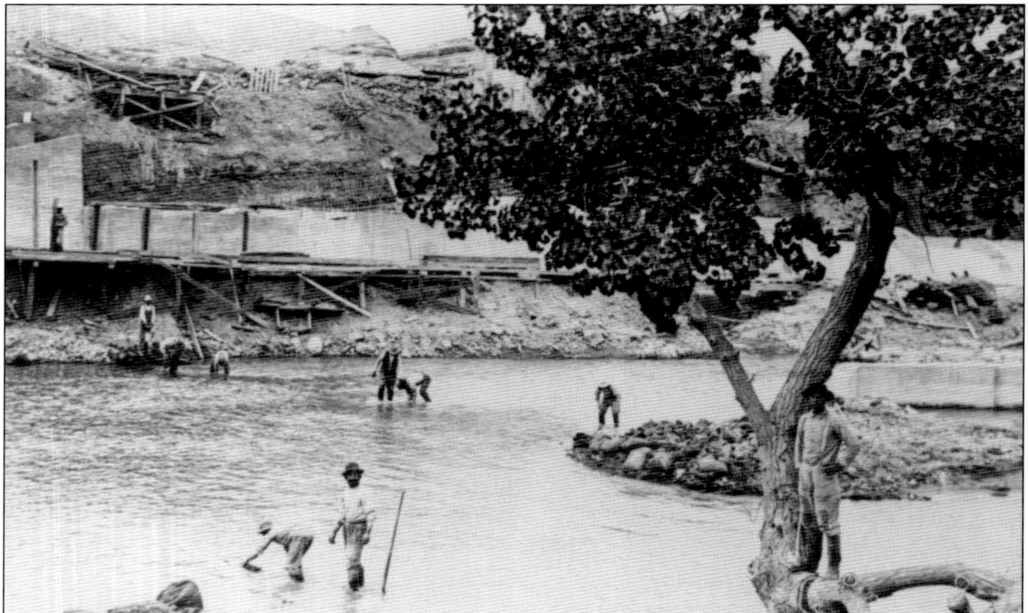

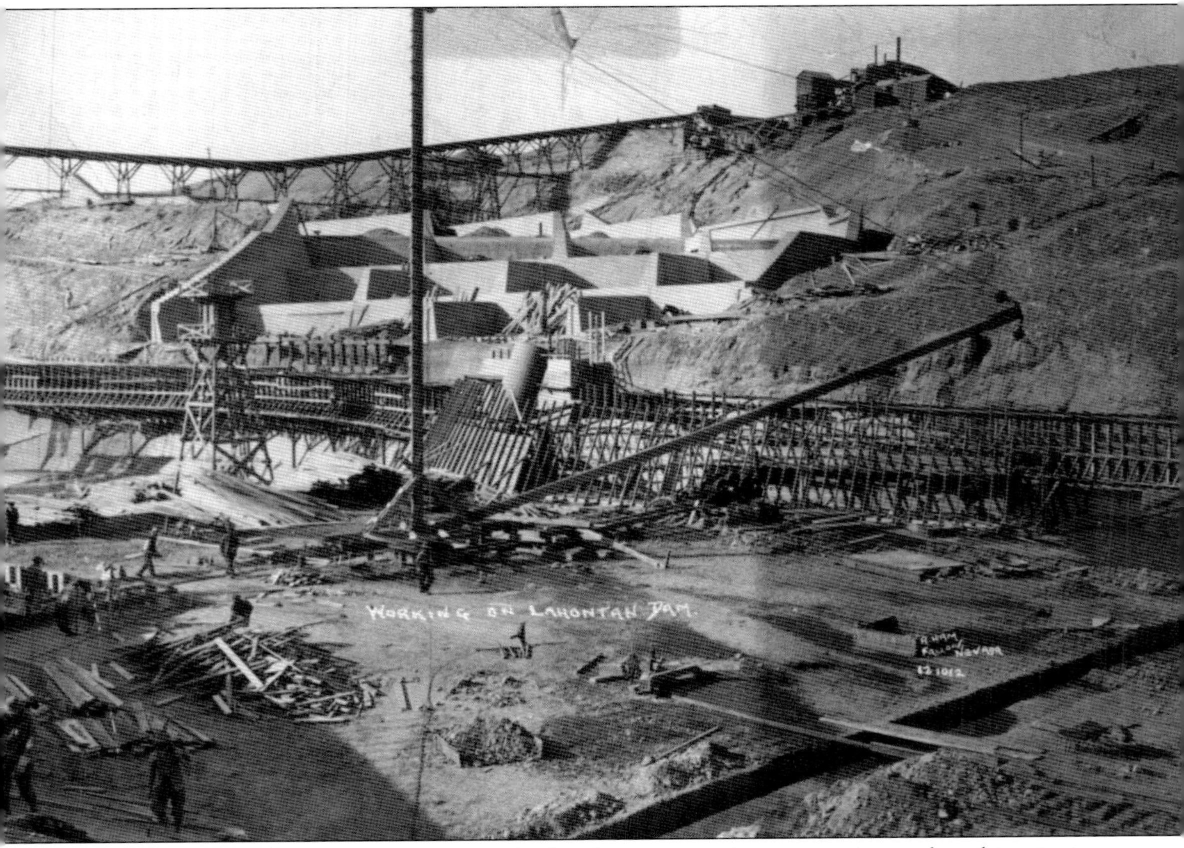

This photograph has the artistic appeal of a photo engraving, evocative and striking in its architectural detail. It reveals the complexity of the construction process, from excavating the land and building the wooden forms to pouring the concrete spillways.

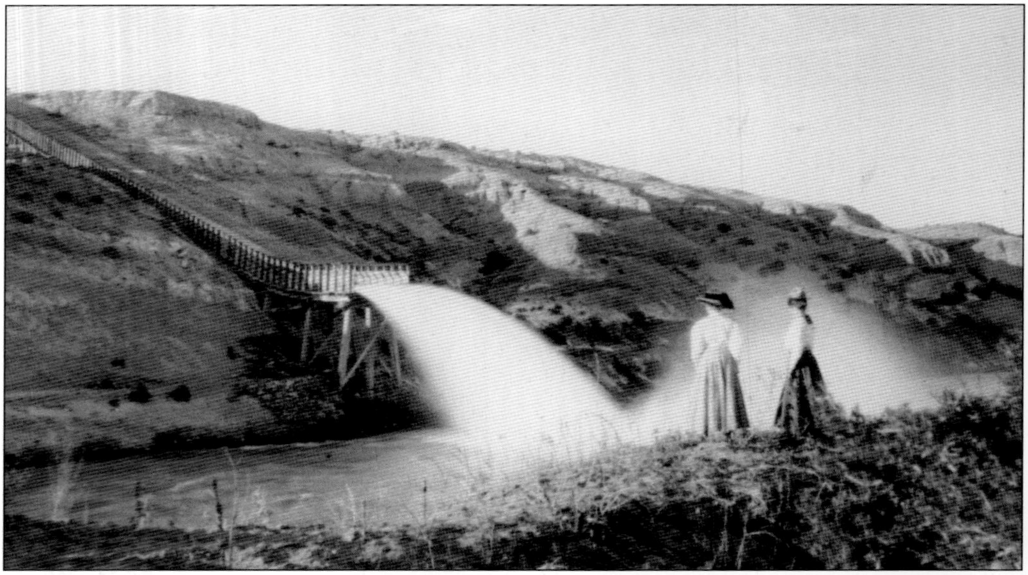

Two unidentified women view a wooden chute carrying water diverted by Derby Dam into the Carson River below Lahontan Dam. This was a temporary structure, removed when the concrete-lined Truckee Canal was completed, allowing the diverted water to flow directly into the Lahontan Reservoir.

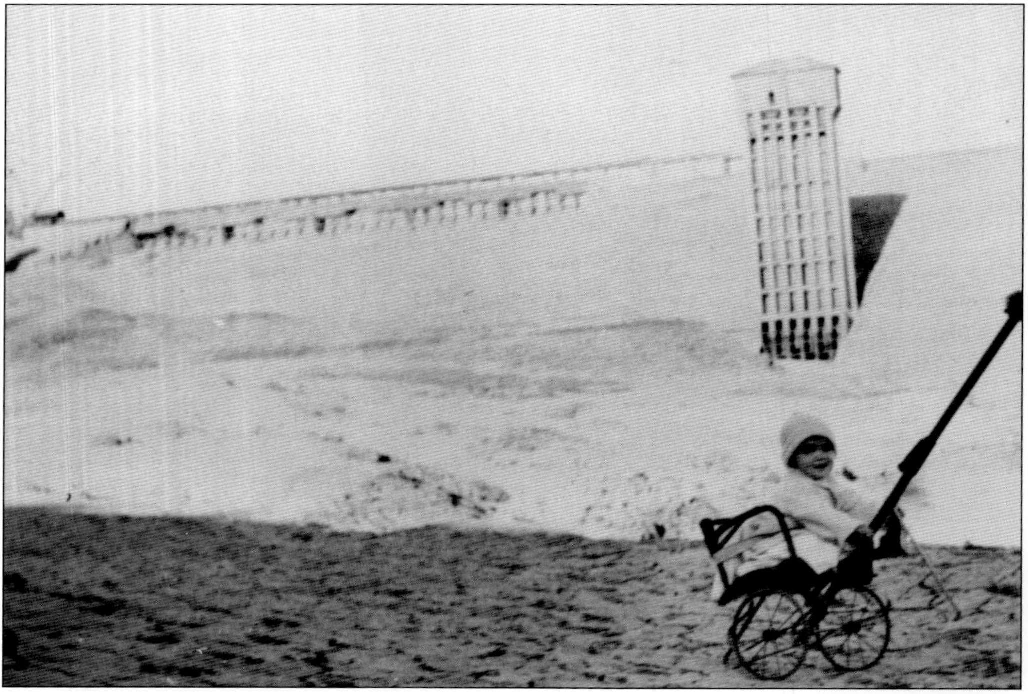

This lucky baby was one of the first to enjoy the new beaches created on the shores of the rising waters of the Lahontan Reservoir.

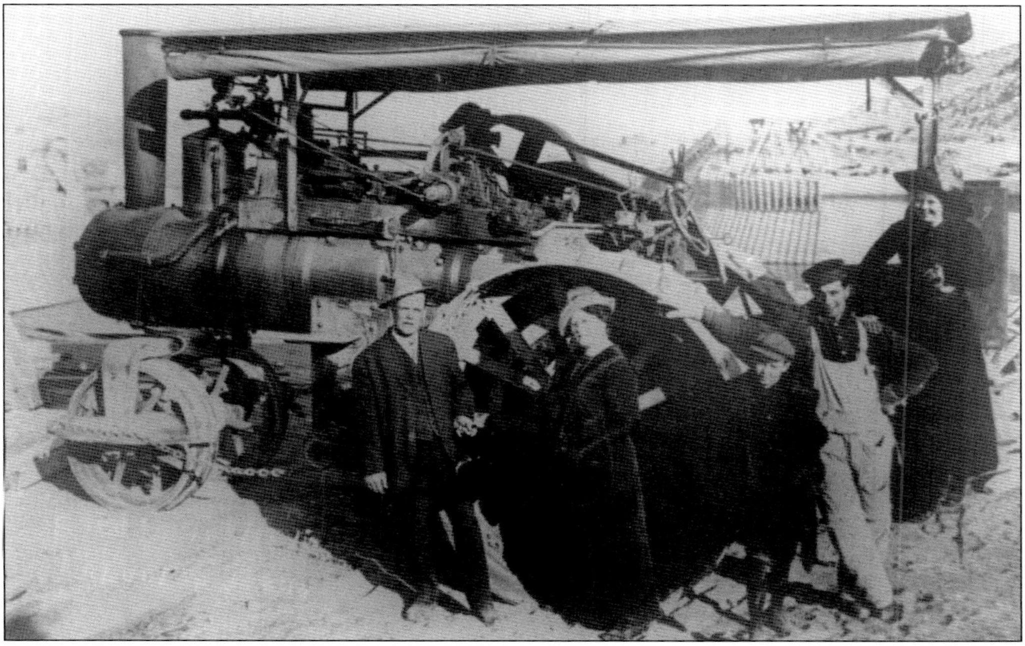

Many curious folks took a day's outing to view the impressive engineering project. On any given workday in 1914, visitors could view 250 men, 52 horses, and 38 mules laboring away. Here, the massive equipment draws attention and provides an interesting backdrop for a photograph.

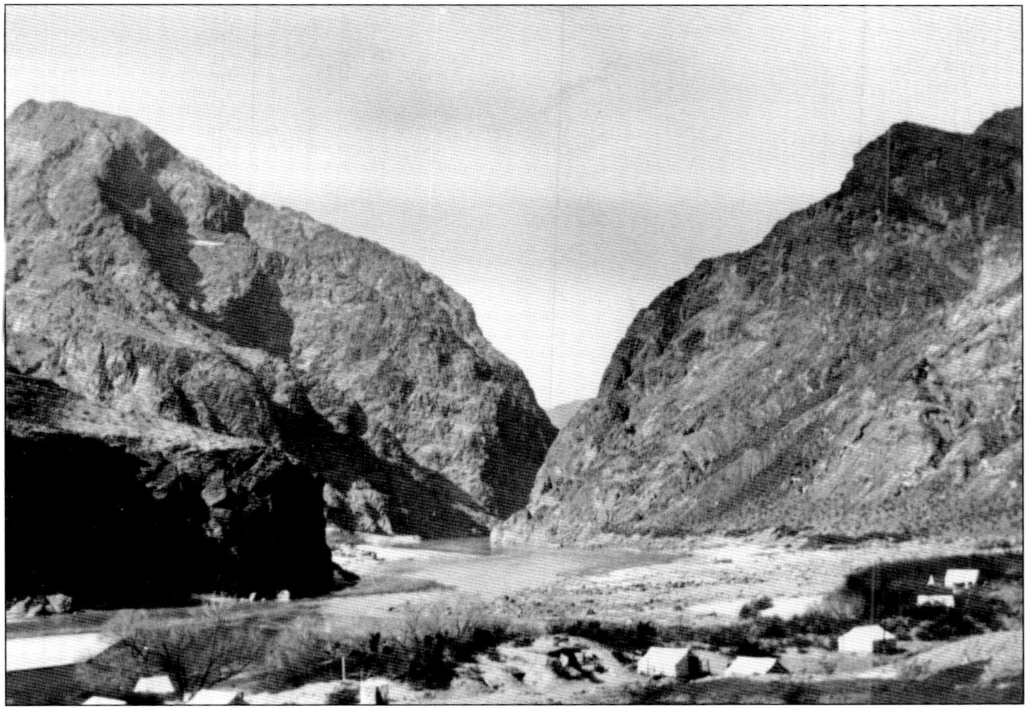

This photograph was taken prior to the construction of the dam. Known as The Narrows, the rocks cliffs were blasted to make way for constructing the pool, spillway, and face of the dam.

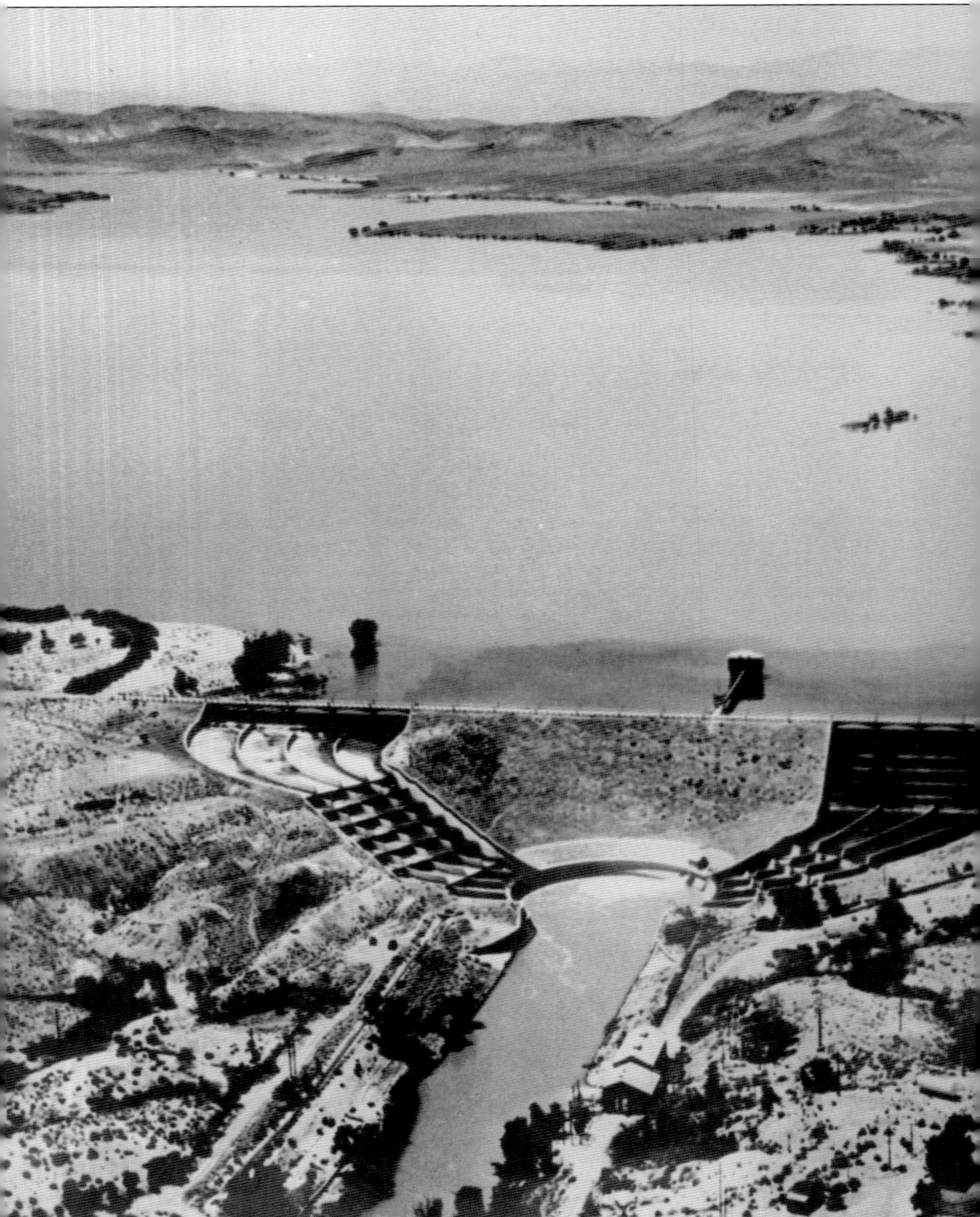

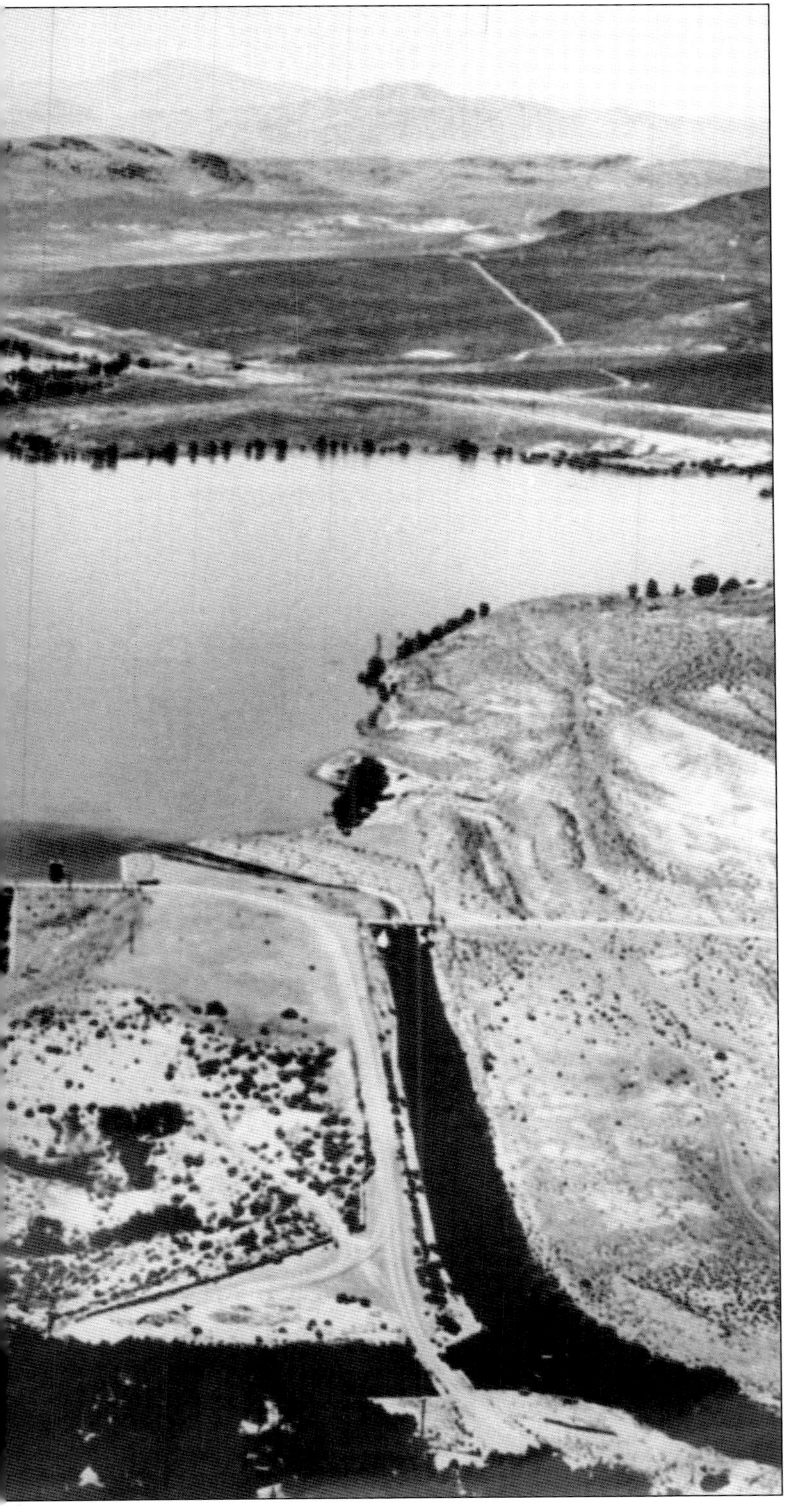

A sweeping view of the finished dam shows the structures, the impounded waters, and the Carson River above and below the dam. The tower that houses the power generators is seen in the center. When at capacity, the dam can store 300,000-plus acre-feet of water. Also visible is the roadway crossing the dam from right to left (north to south), giving swimmers, boaters, and fishermen access to the south side of the dam and reservoir.

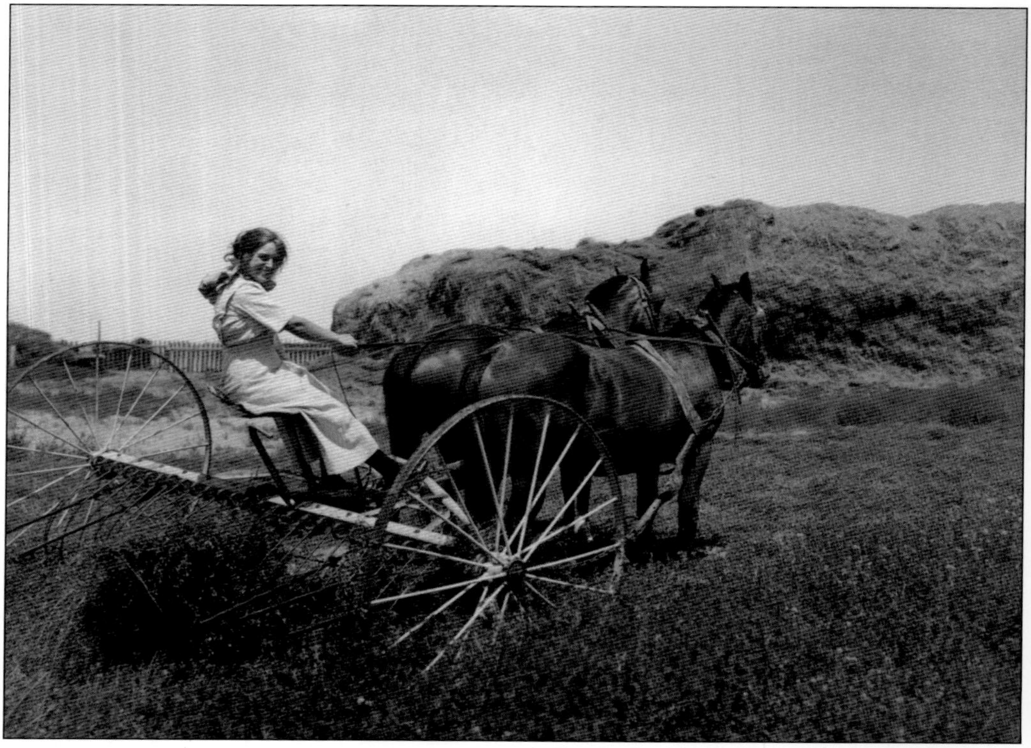

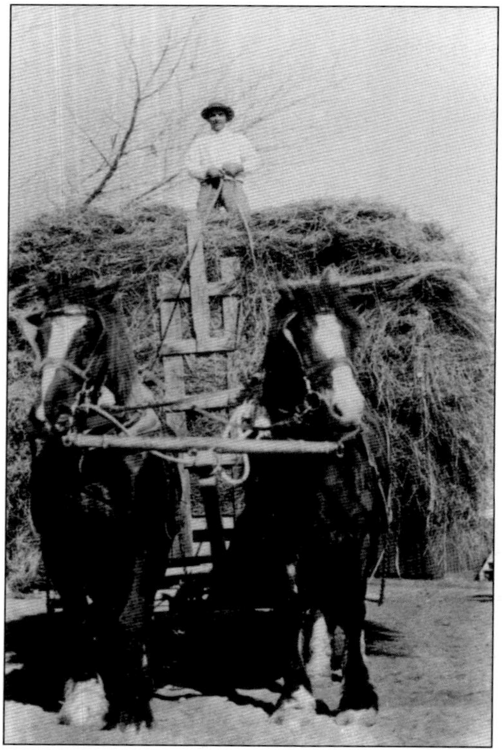

A flood of publicity from the US Reclamation Service drew families to the Newlands Project, where they were offered "the opportunity of a lifetime." Water rights were advertised at $60 an acre, interest free. Title to the land was secured after three years' residency. Despite the many hardships, this young lady seems happy enough to help her family out.

The driver of this hay wagon, Lester "Buck" Kirn, appears to be up to the challenge of balancing an enormous load of hay.

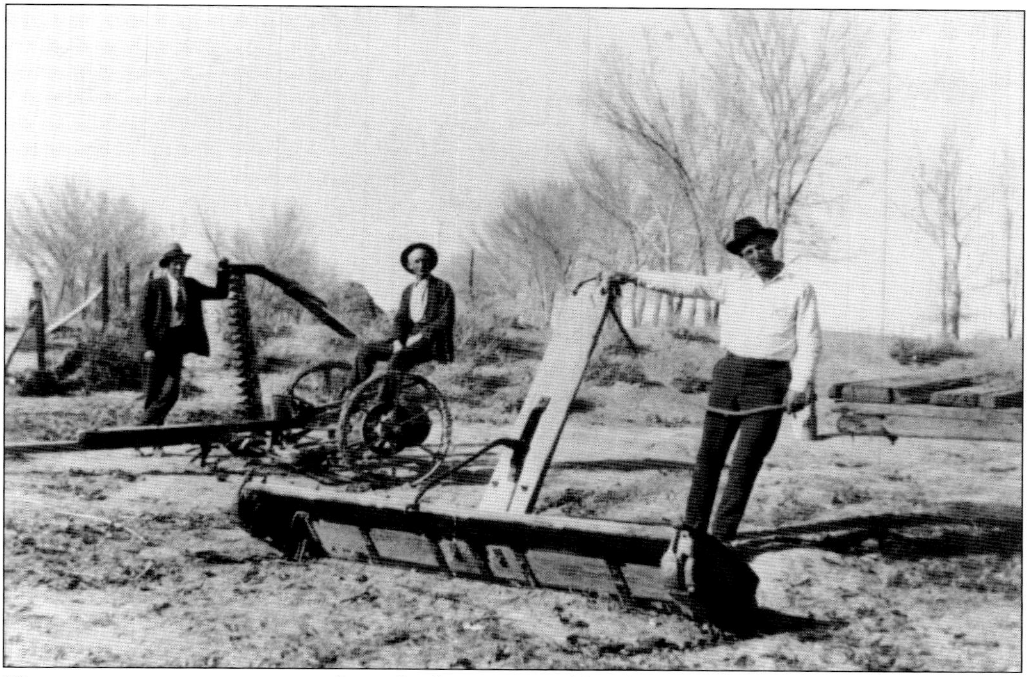

These young men are enjoying the task of scraping and leveling the land, never an easy task given the hard-baked desert floor. One enterprising county resident invented a type of Fresno scraper called the Churchill, designed specifically to tackle and tame local soils.

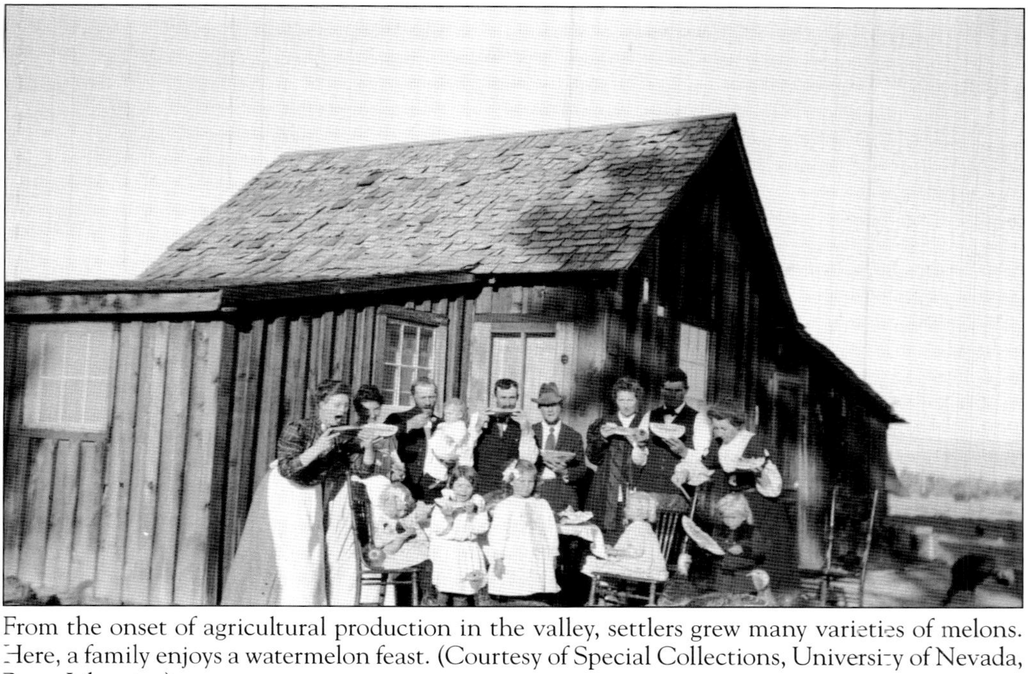

From the onset of agricultural production in the valley, settlers grew many varieties of melons. Here, a family enjoys a watermelon feast. (Courtesy of Special Collections, University of Nevada, Reno Libraries.)

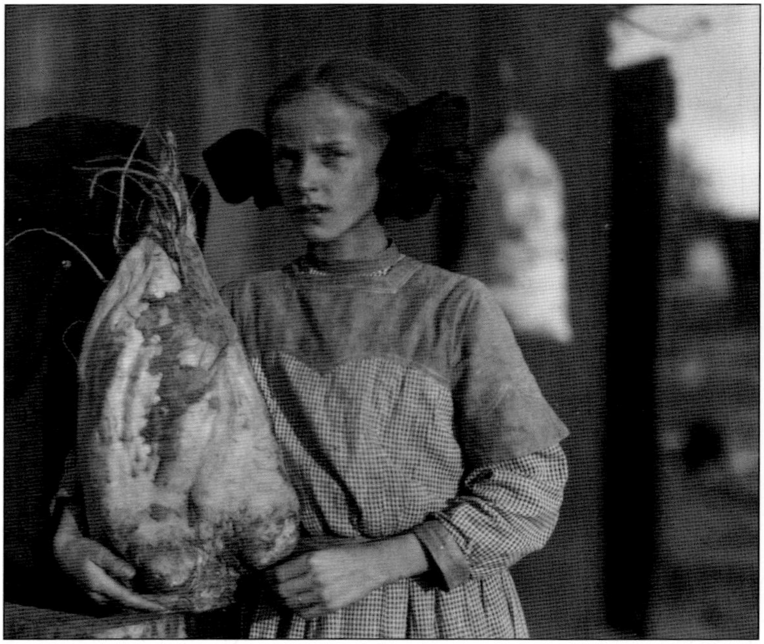

No wonder hopes were high for growing and processing sugar beets in the Lahontan Valley. Note the size of the beet held by this young girl. (Courtesy of Special Collections, University of Nevada, Reno Libraries.)

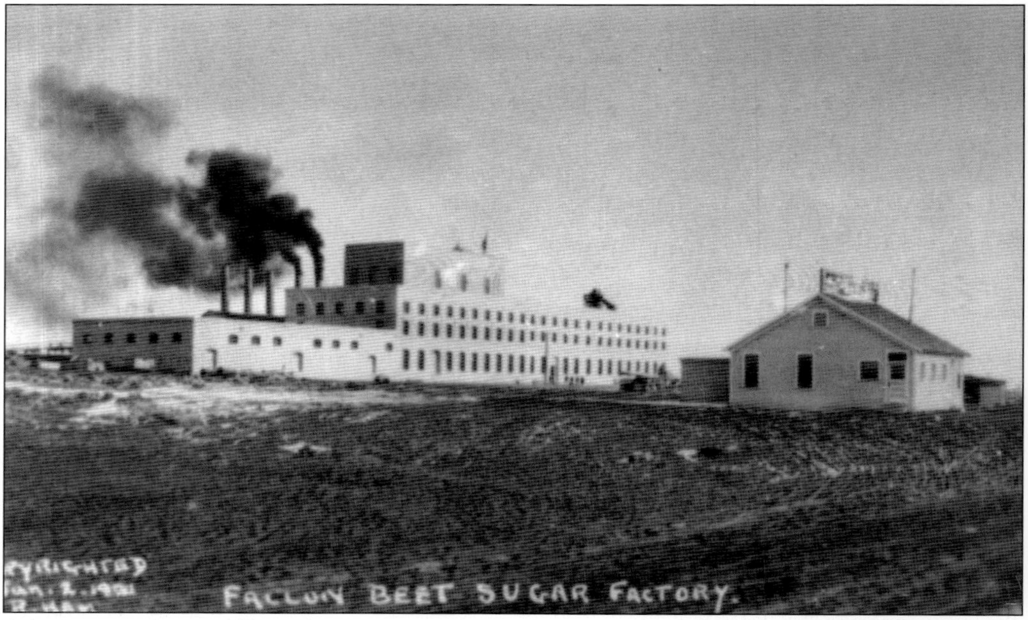

A beet sugar factory, shown here, was constructed in 1910 near Rattlesnake Hill. The company operating the factory declared bankruptcy in 1915 after beet sugar crops suffered from "curly top" disease several years in a row. New owners failed to resurrect the business. During Prohibition, bootleggers entered the abandoned factory and made whiskey from sugar residues. The building was destroyed in 1934.

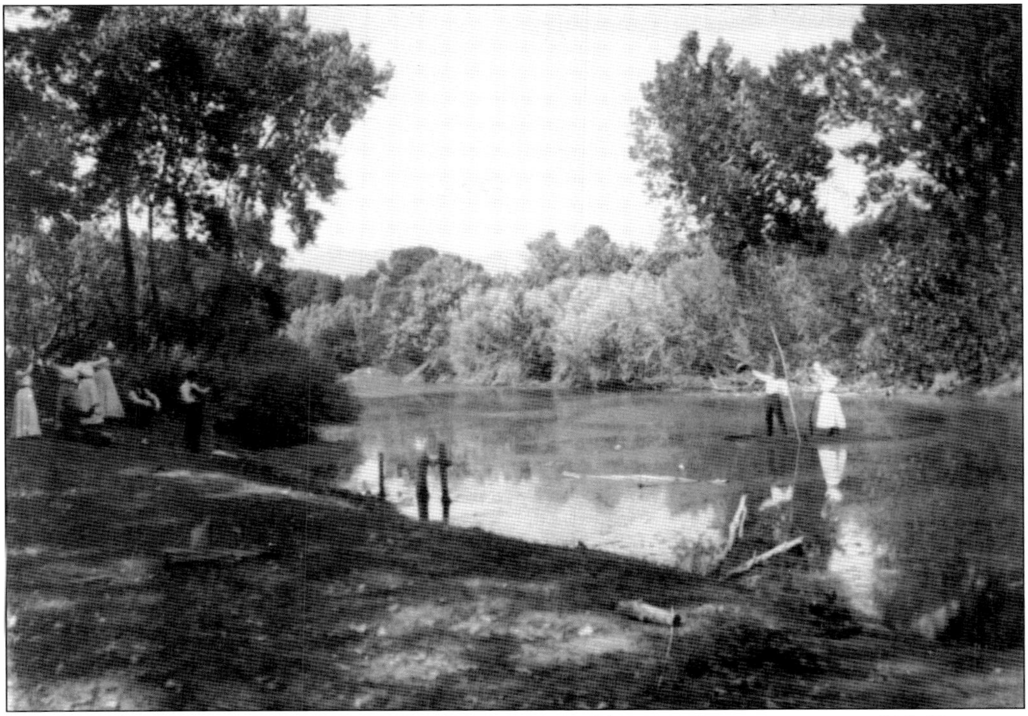

Anticipation ran high that the Newlands Project would "turn this water into gold." However, for many, the Carson River was golden enough on its own, supplying relief from the intense summer heat and providing recreation in both summer and winter. Here, people enjoy the river on a family outing.

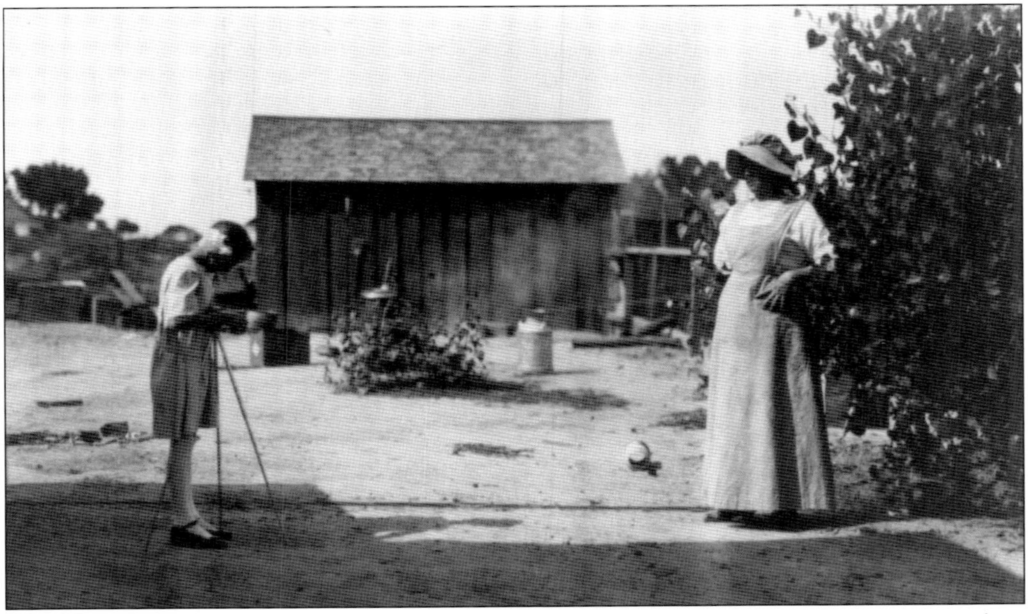

Photographer Rollie Ross Ham captured his daughter, Thelma Ruth, and his wife, Ida, on their Fallon homestead. Note Thelma's camera.

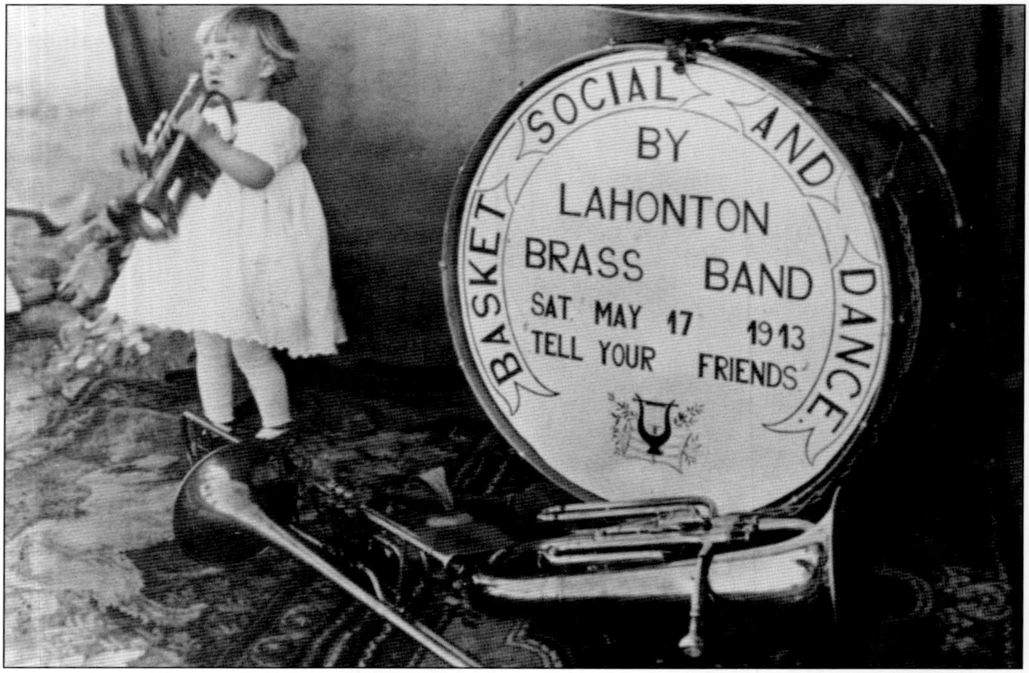

Fallon became the site of the Nevada State Fair in 1915 as the result of an interesting political trade-off. Art Keddie, who represented Churchill County in the Nevada Senate, was a strong advocate of a Nevada Assembly bill moving the state fair from Reno to Fallon. However, he was short on votes in the Senate, so he dropped his opposition to the now-famous Nevada bill legalizing a six months' residency period for a divorce. In return, he gained enough votes to support moving the fair to Fallon. Enthusiastic Fallon boosters constructed a hay palace, seen below. Visitors were presented miniature bales of hay and cookies made from ground alfalfa meal. Above, the Lahontan Brass Band played at parades, rallies, and fairs. (Below, courtesy of Jon Vannoy.)

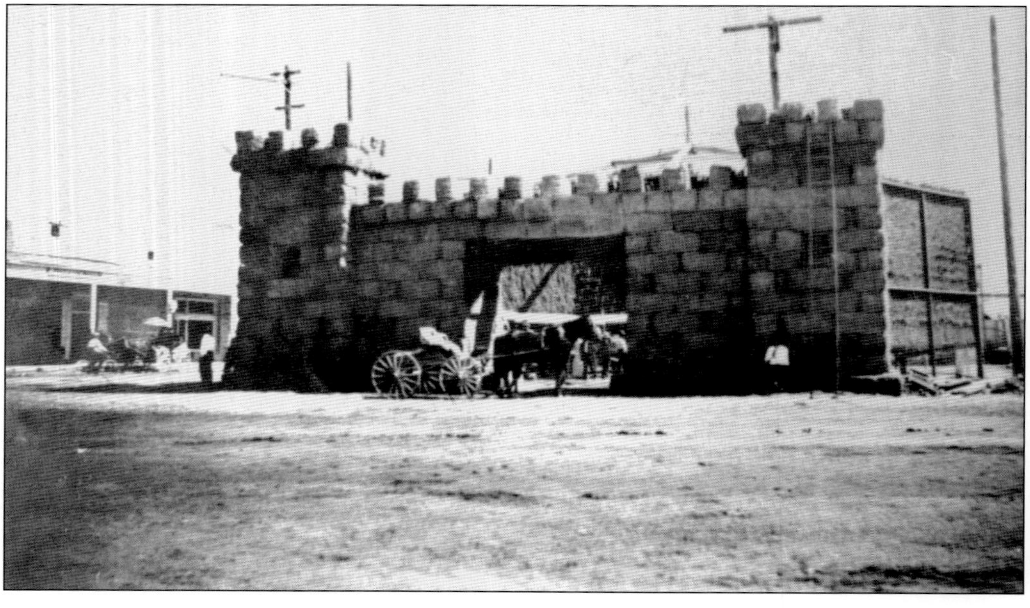

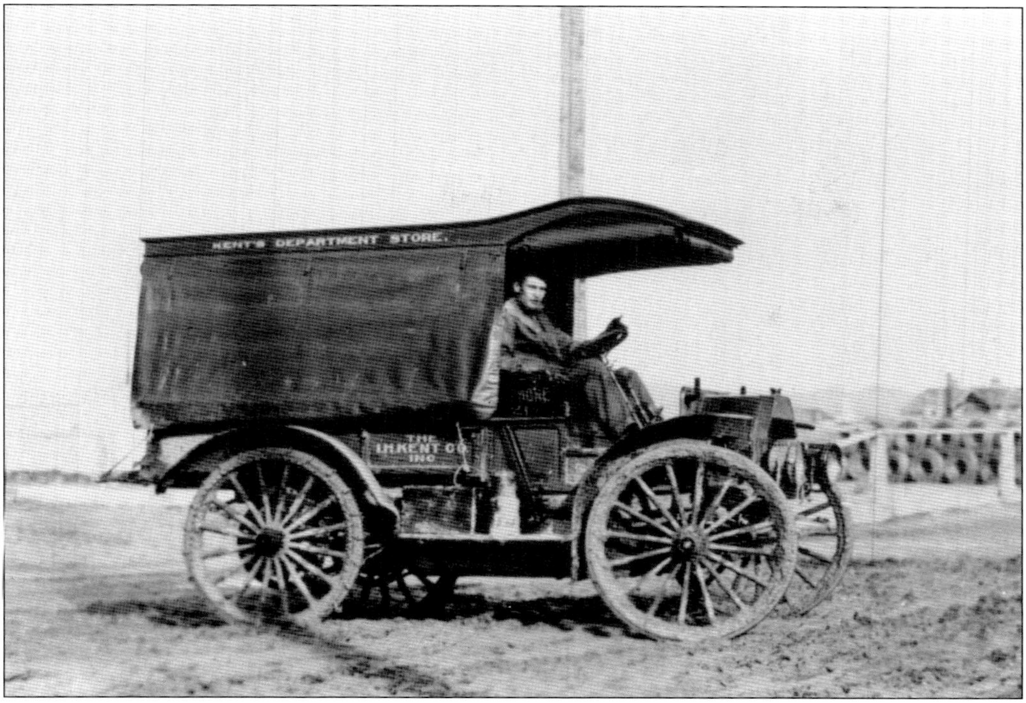

An I.H. Kent company produce wagon makes the delivery rounds.

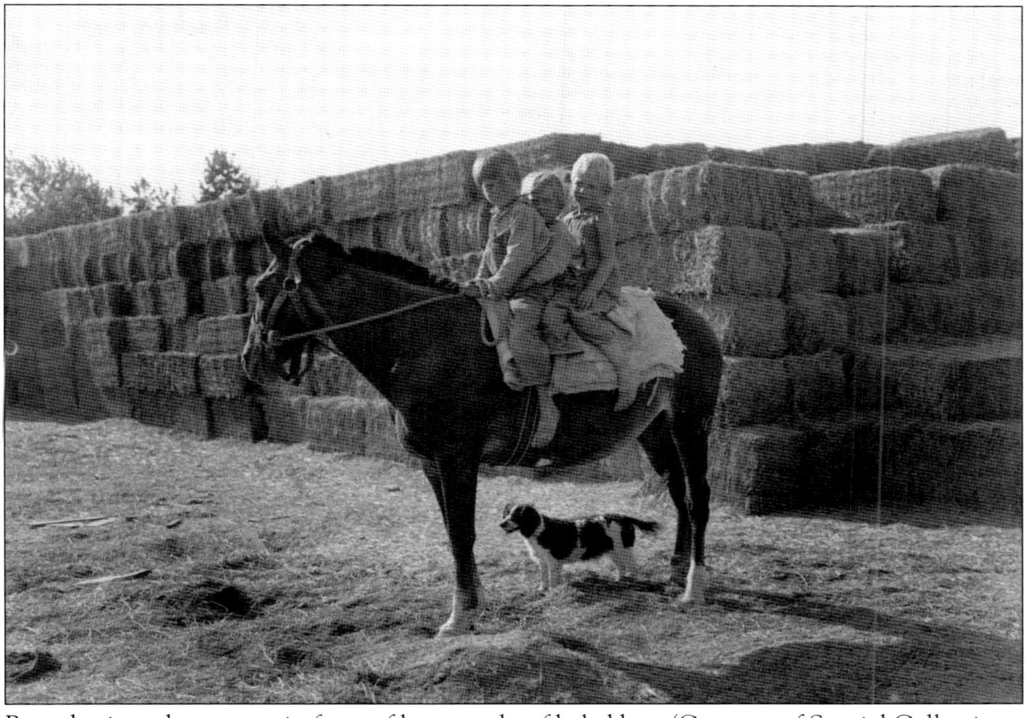
Boys sharing a horse pose in front of large stacks of baled hay. (Courtesy of Special Collections, University of Nevada, Reno Libraries.)

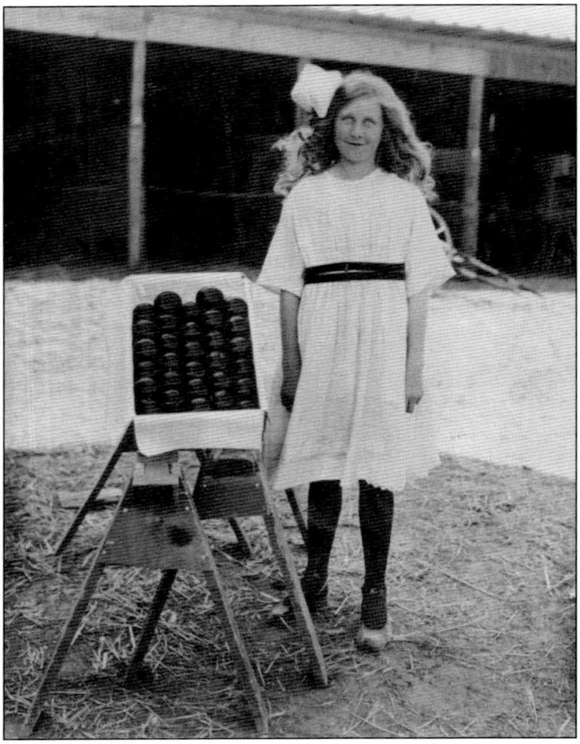

Thelma Johnson won first place for her tomatoes entry in the 1916 Nevada State Fair, held in Fallon.

On horseback, Miss Louise Wendt surveys her Harmon District homestead.

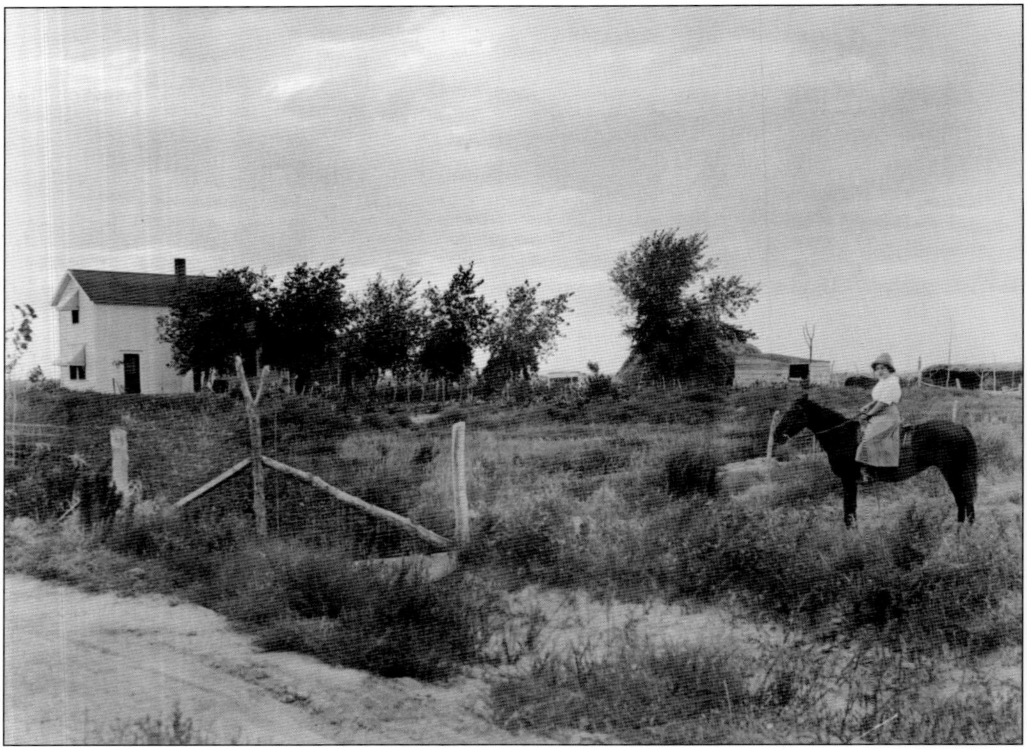

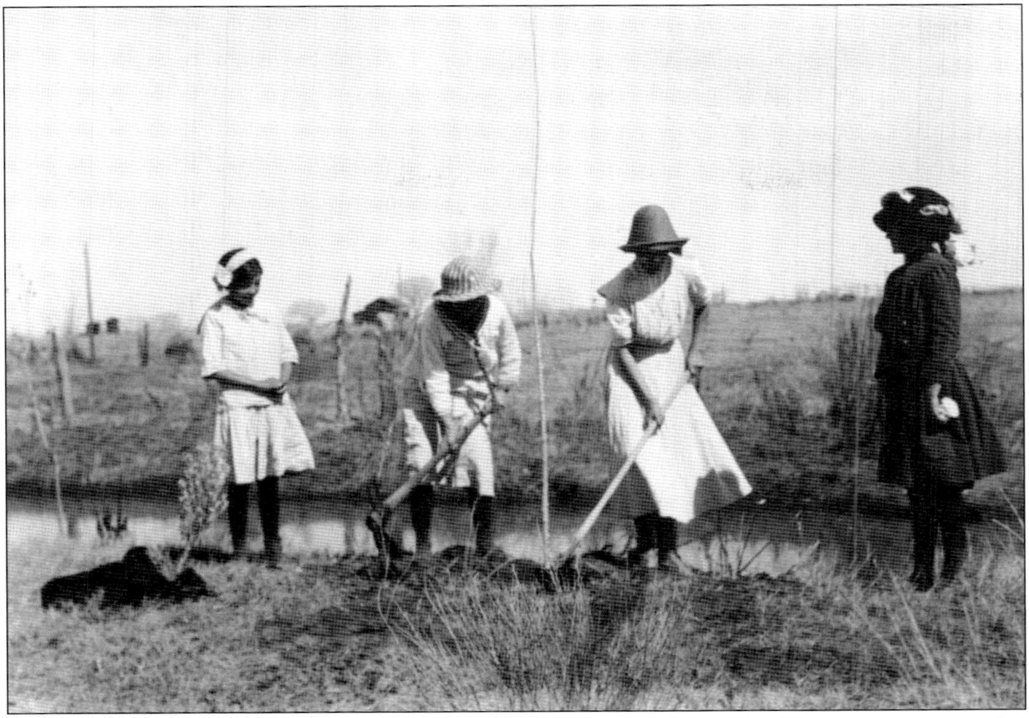

Women work together planting trees in the St. Clair District on Arbor Day. The trees were provided by the Experiment Farm, established by the US Reclamation Service to test seed varieties with a view to increase crop yields and control plant insects and diseases.

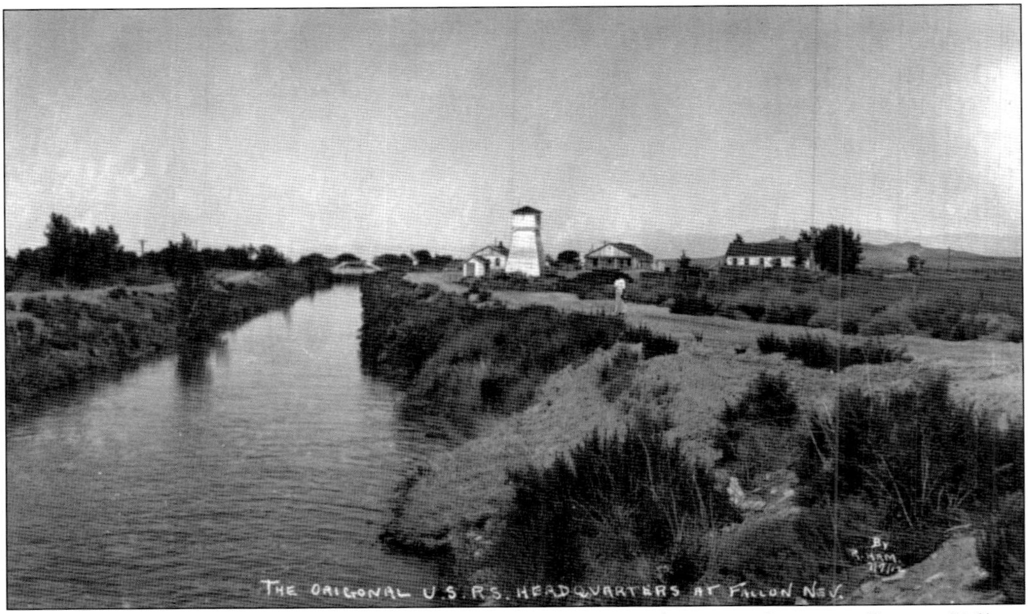

This is a July 1912 view of the earliest location of the US Reclamation Service offices in Fallon. (Courtesy of Special Collections, University of Nevada, Reno Libraries.)

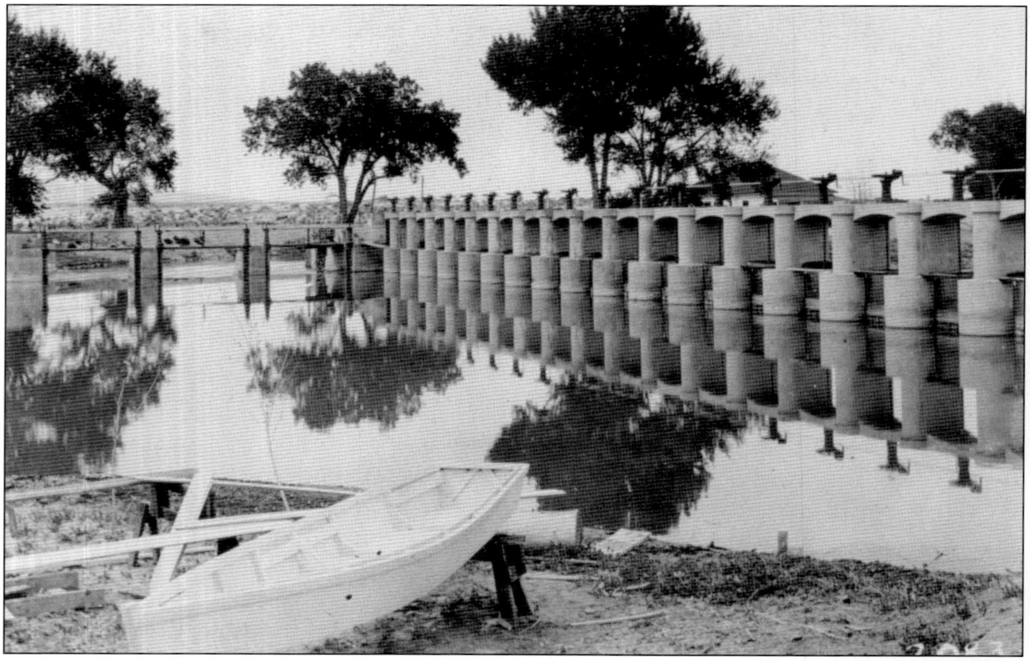

Diversion Dam was built on the Carson River below Lahontan Dam to regulate and direct waters released to downstream users. This photograph highlights the beauty and architectural complexity of the structure.

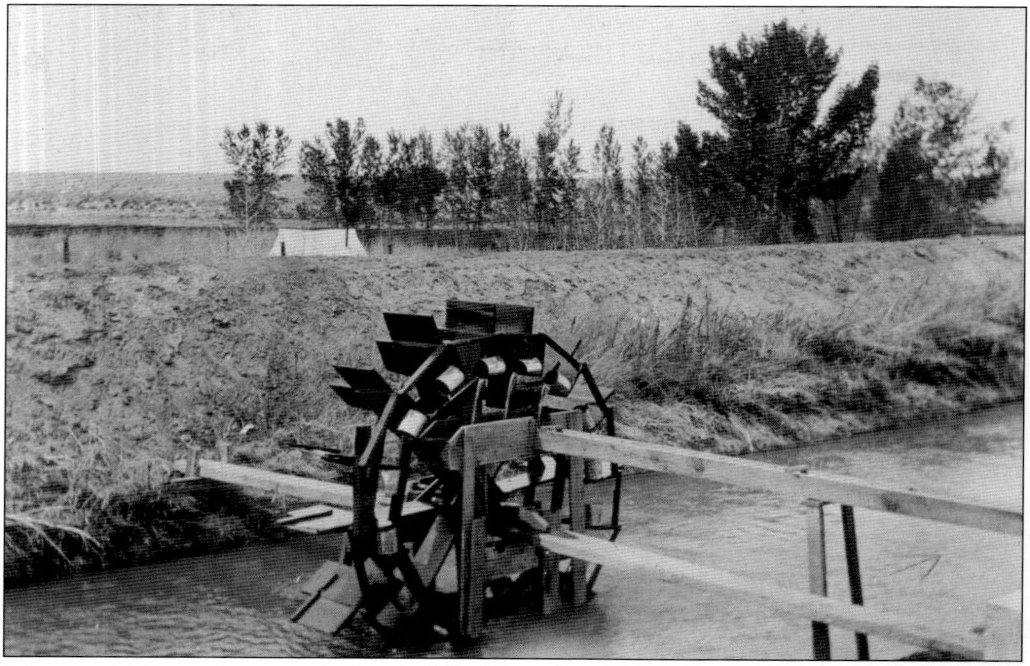

Irrigating in the desert was a challenge for most arrivals on the Newlands Project. Ranchers and farmers quickly learned how to best capitalize on the allocated water. Here, a small water wheel has been installed in a canal.

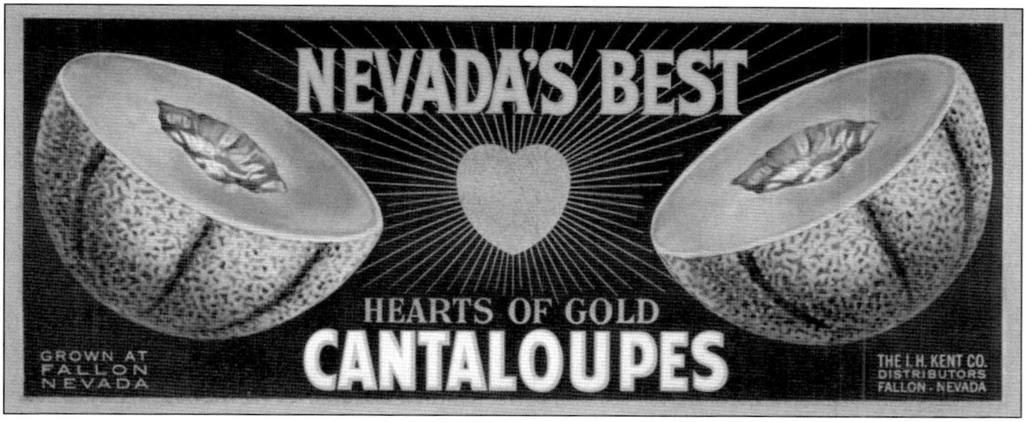

This image shows a label used for shipping and marketing Fallon's Hearts of Gold cantaloupe. The sweetness of the local Hearts of Gold variety has made it marketable throughout the land.

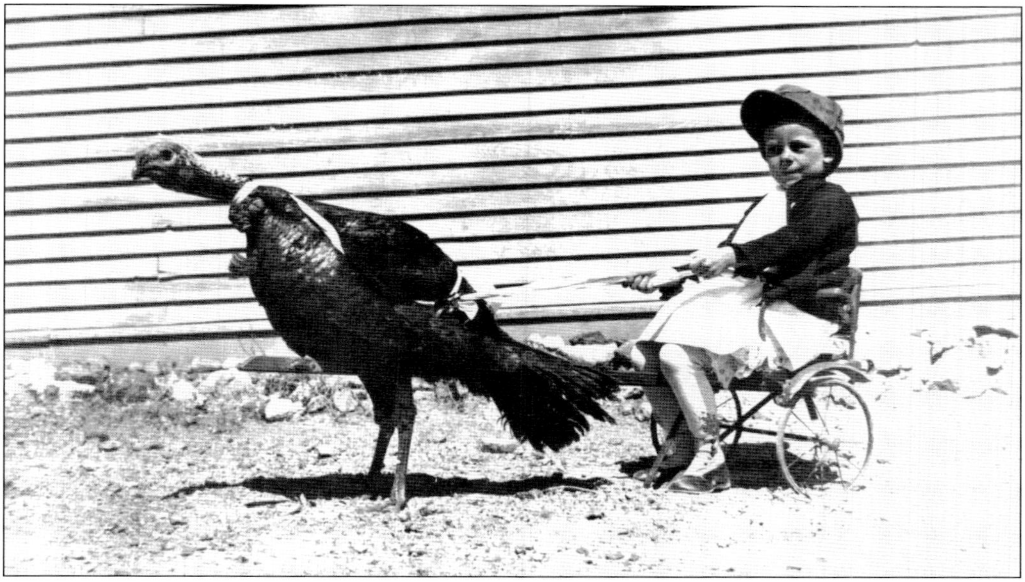

Like the Hearts of Gold melons, Fallon turkeys became nationally known during the 1920s and 1930s. Local folklore circulates that "Fallon Tom Turkey" was featured on the menu of the Waldorf Astoria hotel in New York City and that President Roosevelt was served Fallon turkey on an unspecified Thanksgiving. Here, Helen Blair, daughter of turkey producer Minnie Blair, harnesses the energy of a Fallon turkey.

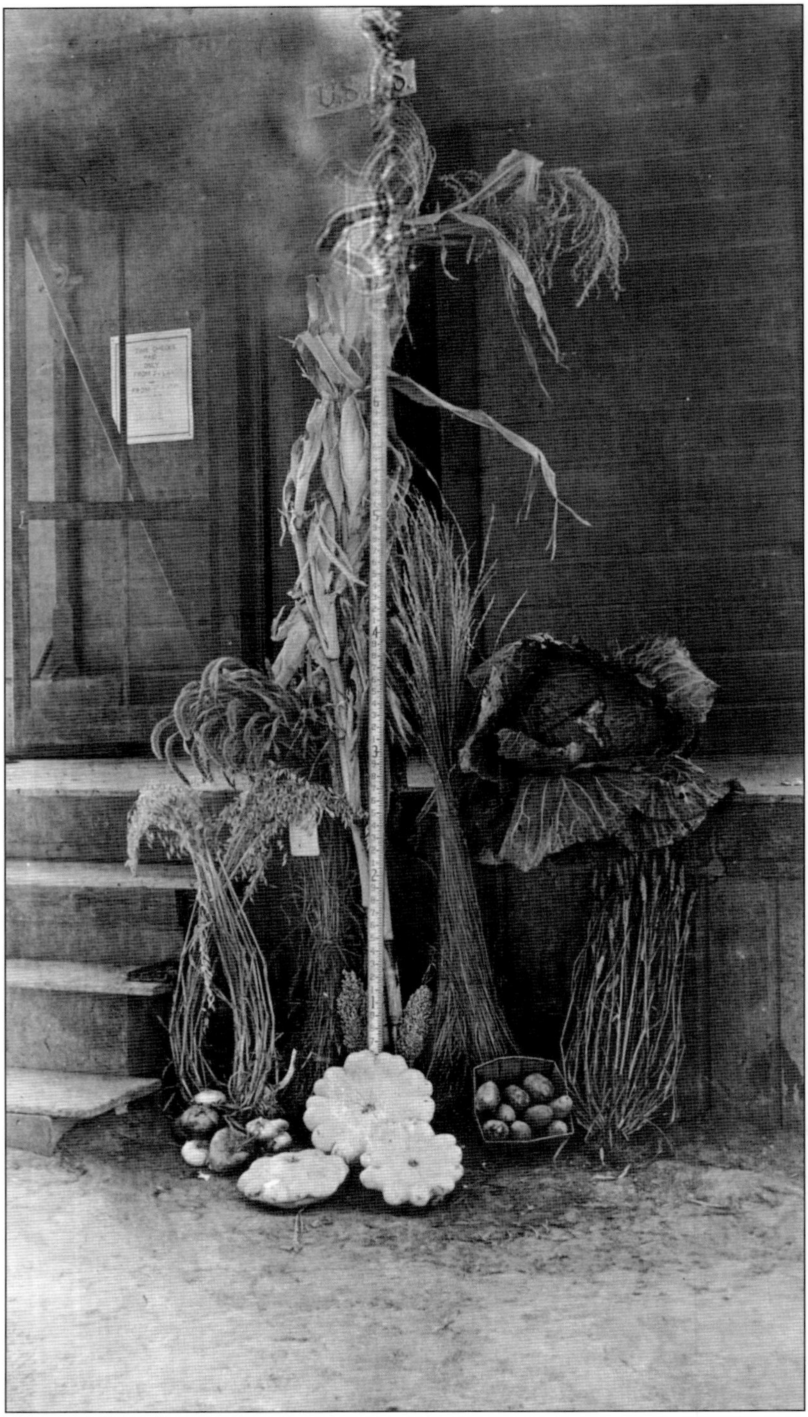

An artistic arrangement of squash, garlic, cabbage, potatoes, corn, and grains suggests the pride this family took in its harvests. (Courtesy of Special Collections, University of Nevada, Reno Libraries.)

Four

The Social Fabric

In the second and third decades of the 20th century, the nation fought a war, won a war, passed Prohibition laws, granted women the right to vote, embraced assembly line manufacturing and entered the worst depression of the country had ever experienced. While Fallon was affected, even changed, by the force of national currents, the area continued to develop and refine a unique local identity.

If someone were to peer into the Lahontan Valley on the eve of the Roaring Twenties, he or she would see the same optimism that characterized earlier times. Yet, most of the dreams of agricultural and business wealth remained elusive. The standard of living was relatively low, even before the Depression years lowered it even further. Rumor surfaced that there was enough oil in the substrata of Stillwater to make everybody rich, but the rumors died a sudden and disappointing death. Despite the economic realities, or perhaps because of them, a strong social nexus evolved, evidenced by increased membership in churches, enthusiastic support for schools, and a remarkable level of participation in clubs and organizations.

Some of the societies were purely local inventions, as their original names suggest. The newspapers of the time are filled with cheery reportage about dances held by the "Bunion Club," boys' nights out held at the "Alfalfa Club," activities for women at the "Artemisia Club," and duck hunts and banquets sponsored by the "Greenhead Club." Residents of the farming districts gathered often, with high spirits. They formed neighborhood sewing circles and women's clubs, several of which still meet. Others held fundraisers for their district schools and planned dances, parties, and rodeos.

Local branches of national organizations thrived. The Masonic orders grew in number and importance, and the literary and cultural club, the Draper Society, built a strong membership. Sporting events were popular in all corners of the community. Churchill County High School men's and women's athletic teams competed for coveted state trophies. City leagues sprung up. Sand lots became practice fields for future baseball stars.

When the Depression and World War II arrived, the community had the advantage of being tightly knit and strong.

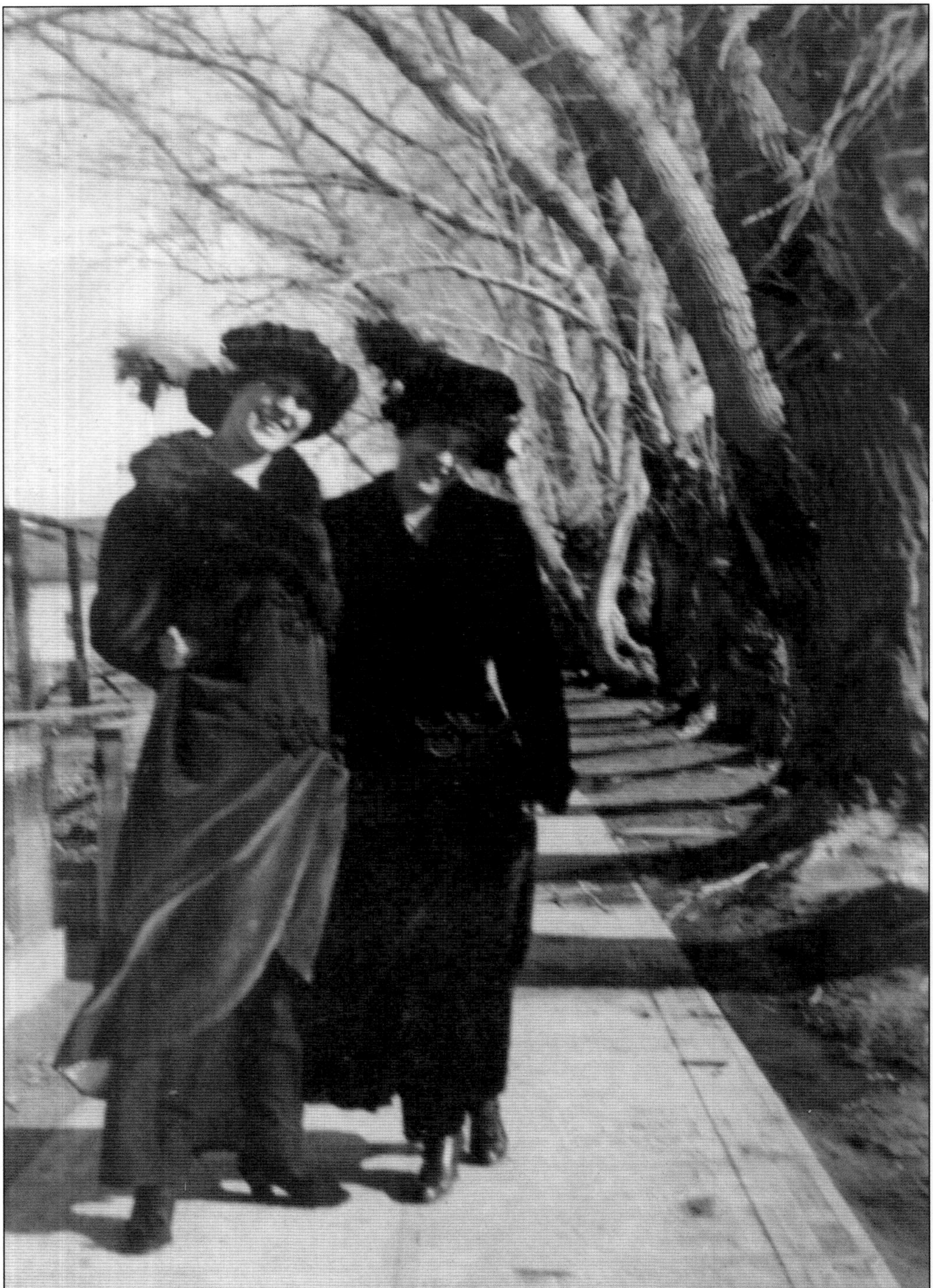

Two Fallon ladies take a stroll down Williams Avenue. The street was shaded by a canopy of cottonwood trees until progress decreed that the traffic lanes should be widened.

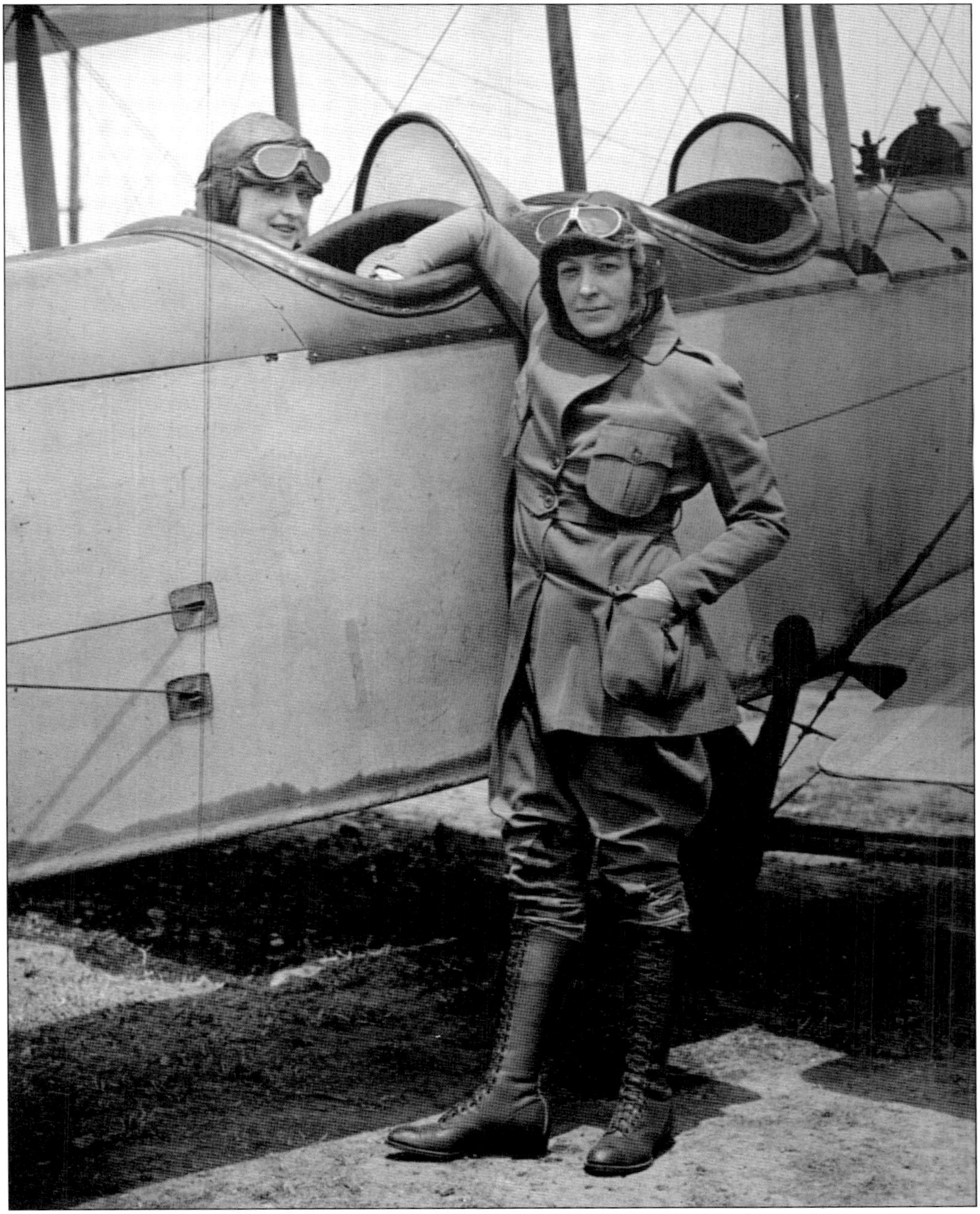

Here, Fallon's Ada Williams Keddie (standing beside the plane), daughter of one of Fallon's founding fathers, Warren Williams, personifies the new woman of the 1920s. She is dressed for flight and ready to soar. Keddie's husband, Arthur Keddie, was a leader in the community and a state senator. Unfortunately, he died young in a tragic accident. Fallon streets Ada and Keddie are named for them.

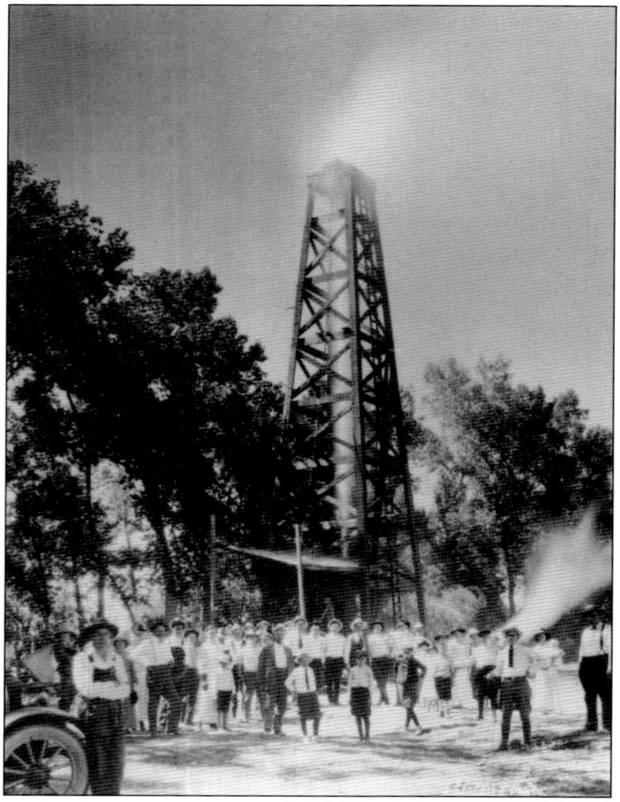

Around 1920, rumors circulated that oil slicks had surfaced in water wells near Stillwater and Sand Springs. By 1921, ten companies were selling oil stocks, their buyers hoping to cash in on Fallon's black gold. Disappointingly, most of the gushers were geysers of hot water. At left, a crowd waits for the elusive gusher. Below, Wheeler Oil Syndicate drills for oil.

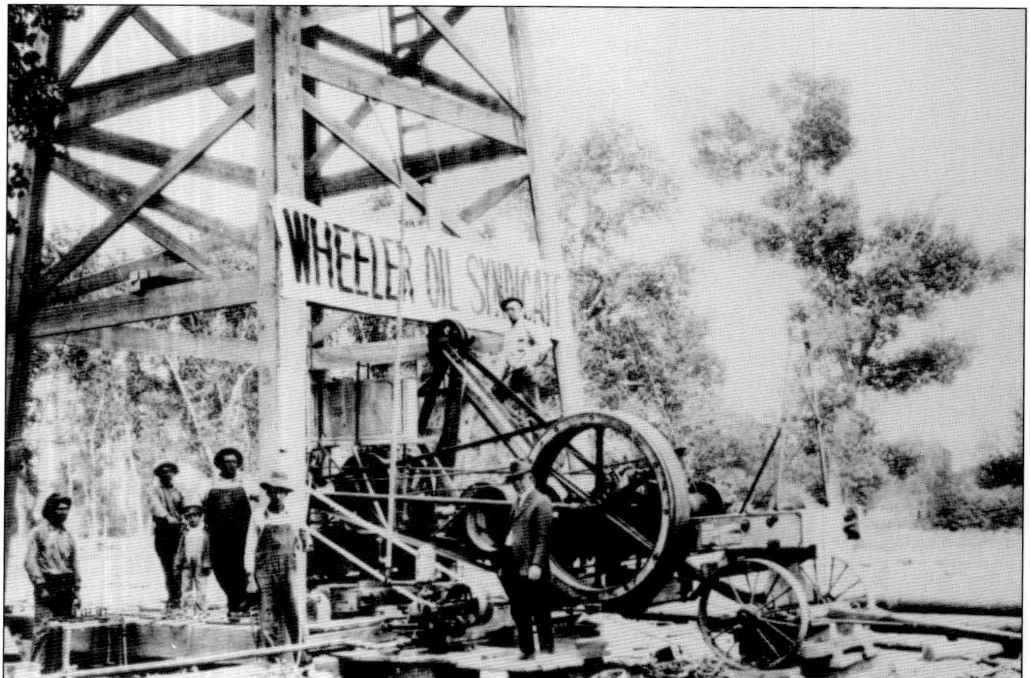

In this pre-Prohibition photograph, new Fallon sidewalks welcome patrons to the Hoffman Bar on Maine Street's west side.

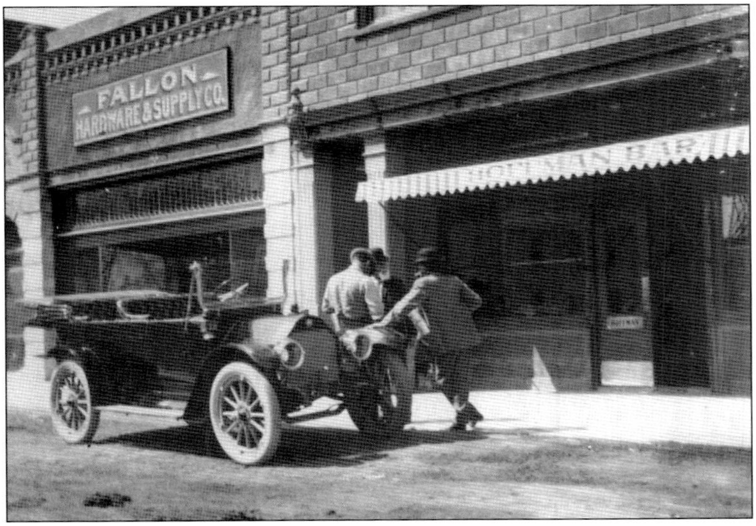

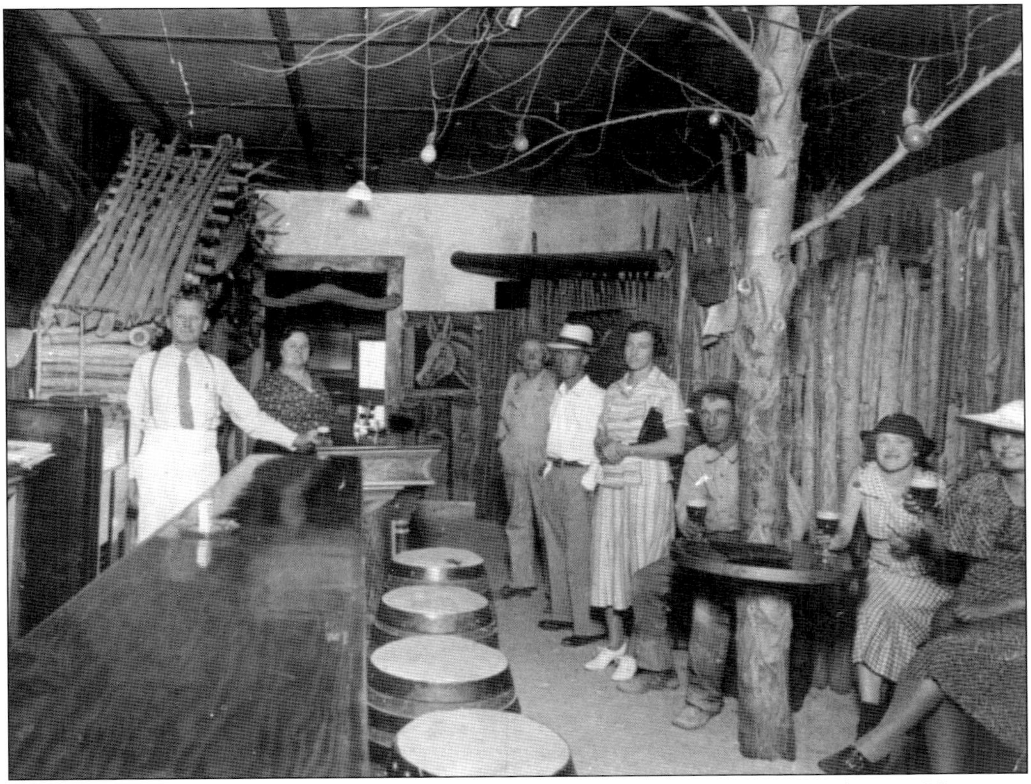

Following the repeal of Prohibition, the Corral Bar became a Maine Street fixture. Historian Frederick Allen observes that after bars reopened across America, there was more "mixed drinking" than ever, referring to female clientele. From left to right are Jack Brite, owner and builder of the bar; Jack's wife, Lillie; unidentified; Chet Douglas, bartender; Edna Erb Douglas; Roy Tucker; Babe Tucker; and unidentified.

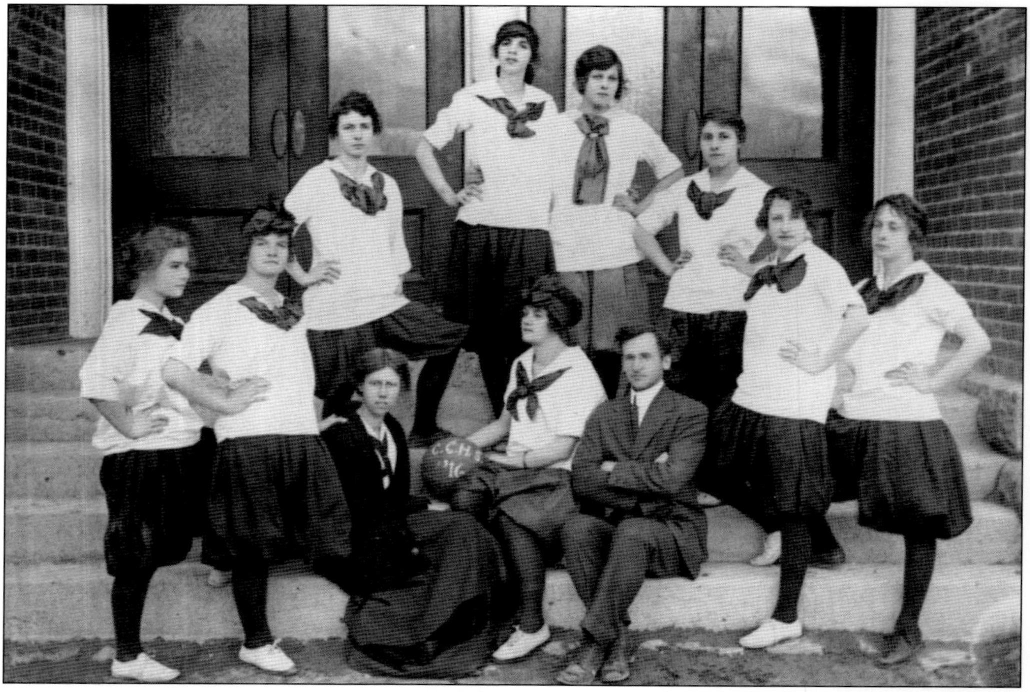

Pictured here is the Churchill County High School girls' basketball team of 1916. From left to right are (first row) Ruth Mary Geissler, Mattie Steinbrook (captain), and Professor McKillop; (second row) Blanche Ferguson, Evelyn Steinbrook, Clare Melton, Inez Laveaga, Fay Moody, Margaret Dolf, Vera Wickland, and Irma Bendle.

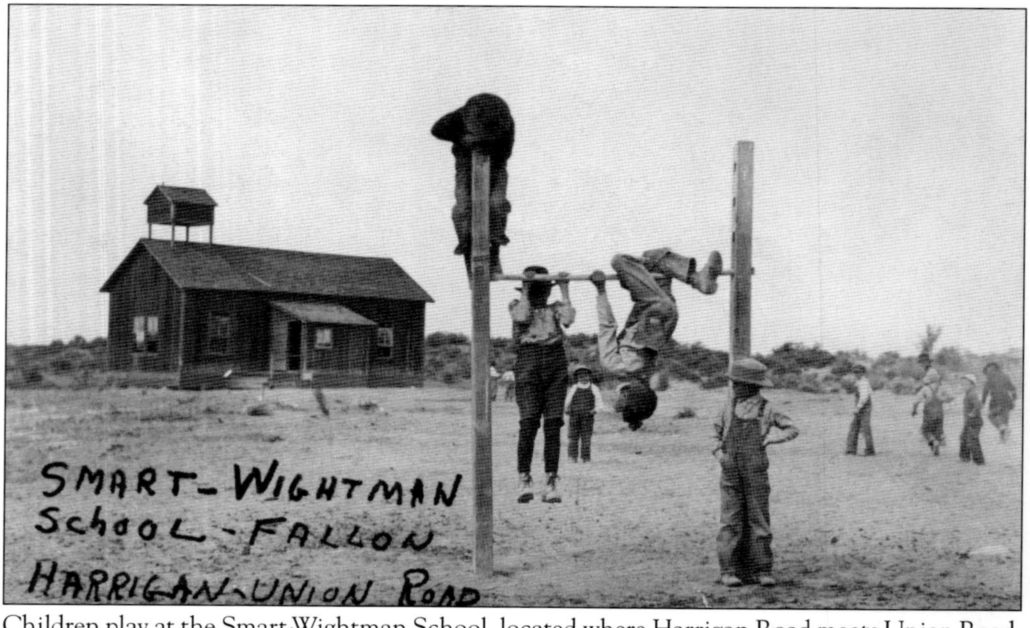

Children play at the Smart-Wightman School, located where Harrigan Road meets Union Road. Each rural farm district built and maintained an elementary school. The schools were gradually consolidated, and by the mid-1950s all rural children were bused to Fallon schools.

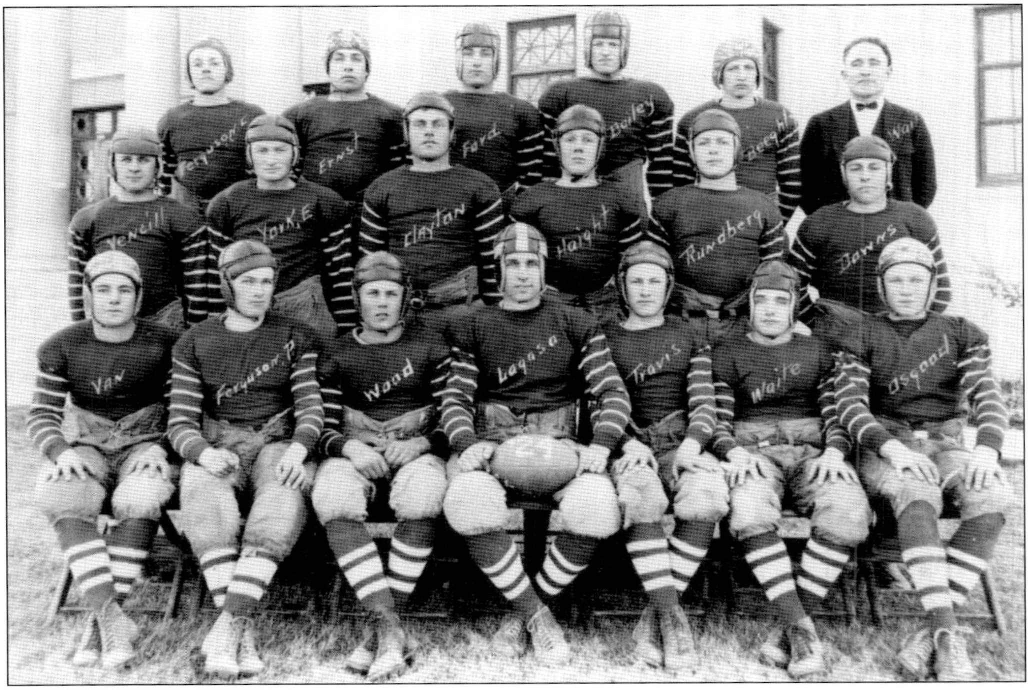

Pictured here is the 1924 Churchill County High School football team. The last names of the players are affixed to their jerseys.

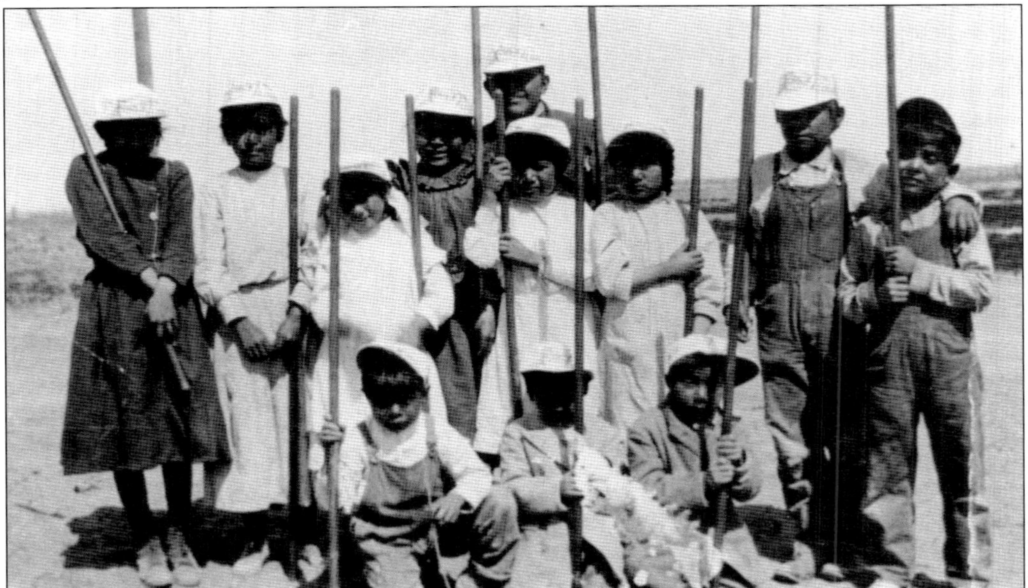

Children participate in a drill of some kind at the Immanuel Indian Mission School. An Indian Day School, run by the Indian Service, and an Indian Mission, run by Baptists, were both built in close proximity to the Stillwater Indian Reservation in 1908 and 1913, respectively. The Baptist missionaries held classes in religion and domestic arts, apparently attended by the day school students.

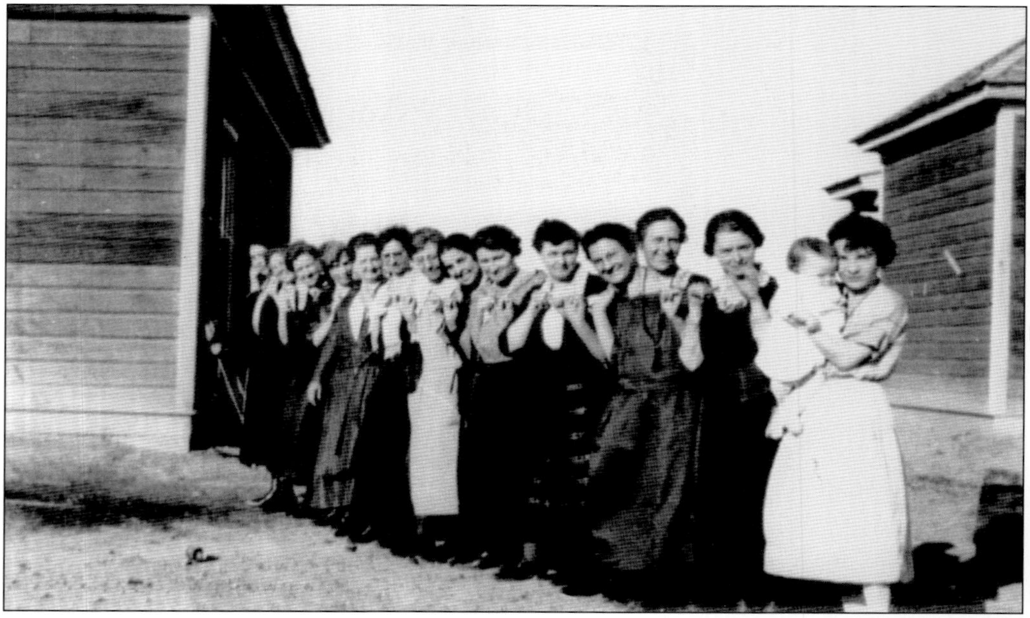

Rural districts funded and built schools, but they also formed social clubs where neighbors met to sew, quilt, bake, and dance. Pictured here are members of the Stillwater Ladies Friendly Club.

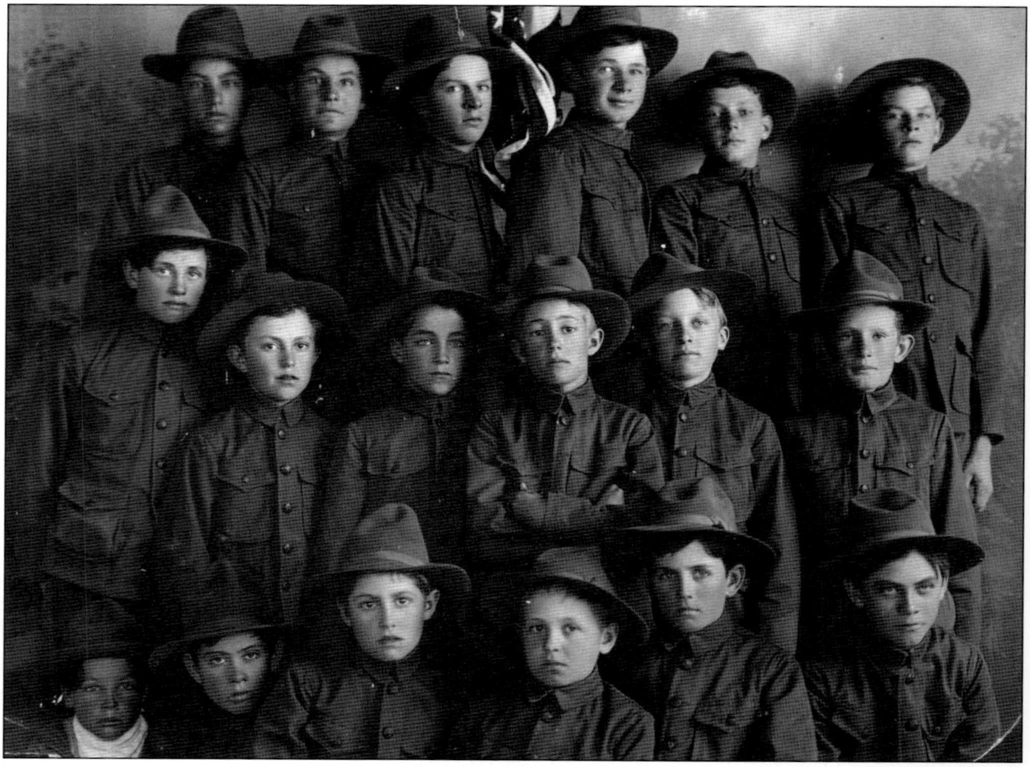

This 1908 photograph shows Fallon's first Boy Scout troop. Third from the left in the bottom row is Ernest J. Maupin Jr.

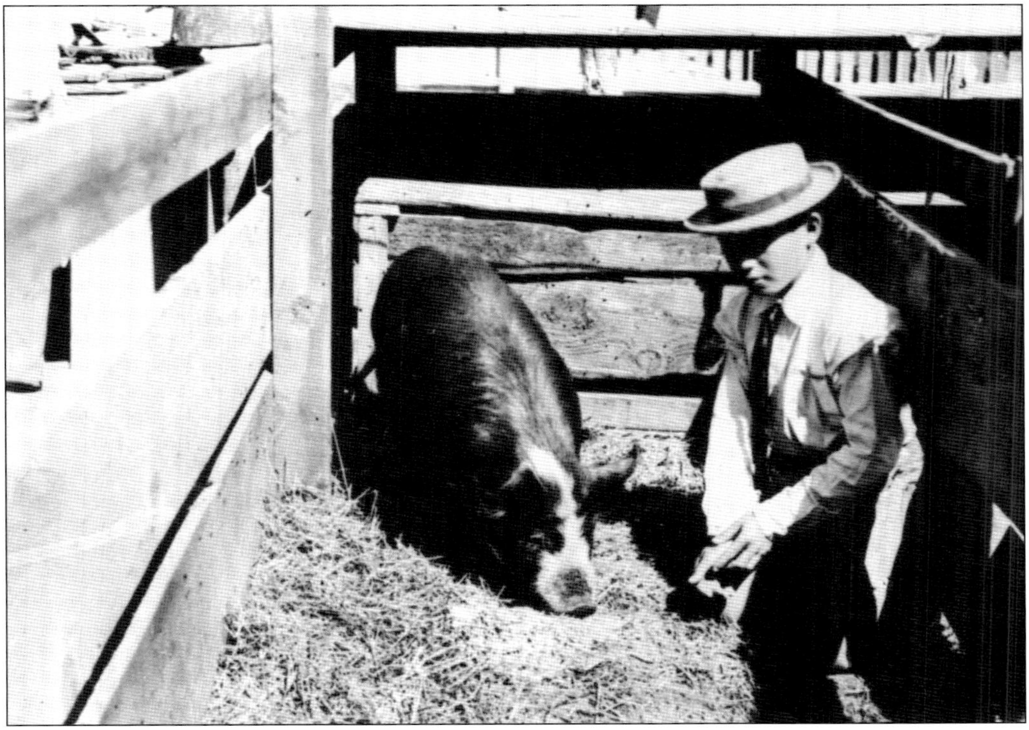

Leslie Sanford, a member of the Boys' Better Livestock Club, shows off his prize-winning pig.

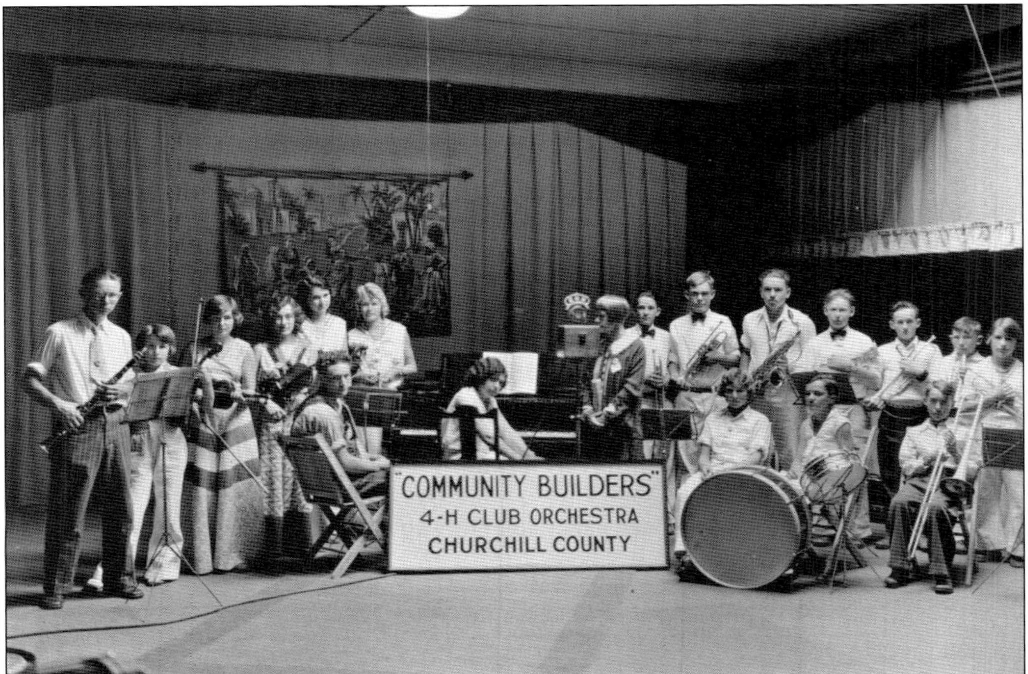

The members of the Community Builders 4-H Club Orchestra pose for this photograph.

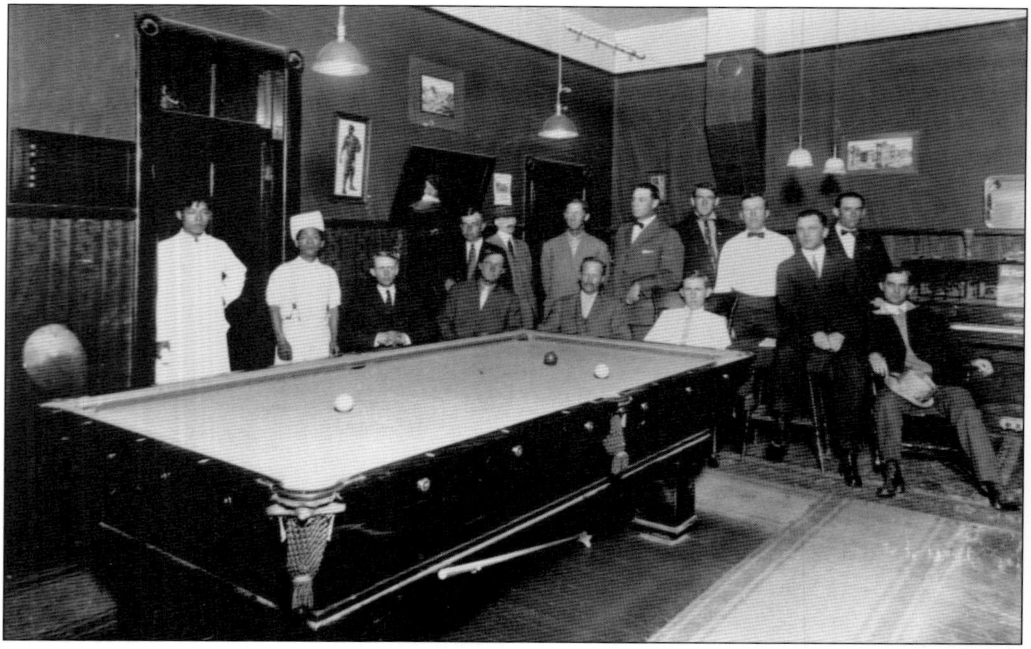

Single young men in Fallon banded together around 1906 to form the Alfalfa Club. Many of them boarded at the Allen House, where they are shown in 1911 gathered around their locally famous large and perpetually busy pool table. The Japanese cook, Eddie, was known throughout town for helping the Alfalfa Club's members host the single ladies.

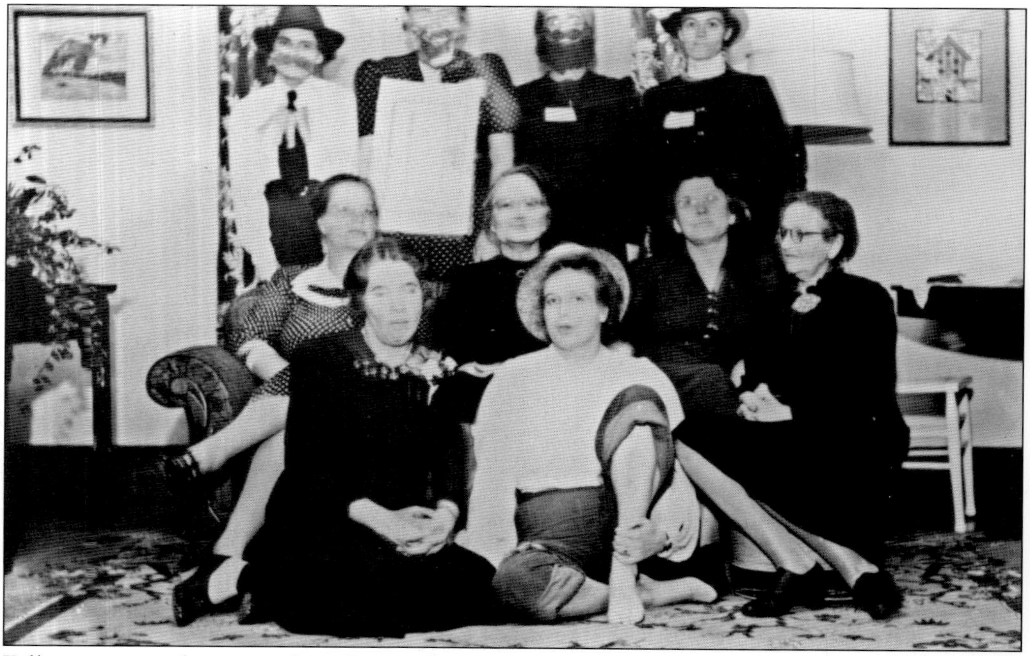

Fallon women who enjoyed reading and writing were encouraged to join the Scribblers' Club. Here, members are dressed to hint at a book title. Readers are invited to guess the titles of any of their books.

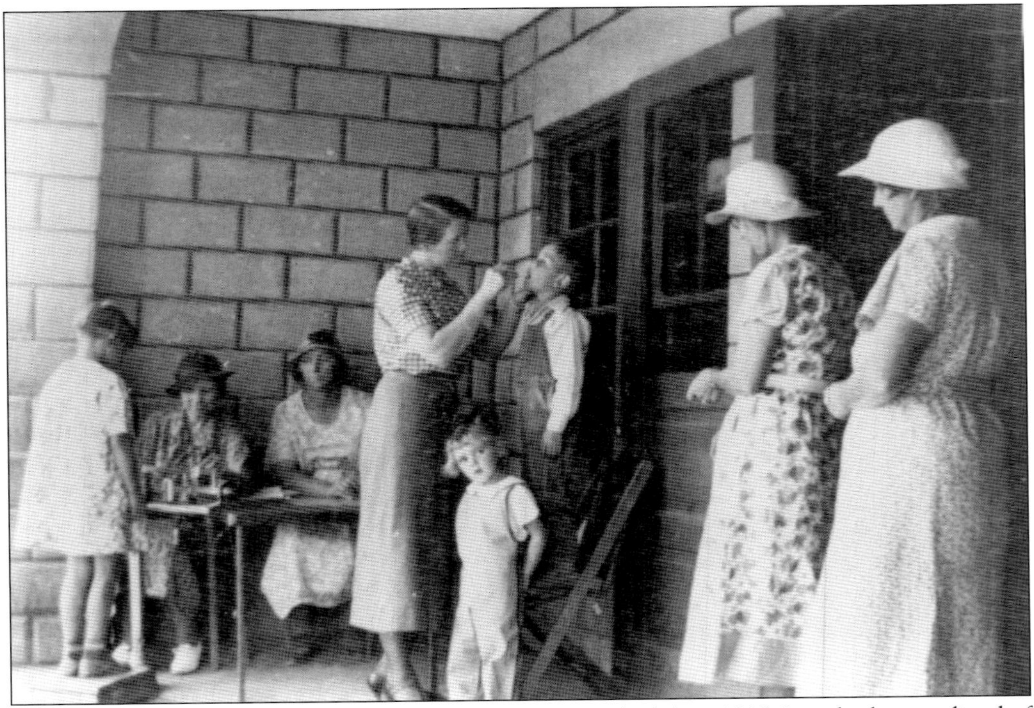

Members of Harmon District formed the Harmony Social Club in 1915. It is the longest lived of the district social organizations and has current membership. Here, Lina and Jessie Freeman are seated at a card table while monitoring a "Keep Growing Contest."

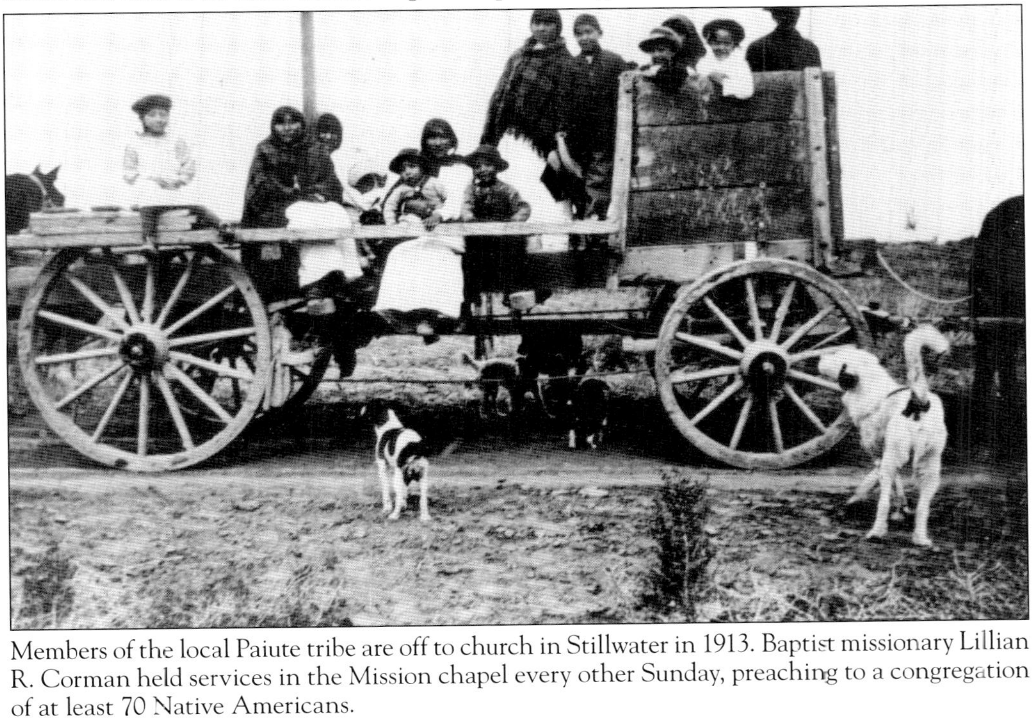

Members of the local Paiute tribe are off to church in Stillwater in 1913. Baptist missionary Lillian R. Corman held services in the Mission chapel every other Sunday, preaching to a congregation of at least 70 Native Americans.

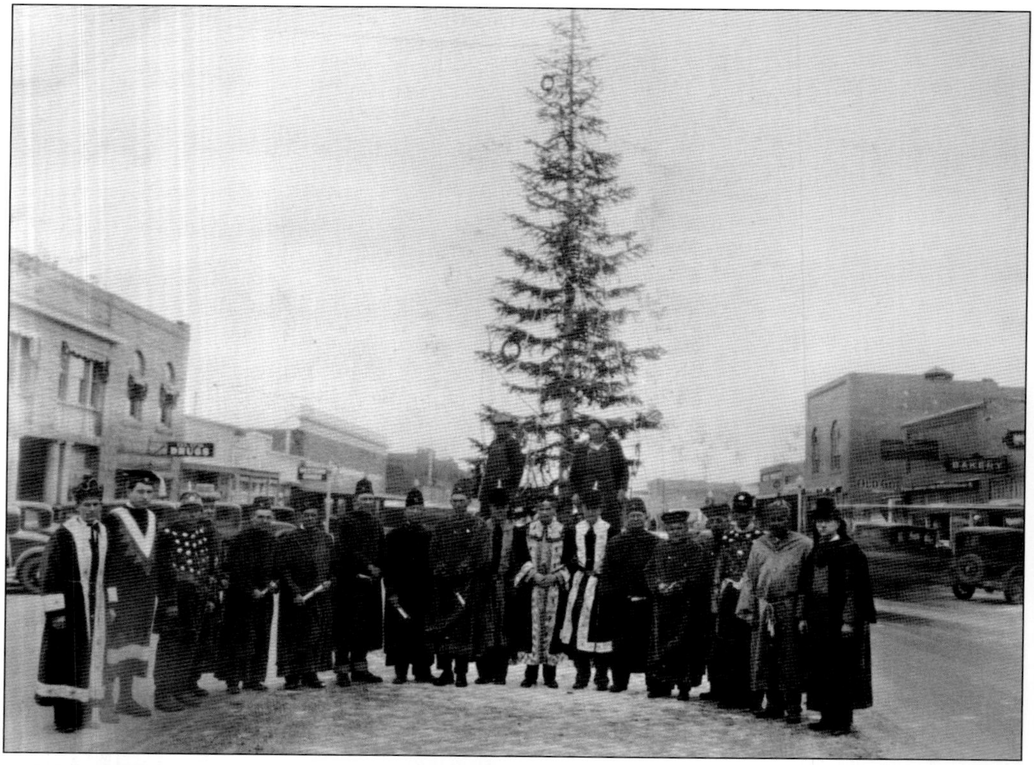

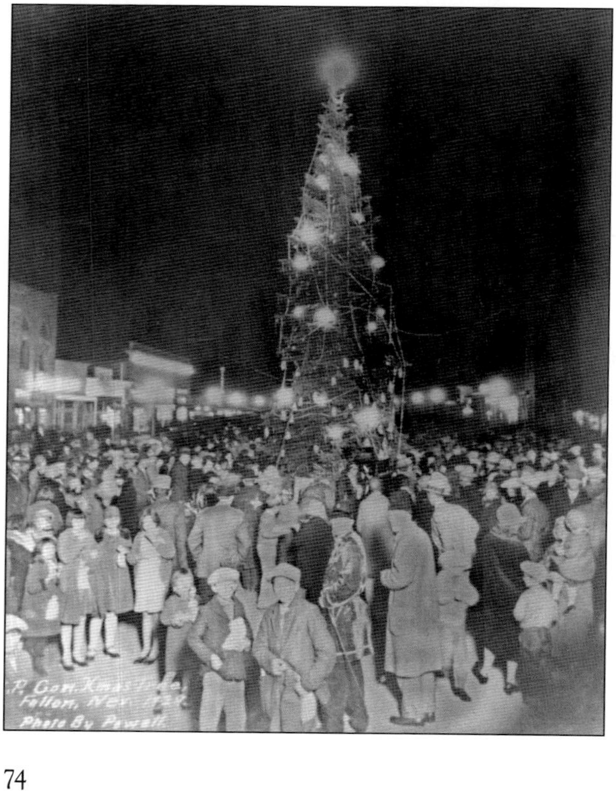

Members of the Fallon Knights of Pythias began a long-standing tradition in 1929 when they held a ceremony to light a Christmas tree raised in the center of Maine Street. A 50-foot tree is still erected each year in the same spot. The city sponsors a lighting ceremony attended by many hundreds of celebrants.

Here, the Knights of Pythias light the Christmas tree in 1930. Following national trends, membership in local branches of national fraternal organizations flourished until recently. Fallon's Fraternal Hall, on Maine Street, was designed to provide stylish meeting rooms and a banquet hall for members of the Knights of Pythias and Masonic orders.

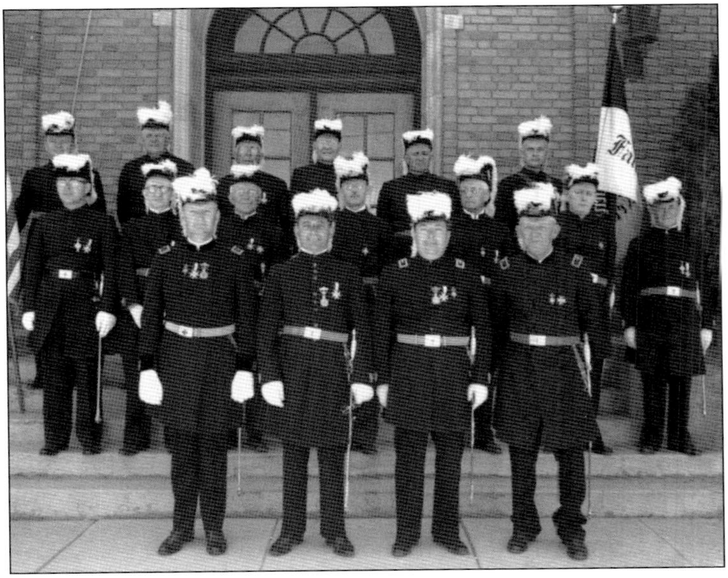

Seventeen of the sixty members of the Lahontan Commandary of Knights Templar stand in front of city hall in 1954. From left to right are (first row) Carl Dodge, Lester Kirn, Frank Woodliff, and H.R. Atkinson; (second row) Don Cooper, Percy A. Bailey, Roy Krukenberg, A.B. Andrews, Dale Reed, C.L. Evans, and Alfred Luke; (third row) Dr. C.P. McCuskey, J.W. Johnson, Charles Ogee, E.H. Hursh, W.W. Whitaker, and Loring Primeaux.

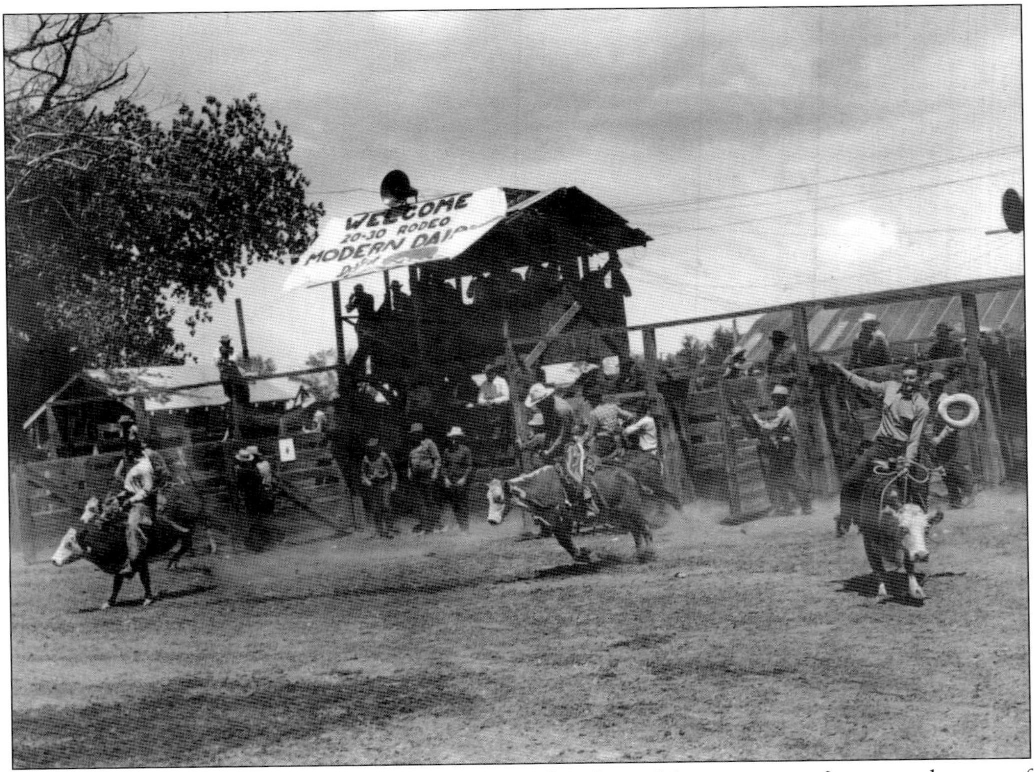

Fallon's 20-30 Club was organized, as the name implies, by and for young men between the ages of 20 and 30. Formed in the 1920s, they were very active in the community, holding fundraisers for civic projects and sponsoring the popular 20-30 Club rodeo, shown here at the "old" fairgrounds on Williams Avenue west of Venturacci Lane. (Courtesy of the Nevada Historical Society.)

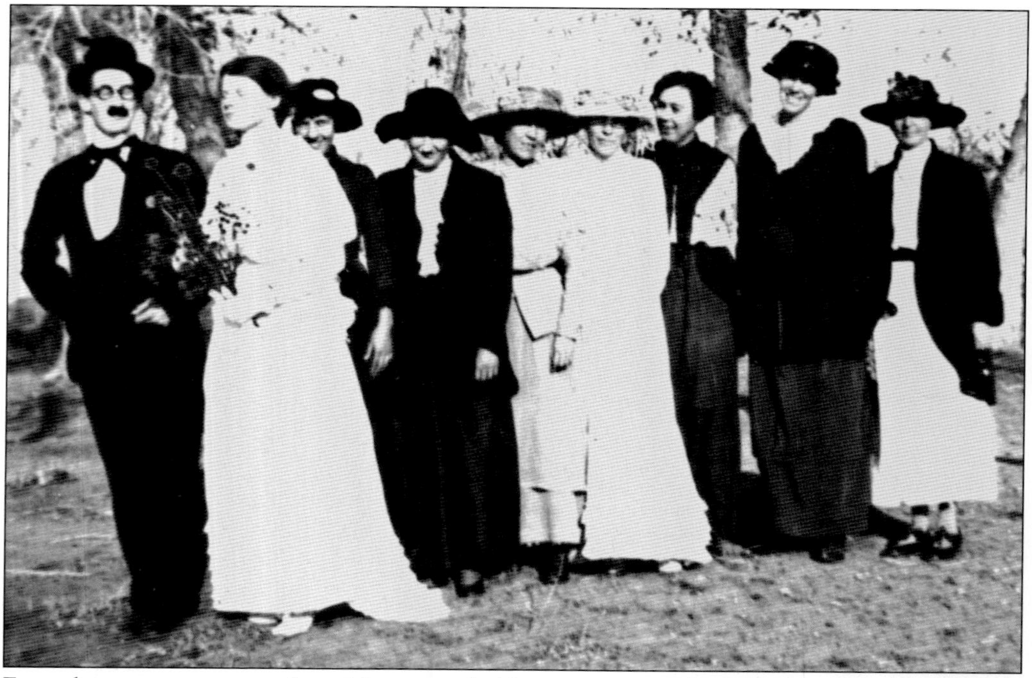

For unknown reasons, mock weddings were held at meetings of the Stillwater Friendly Club and the Harmony Club. Pictured is a 1939 mock wedding held at the Stillwater Friendly Club.

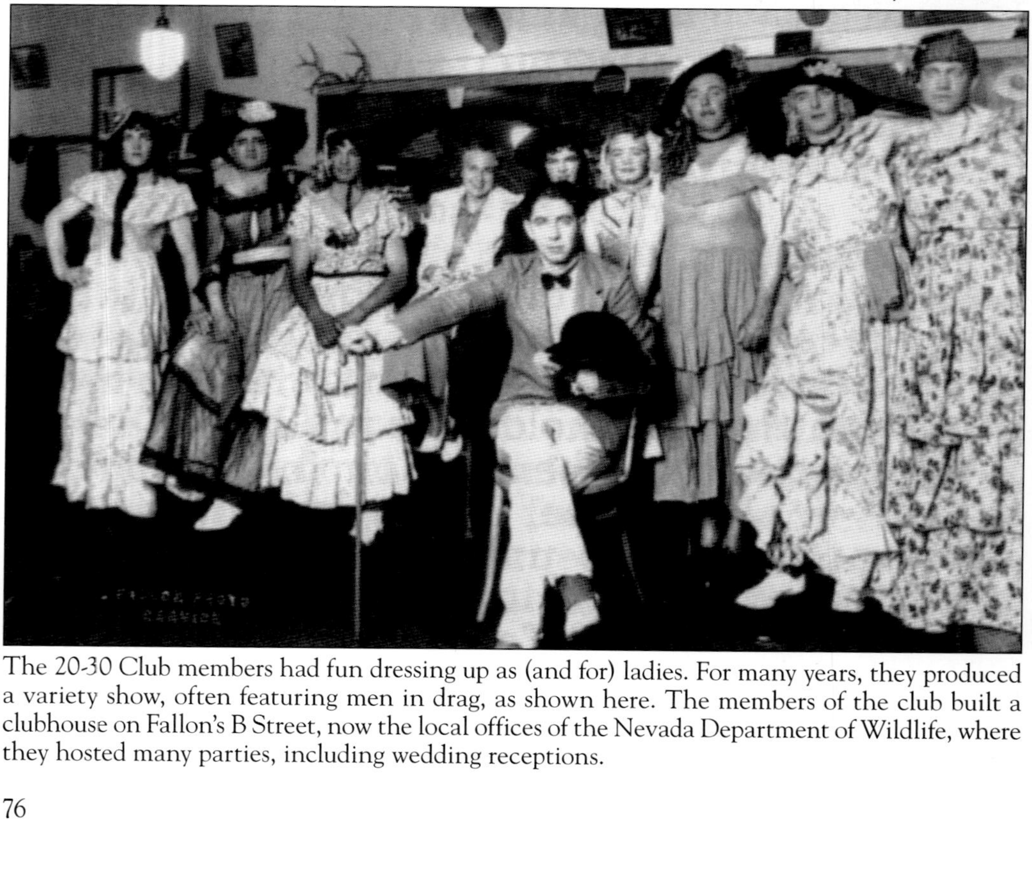

The 20-30 Club members had fun dressing up as (and for) ladies. For many years, they produced a variety show, often featuring men in drag, as shown here. The members of the club built a clubhouse on Fallon's B Street, now the local offices of the Nevada Department of Wildlife, where they hosted many parties, including wedding receptions.

St. Patrick's Catholic Church was built in 1913. Prior to then, Mass was celebrated in the upper-floor chambers of the courthouse, and the priest came by stage from Hazen.

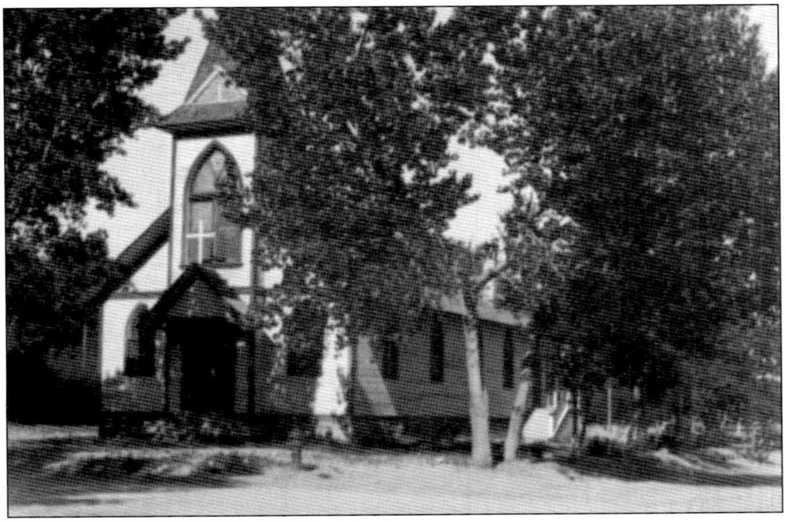

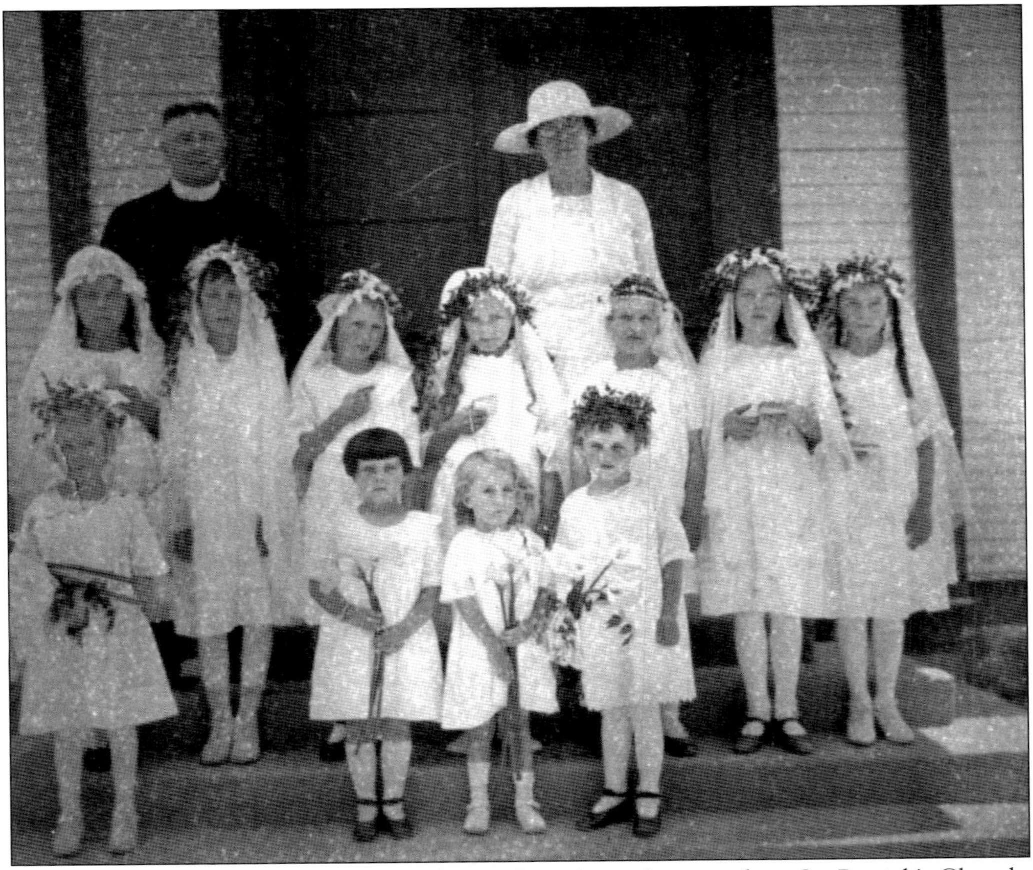

In 1921, the First Holy Communion class gathers for a photograph at St. Patrick's Church. Pictured are Helen Murphy, Helen Jesch, Marguerite Covell, Frances Jesch, Grace Hannifan, Agnes McDonnell, Eileen Hannifan, Agnes Brown, Kathleen Mason, Dorothy Mason, and Mollie Donovan. Father Meehan and Elsa Dietz stand behind the class members.

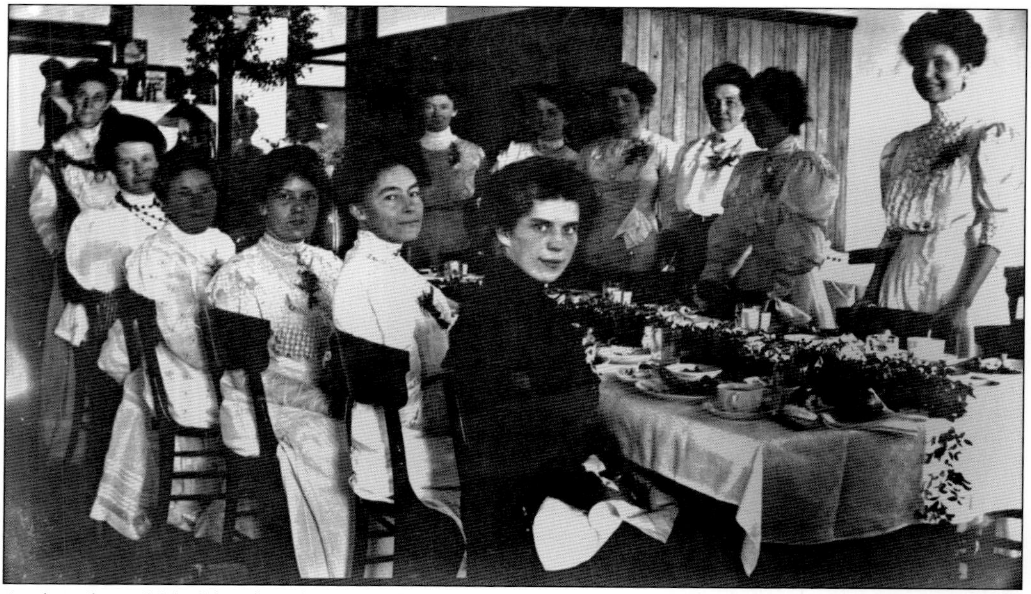

A church guild holds a luncheon at the Ernie Loring home on East Richards Street.

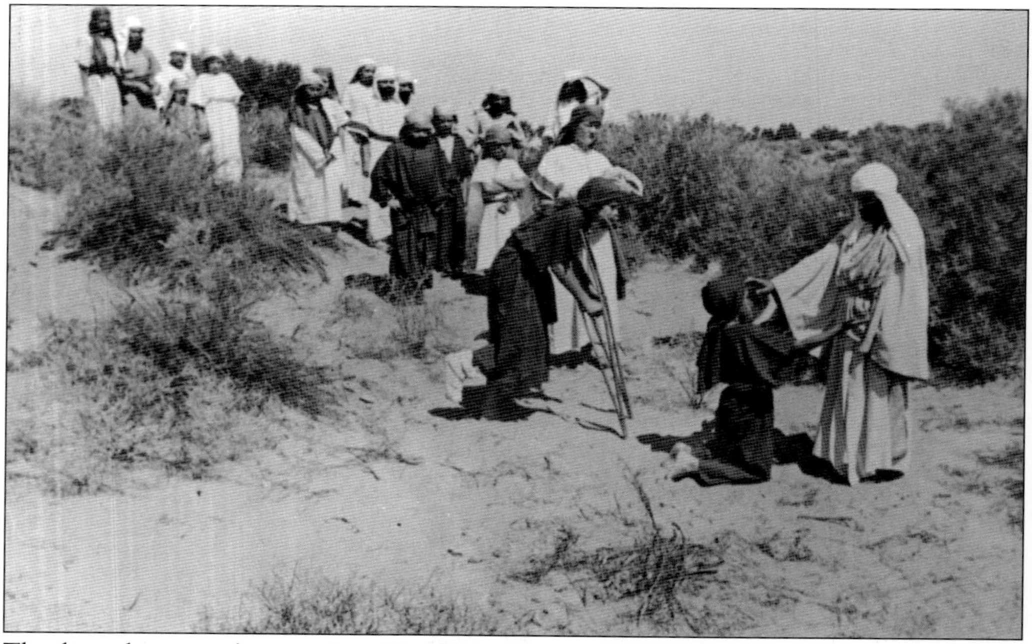

The desert becomes the stage for a New Testament pageant presented by a Sunday school class of the Fallon Methodist Church. As part of the dramatic action, a child on crutches stands in line to be healed by Jesus.

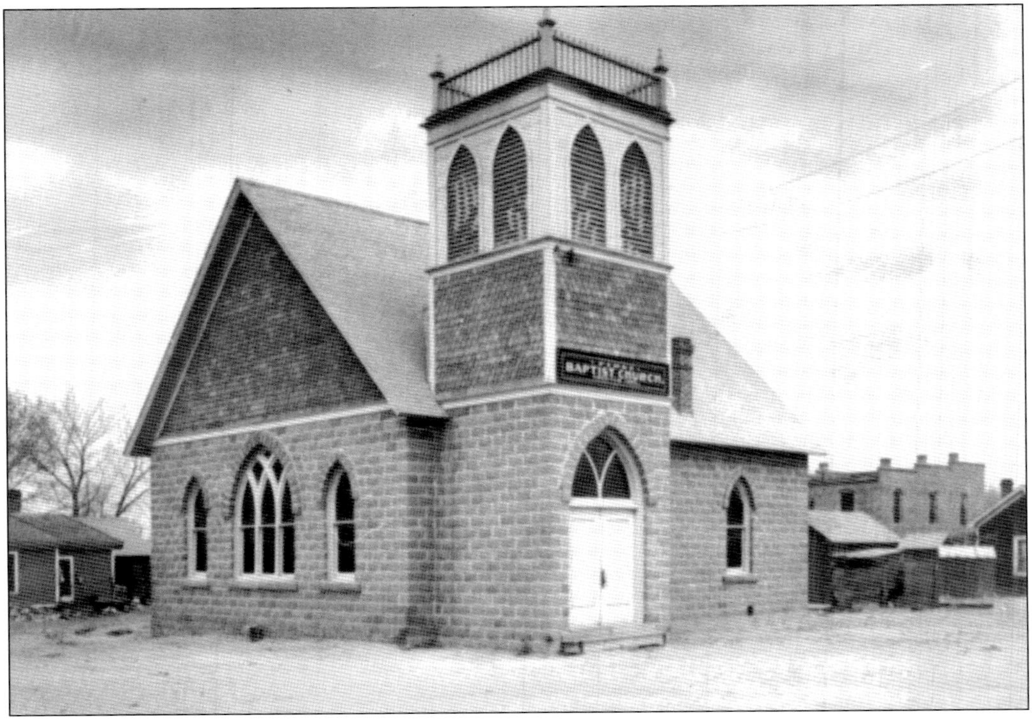

The Fallon Baptist Church was built on First Street in 1908. The City of Fallon now owns the building.

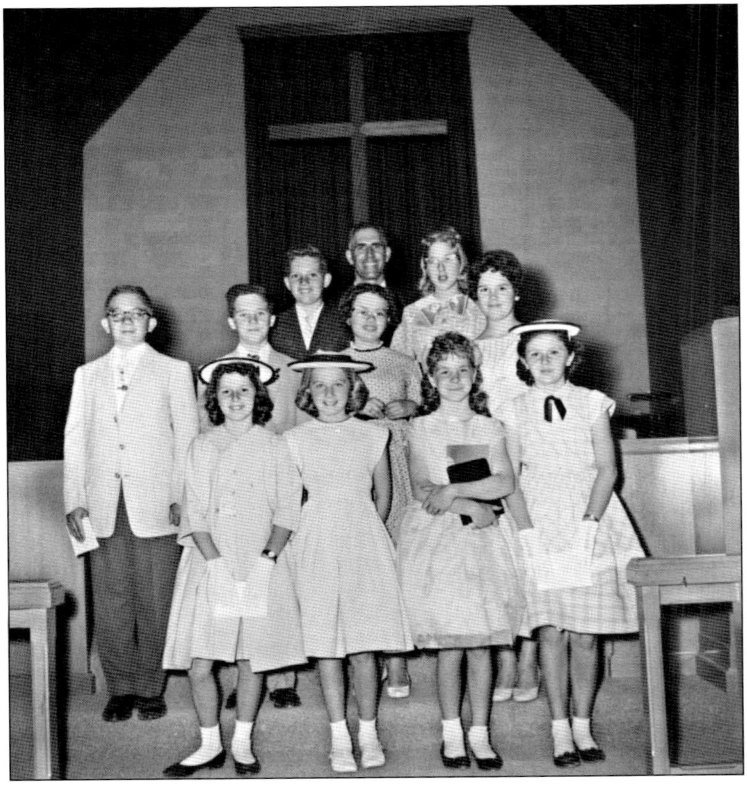

A youth group stands before the altar of the Fallon Methodist Church.

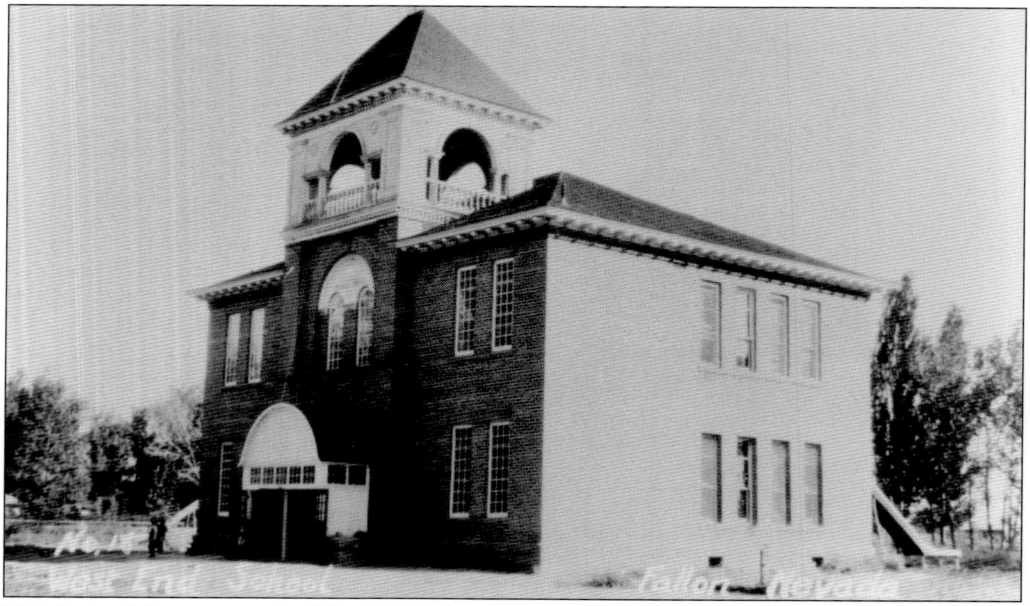

This beautiful structure, the West End School, was built in 1908 at a cost of $15,000. It was torn down in 1940 and replaced first with "cottage-style" buildings and then eventually with the one-story building now known as West End School.

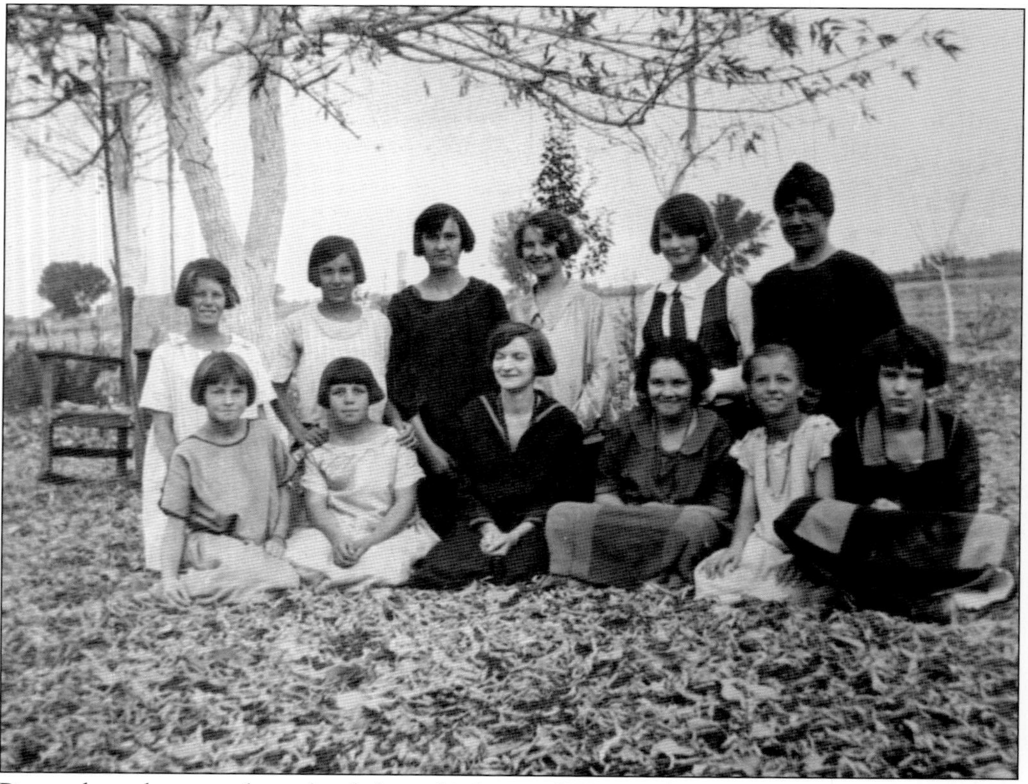

Pictured are the seventh- and eighth-grade classes of West End School in 1913.

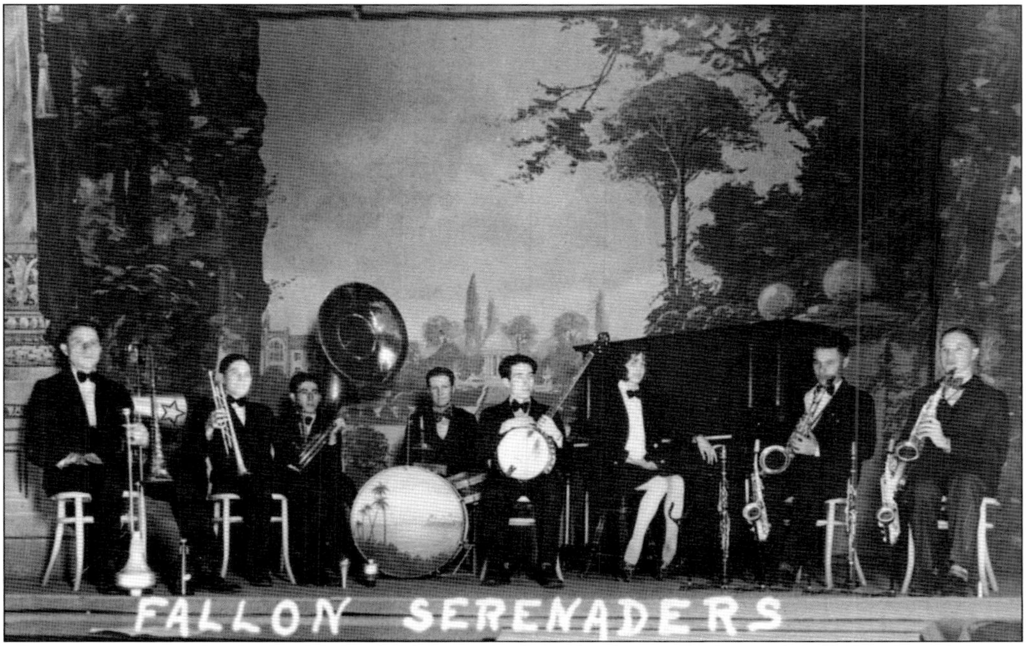

The Fallon Serenaders project professionalism in this 1927 photograph. From left to right are George Bunton, Darrel Berry, Bill Winder, Gary Callahan, Frank Woodliff, Louise Witherspoon, Vernon Mills, and Clarence Byrd.

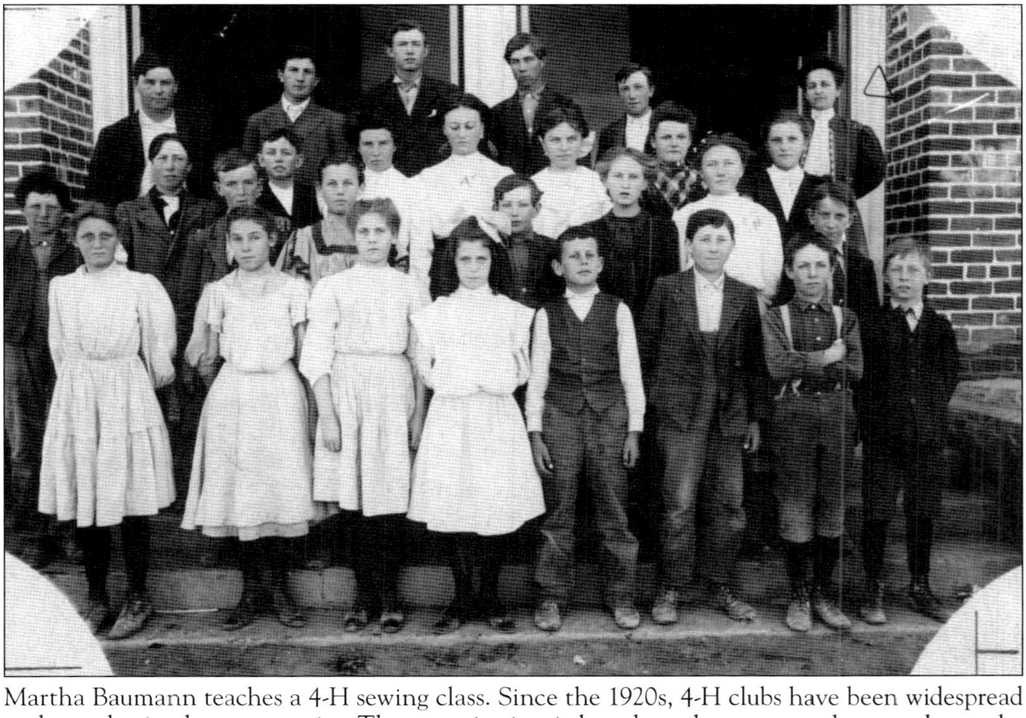

Martha Baumann teaches a 4-H sewing class. Since the 1920s, 4-H clubs have been widespread and popular in the community. The organization is based on the concept that one learns by doing, and equal attention is given to both genders.

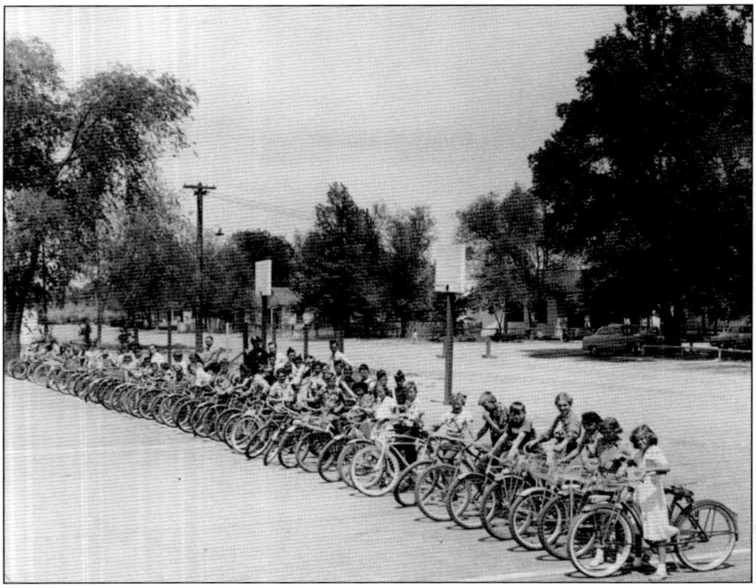

A Bike Patrol lines up for Safety Day at Oats Park School around 1945. Shown with the students are Al Seeliger, superintendent of schools, and George Wood, chief of police.

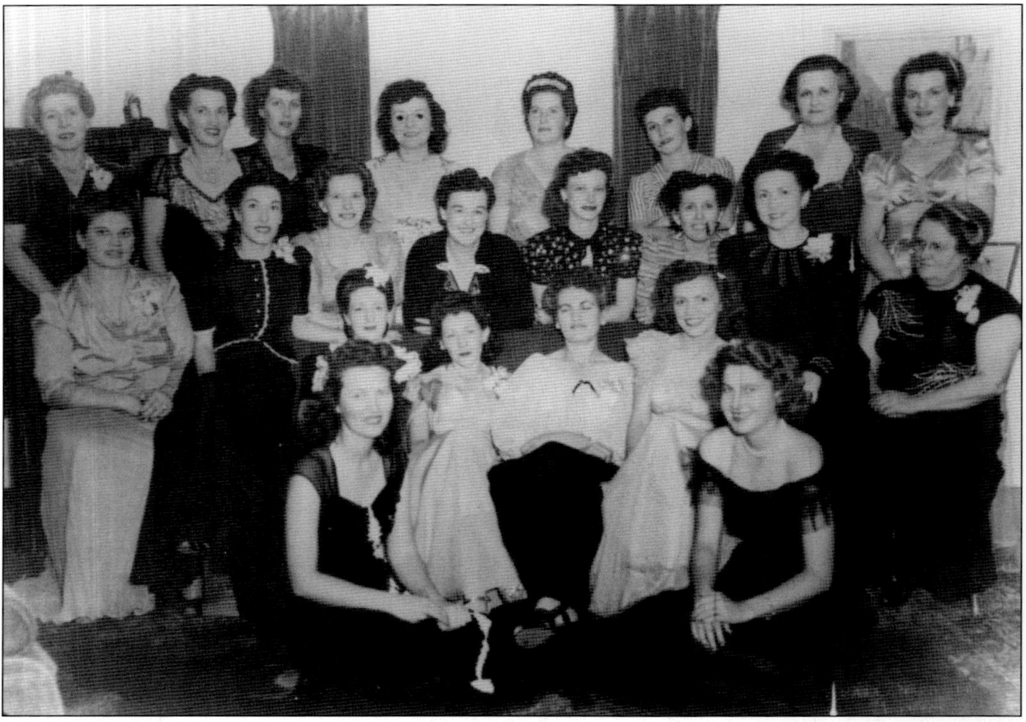

Ladies of Beta Sigma Phi meet in the living room of Clarita Davis's home on Williams Avenue. From left to right are (first row) Velda Ronnow, Irene Hennen, Mae Elllison, Dorothy Durbin, Sis Miller, and Sis Winder; (second row) Ethel Rogers, Nola Biggs, Margery Dodge, Fran Arrizabalaga, Roma Wood, Mary Ryan, Ruth McCuskey, and Gladys Saunders; (third row) Clarita Davis, Jessie Whitaker, Bea Ogden, Judy Frey, Maxine Elliot, Virginia Jones, Gladys Bowler, and Eileen Cooper.

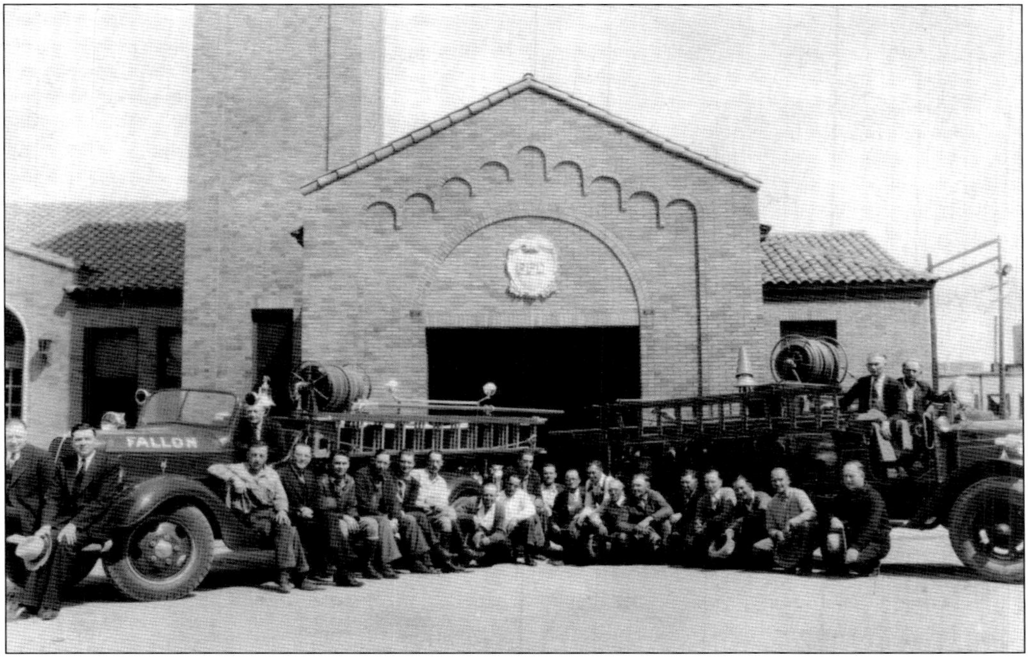

Fallon organized a volunteer fire department in 1915 following several devastating fires. The 1910 fire almost destroyed the Maine Street business district. The department stays current with the shifting technologies of firefighting and earns consistently high national ISO ratings. Shown here are volunteer firemen with trucks in front of the Fallon Fire Station, then located at Fallon City Hall, around 1948.

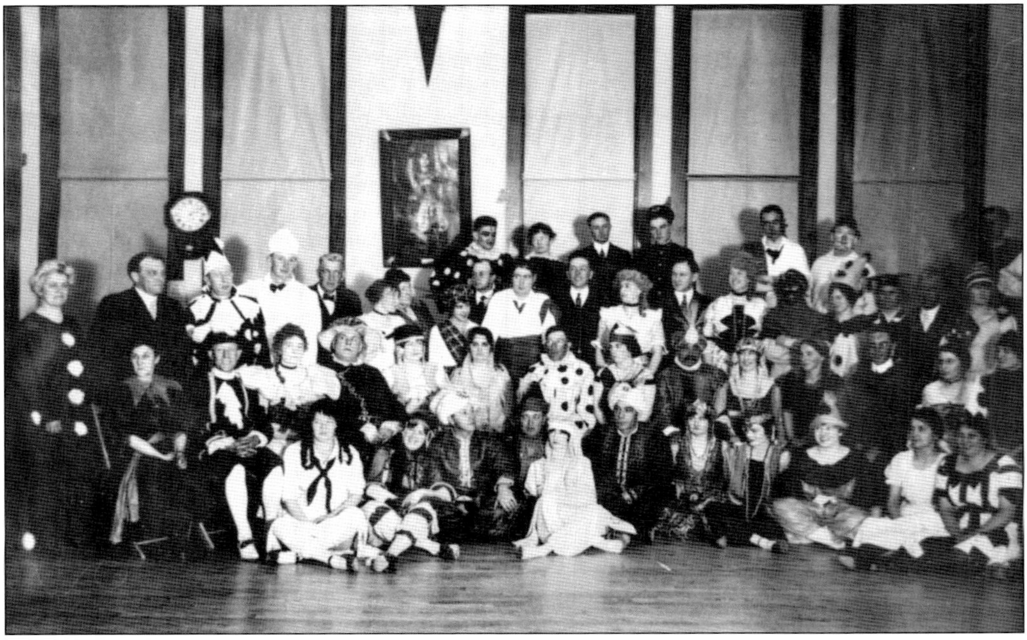

This photograph brings meaning to the phrase, "Send in the Clowns." The undated image suggests that Fallon families have always loved a good time; costumes are optional but nonetheless appreciated.

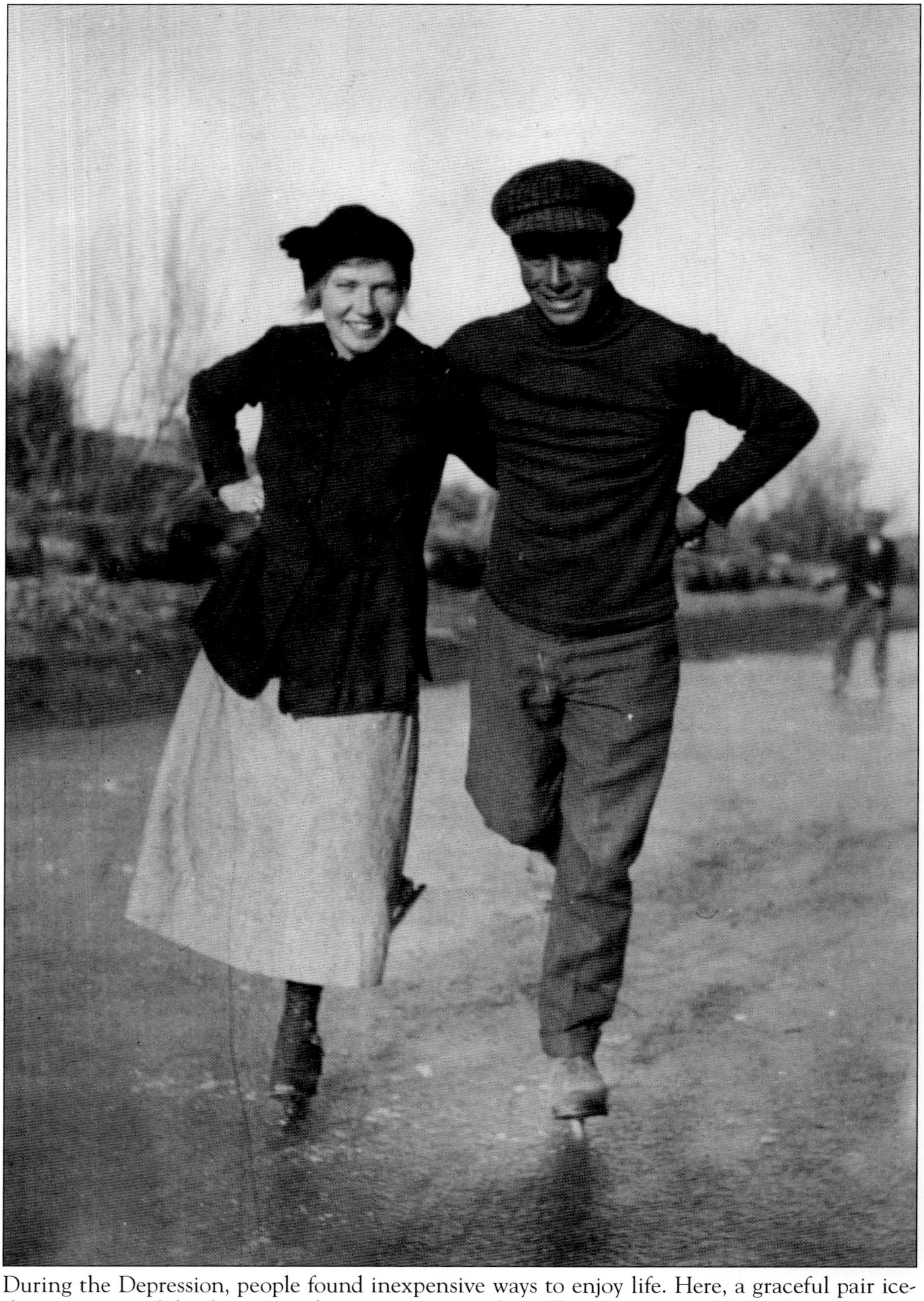

During the Depression, people found inexpensive ways to enjoy life. Here, a graceful pair ice-skates on one of the frozen ponds or reservoirs in the valley. (Courtesy of Special Collections, University of Nevada, Reno Libraries.)

Five

Moving toward Mid-Century

In the Lahontan Valley, the Great Depression affected the local mood and economy in many ways. To use just one example, the bottom dropped out of the turkey market. Across the country, poultry and other products (alfalfa, melons, tomatoes, wheat, and milk) on which the Fallon farmers and ranchers had staked their fame and fortunes suffered to some degree in the marketplace; however, the valley continued to maintain its agricultural base. One contributing factor was the cultural diversity of the rural population, where ethnic friends and neighbors helped valley residents survive the worst and offered differing approaches to seeding and growing techniques. By the 1930s, the area had become home to emigrants from Italy, Portugal, Spain (especially the Basque region), Germany, and the Eastern European nations. Particularly notable were the contributions made by Japanese American farmers, who were assimilated into the community and protected by it during the war.

Fiscal health was improved somewhat by New Deal programs. In particular, the Civilian Conservation Corps added to the economy and improved the infrastructure of the Newlands Project.

When the United States entered World War II, Fallon was fairly well positioned to contribute to the war effort. Markets and prices for agricultural goods expanded quickly, and local farms increased production. Victory gardens were planted to supplement local food supplies. Fallon men and women lined up to serve.

Historians would most likely agree that the most fundamental and lasting change the war brought to Fallon came in 1942 with the opening of an Army Air Corps facility on a strip of land eight miles east of Fallon. Originally an inland continental defense base, in 1944 the small military complex became the Fallon Naval Auxiliary Station (NAAS). In 1951, the station was expanded to include a landing field for Naval Air Station Alameda. The social and economic importance of the facility, now a Naval Air Station (NAS), has continued to grow. Today, many local retirees can trace their first acquaintance with the valley to a military assignment at "the base." The fact that so many have returned speaks to the welcoming and diverse nature of the community.

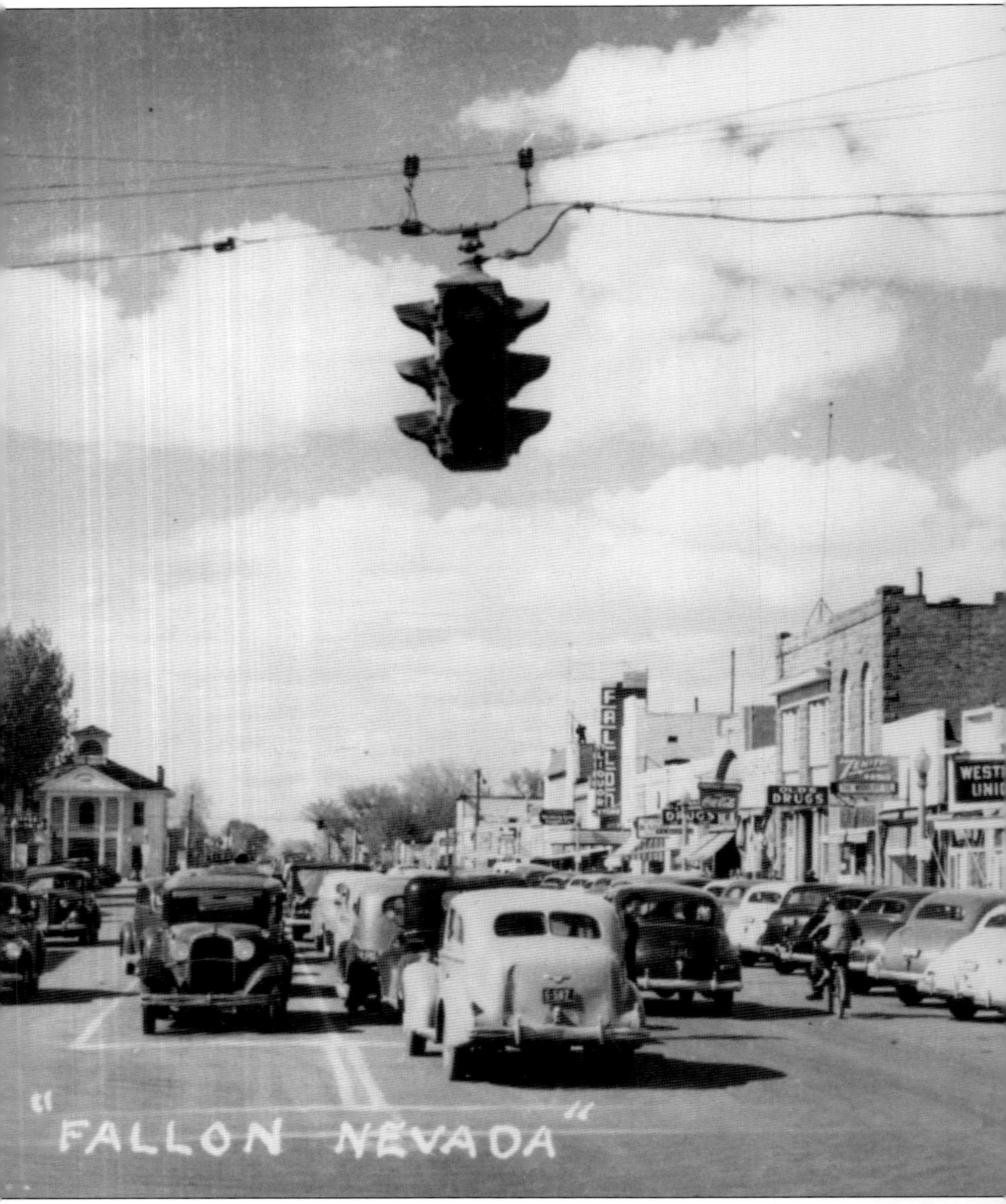

Maine Street, Fallon, in the late 1930s is shown with its distinctive parking pattern. Vehicles could be parked down the meridian as well as in front of businesses. This view showcases the courthouse, the Fallon Theater sign, and the stoplight at Center Street and Maine.

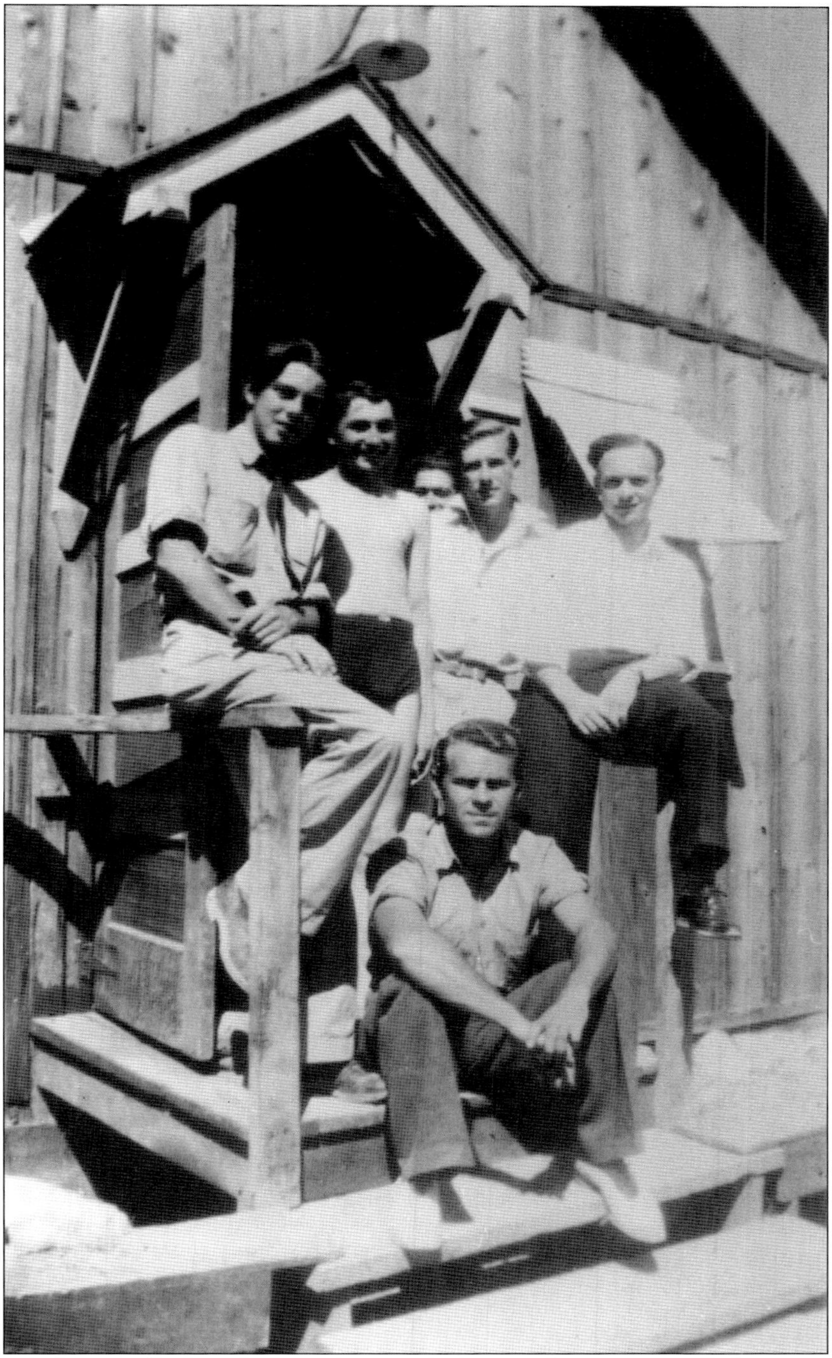

As part of Pres. Franklin D. Roosevelt's economic recovery plan, the Civilian Conservation Corps (CCC) was formed. Unemployed young men were stationed in CCC camps, primarily in rural areas, where they were assigned conservation work dictated by local conditions. Two camps were formed in Churchill County. Here, CCC workers pose at Camp Newlands, built on North Taylor Street.

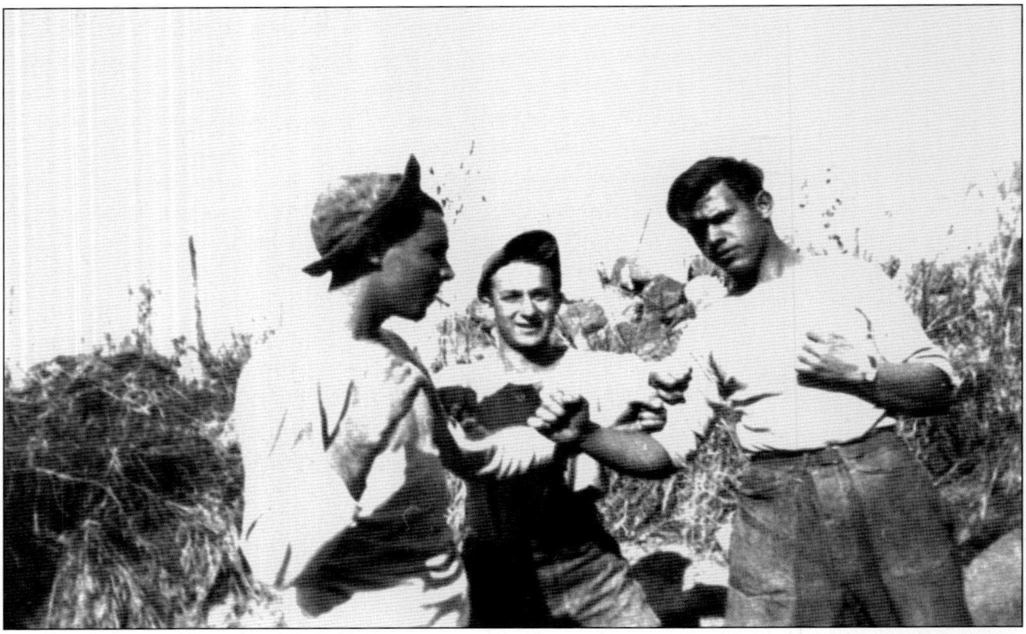

Camp Carson River was built between West Williams Avenue and Auction Road. The camp structures were temporary, but each camp employed a cook. The men were encouraged to join in local activities, and many of them played on sports teams. These men stayed in shape.

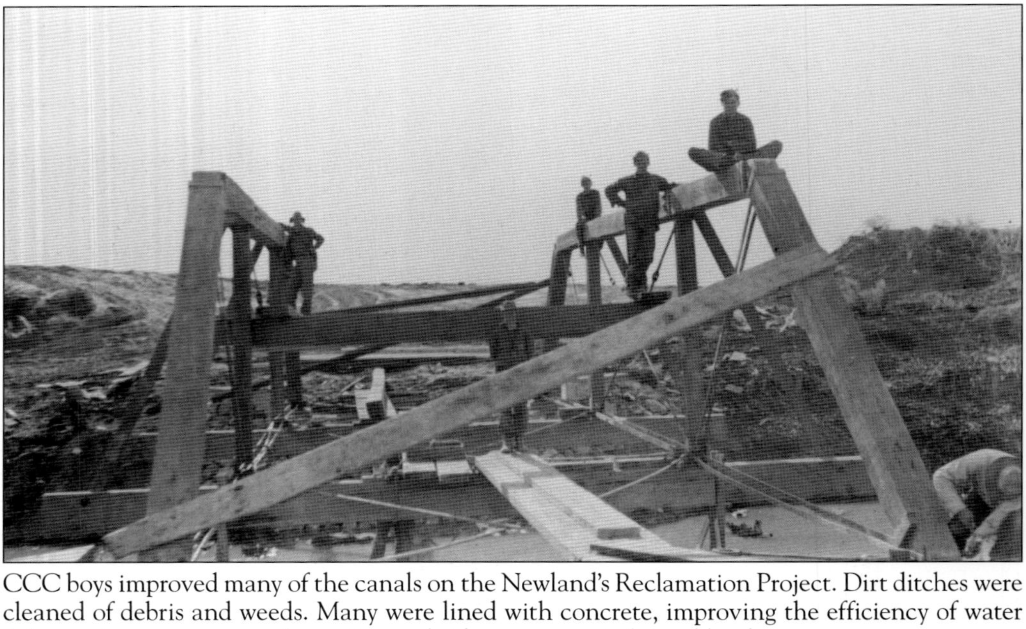

CCC boys improved many of the canals on the Newland's Reclamation Project. Dirt ditches were cleaned of debris and weeds. Many were lined with concrete, improving the efficiency of water delivery from reservoir to farm. Here, a bridge structure is framed by the crew.

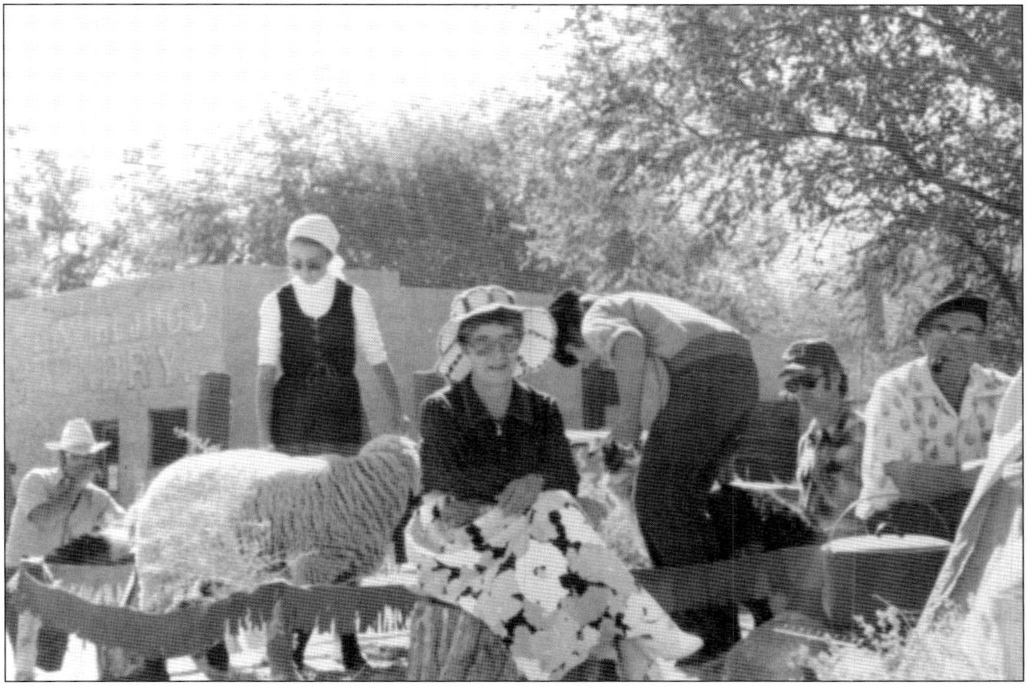

Basque ranchers and sheepherders emigrated from the mountainous regions of France and Spain to the mountains and valleys of Nevada very early in the state's history. The Basque culture is celebrated throughout the state in festivals and parades.

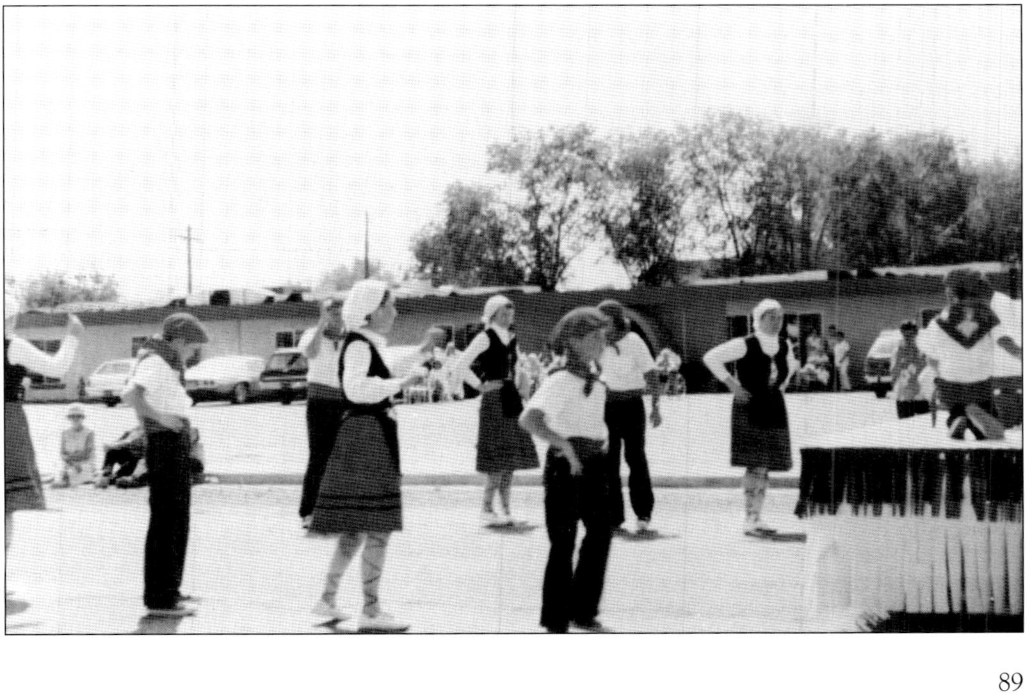

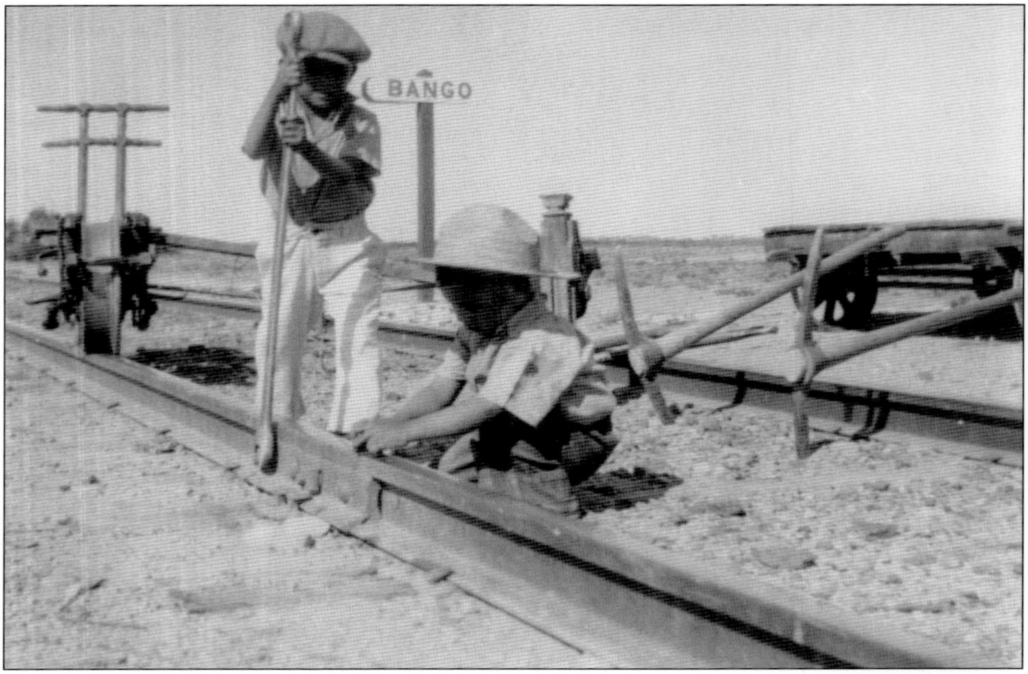

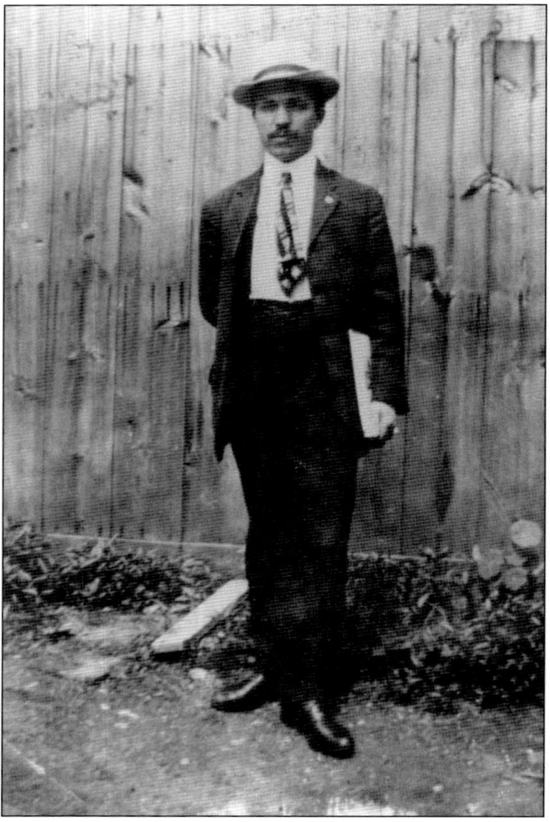

Italian immigrant Julios Ratti, a railway employee, and his wife, Ruby Ruiz Ratti, arrived at Bango, a railway maintenance station in the desert north of Lahontan Dam, in 1929. The self-proclaimed "Mayor of Bango" and his wife built a rich life there. In this photograph, their children comprise a small crew to work on the tracks.

Nicholas Jesch arrived in New York from Austria-Hungary in the early 1900s. After reading about the Newlands Project, he and his brother journeyed to Lahontan City in 1911 or 1912, where Nick established a barbershop. He met and married Bertha Dietz, whose parents were German immigrants. They moved near Fallon and raised their family there.

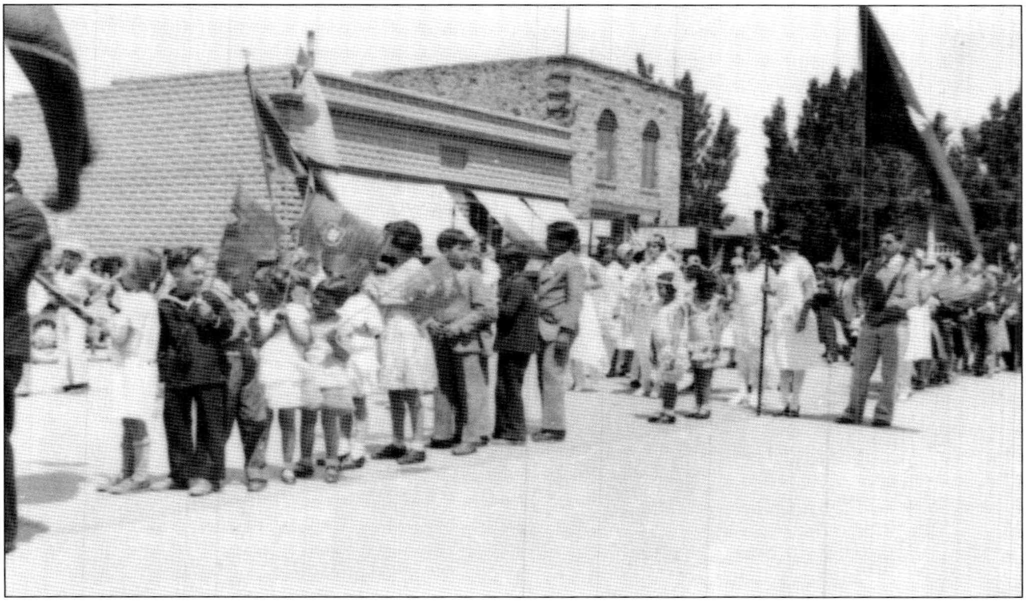

Portuguese Americans in Fallon celebrate Festa each May. Festa celebrations originated in Portugal to honor the heartfelt efforts of Queen (Saint) Isabel to feed her nation's poor. According to legend, she pledged her crown to the Holy Spirit in exchange for food for her people. Above, 1939 Festa queen Ellie Armas wears the symbolic crown and carries a scepter, representing the people. Below, the Festa procession moves toward St. Patrick's Catholic Church.

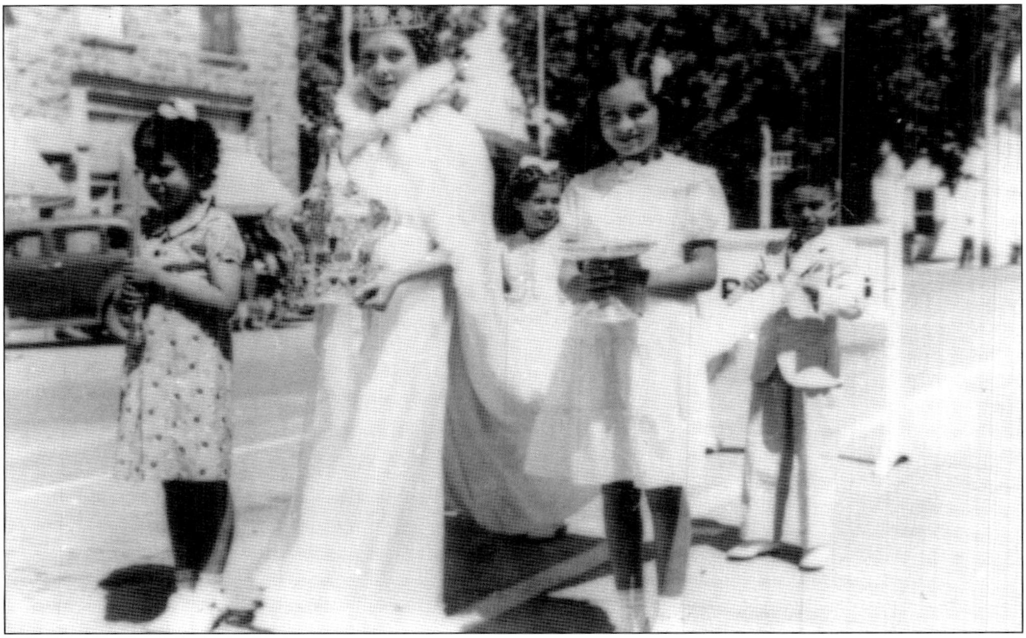

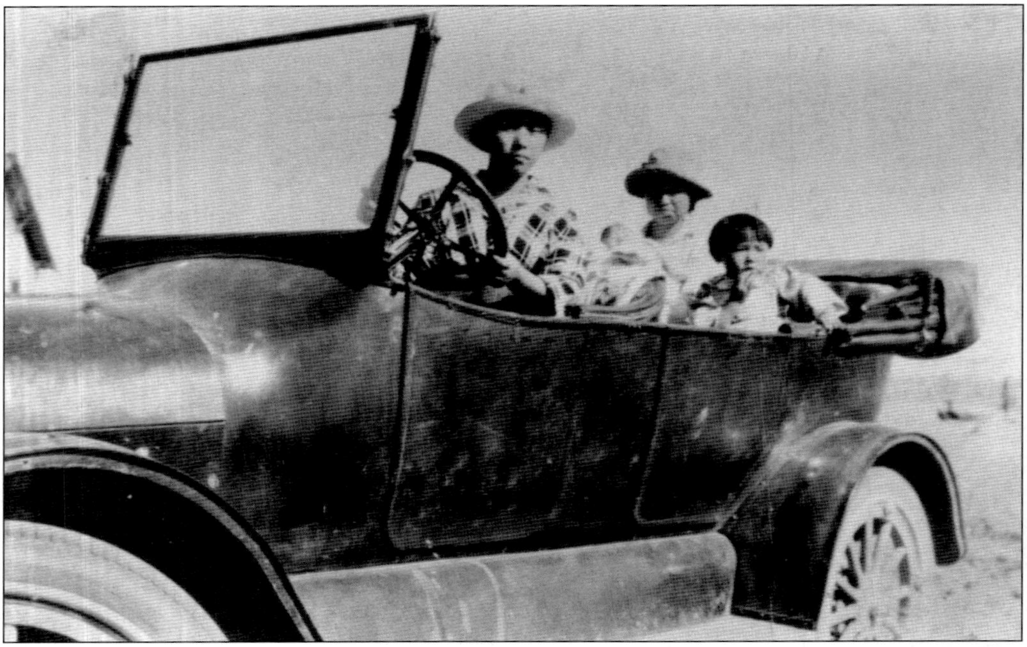

The Juichi Kito and Kensuke Ito families began raising cantaloupe in the valley in 1922. They also produced alfalfa, vegetables, and milk products and raised turkeys, chickens, and livestock. All their children graduated from the local high school and pursued advanced degrees. As to how these two families fared during the war, Masa Kito, daughter of Joichi Kito, recalled, "A group of prominent townspeople came to our defense and persuaded federal authorities that the Japanese of this area were loyal."

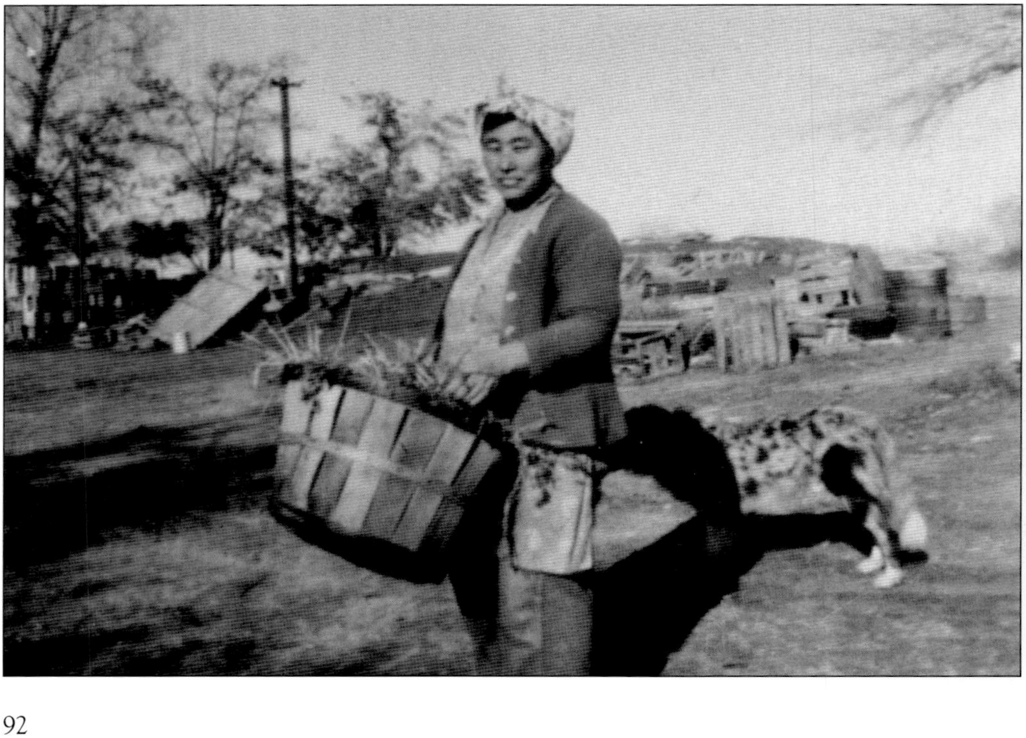

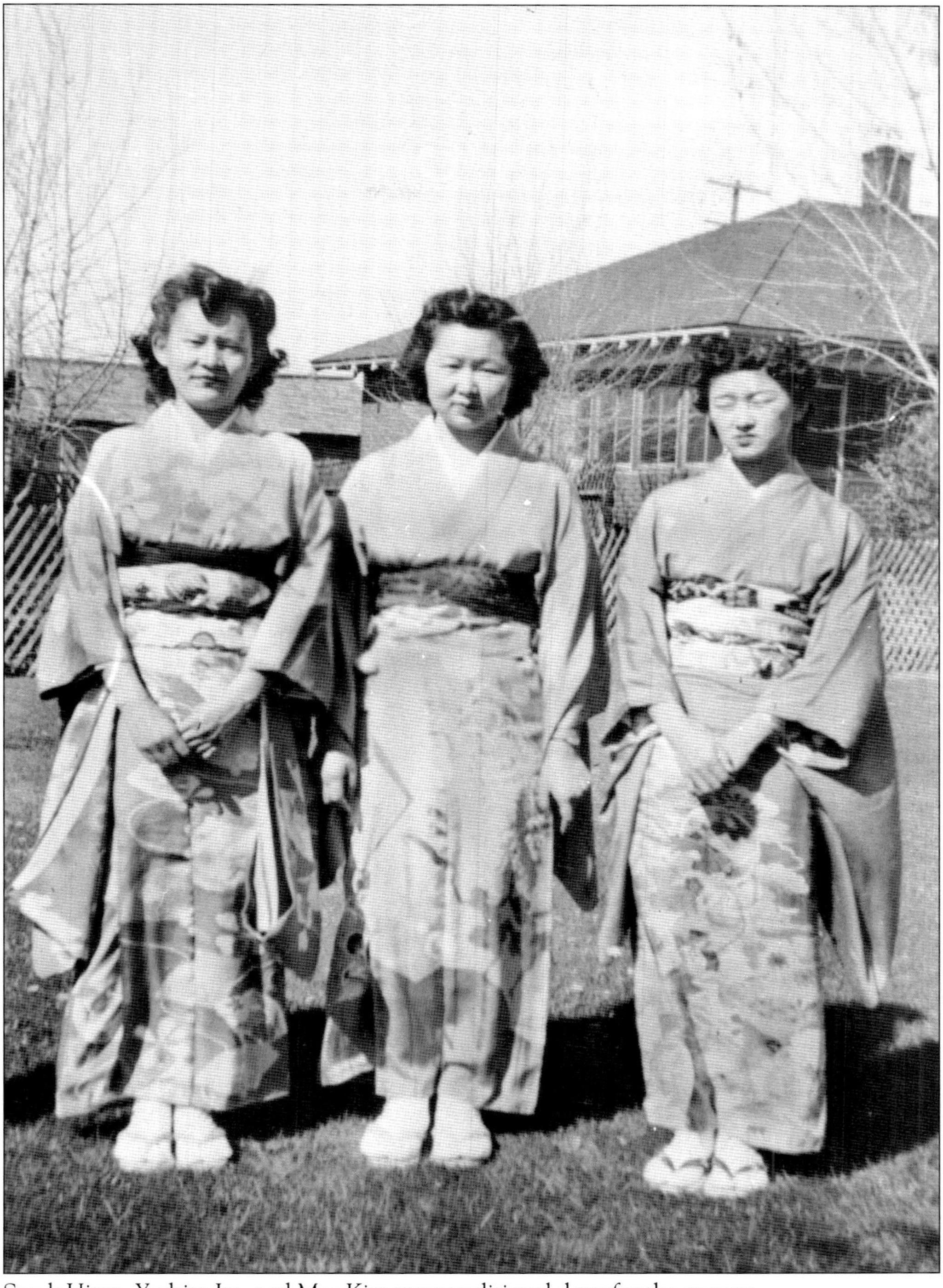

Sasak Hiten, Yoshito Ito, and May Kito wear traditional dress for the camera.

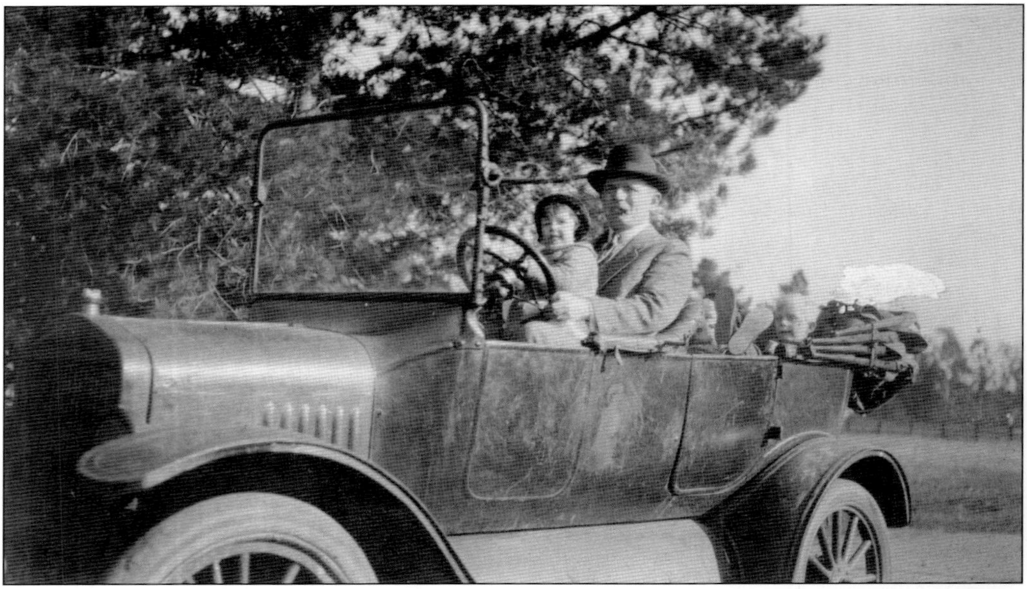

Many German immigrants settled on the Newlands Project. During World War II, security patrols were dispatched to guard Lahontan Dam because of a few expressions of anti-German sentiment. However, most of the valley's families knew that the German settlers, like the Prudler family shown here, were loyal Americans.

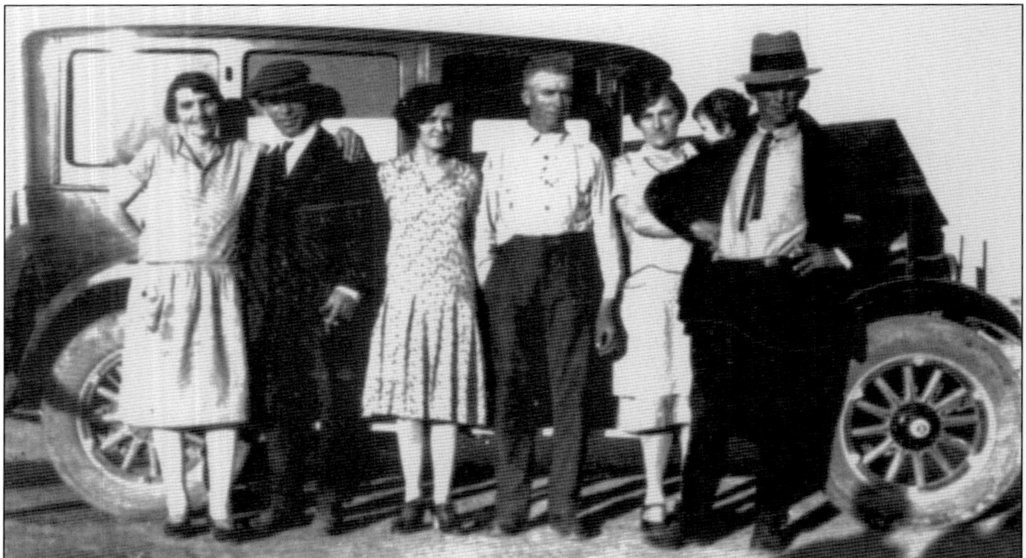

In 1908, Andrew and John Getto emigrated from Italy, eventually settling in the Lahontan Valley in 1911 to farm and raise dairy herds. From left to right are Mary Getto Bria, Mike Bria, Desolina Getto, Andrew Getto, Carolina Getto, Elena Getto (child), and John Getto.

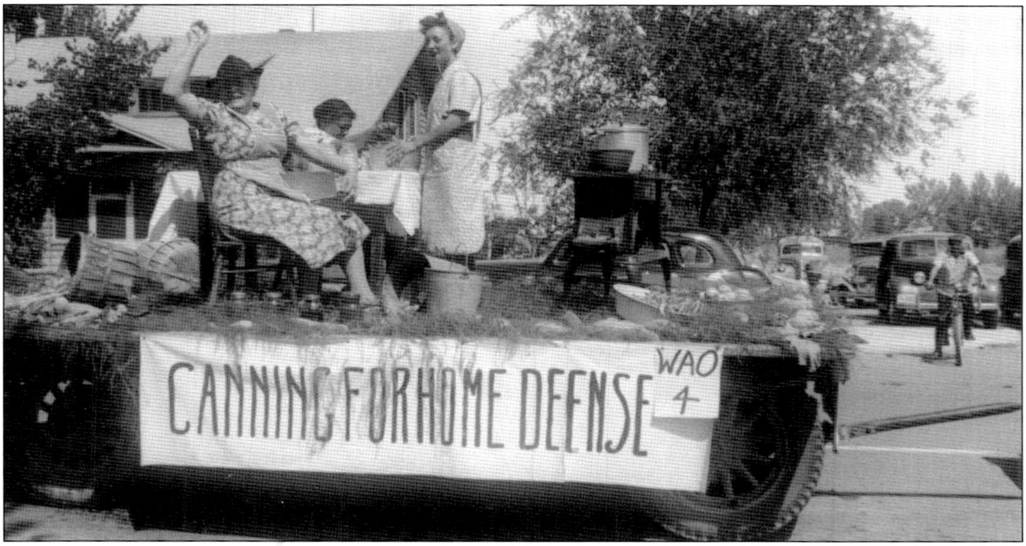

A float entered in a 1943 Fallon parade proclaims the virtues of home canning, promoted by the government as vital to the war effort.

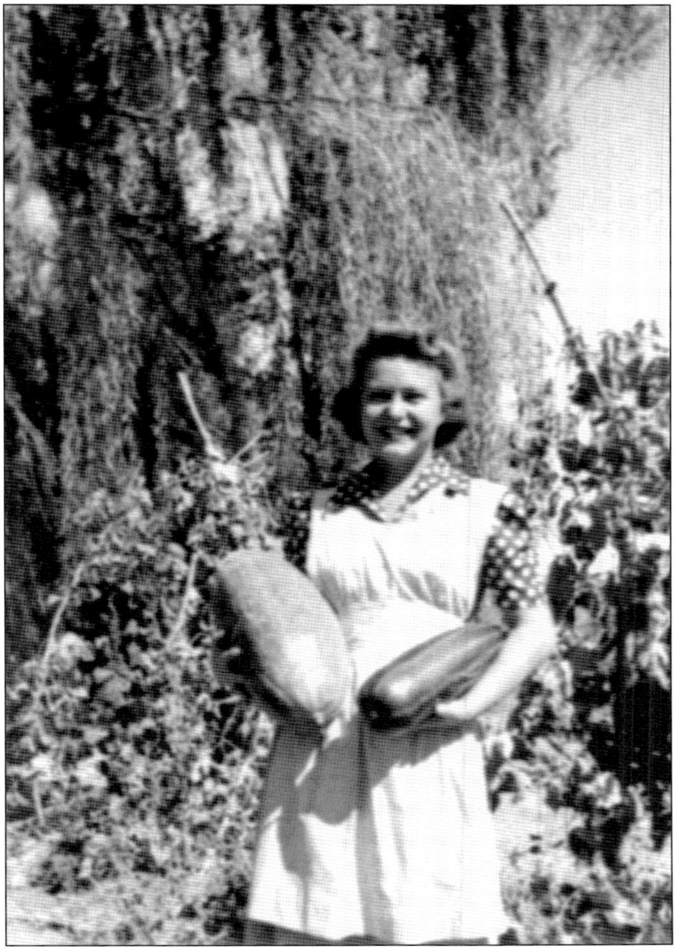

During the war, Americans were encouraged by the government to plant victory gardens. Almost 20 million gardens were planted, producing 40 percent of the vegetables consumed in the United States. One US poster read, "Our food is fighting." Shown here is one of many victory gardens planted in the valley.

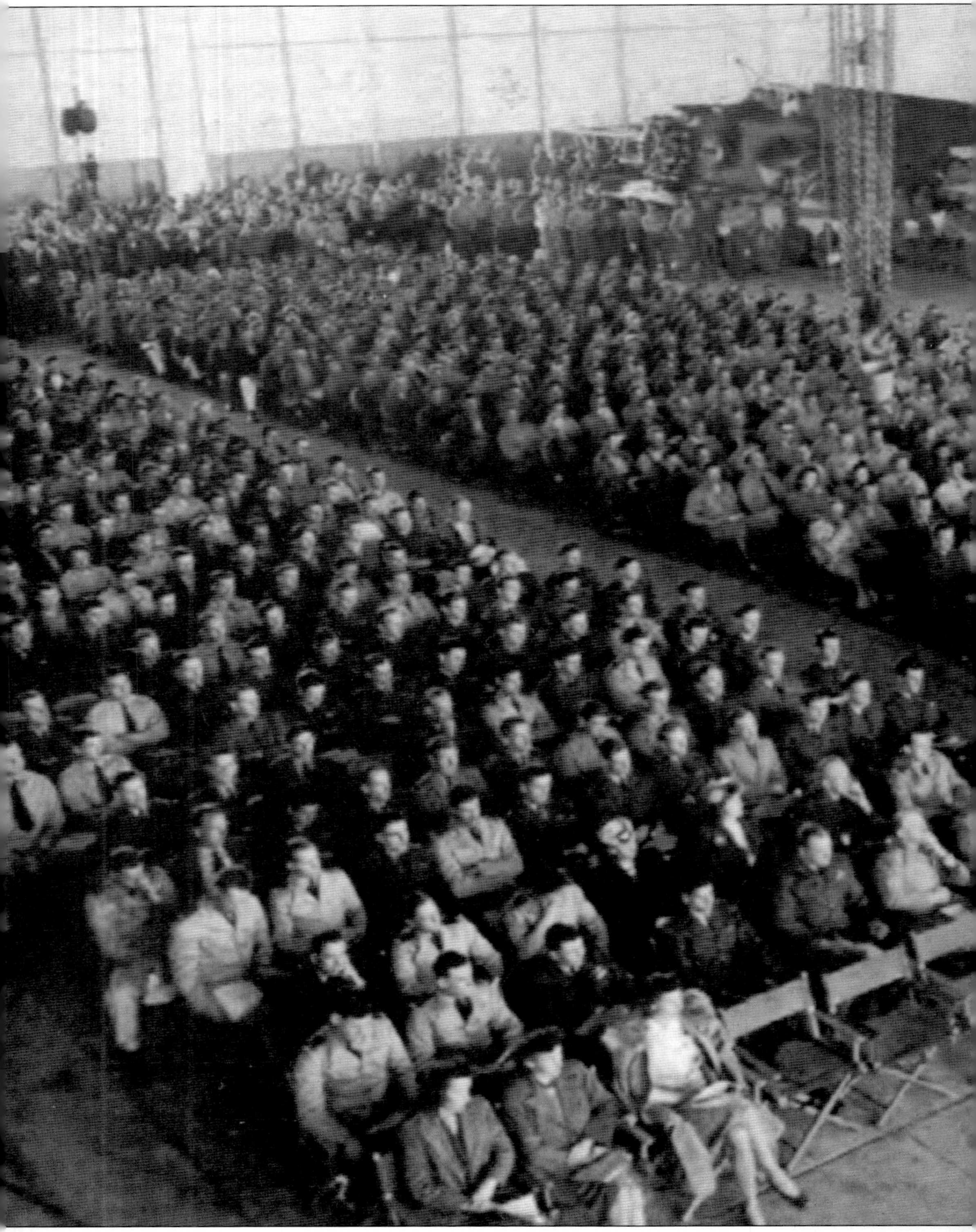

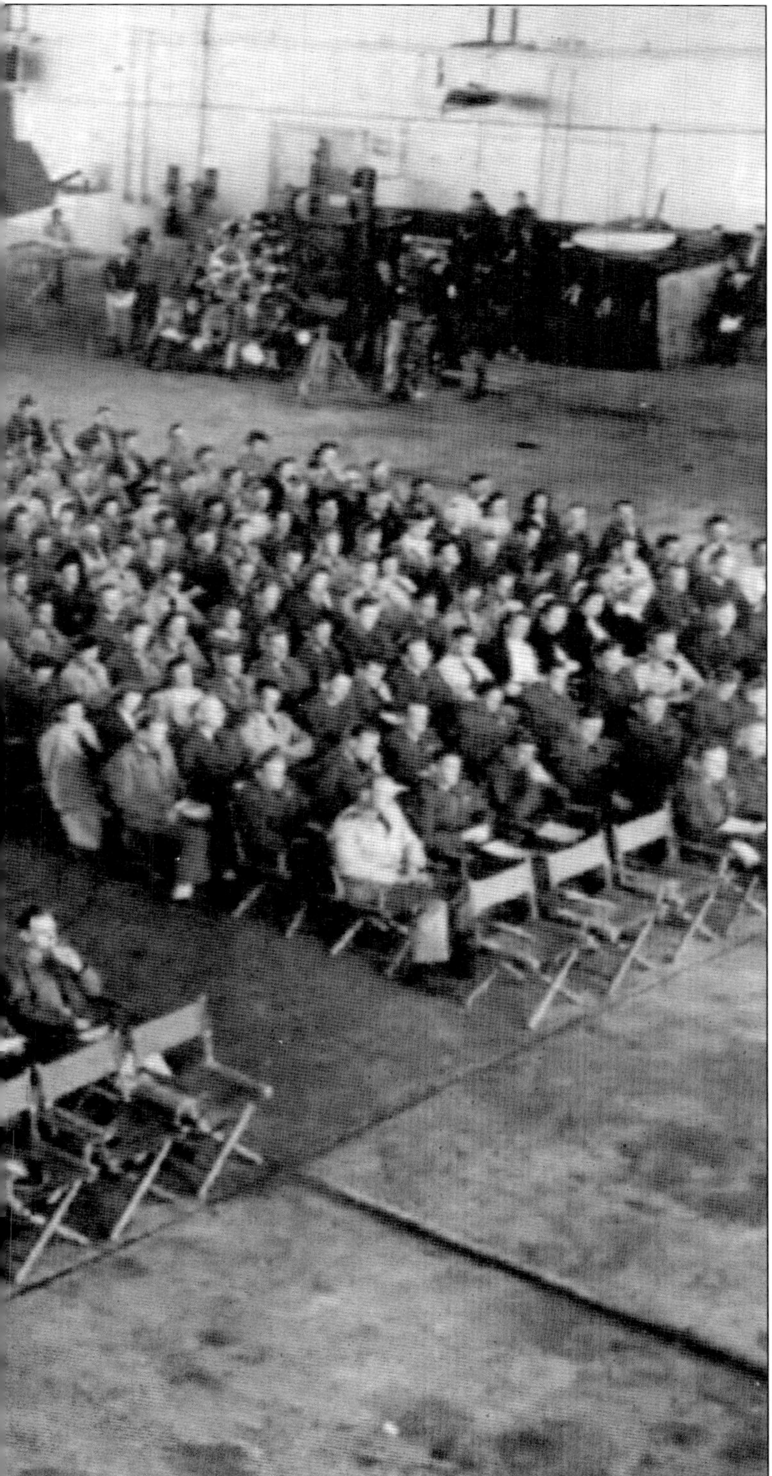

A memorial service for Franklin Delano Roosevelt was held in Hangar 1 at the Fallon Naval Air Station in 1945. (Courtesy of Naval Air Station Fallon.)

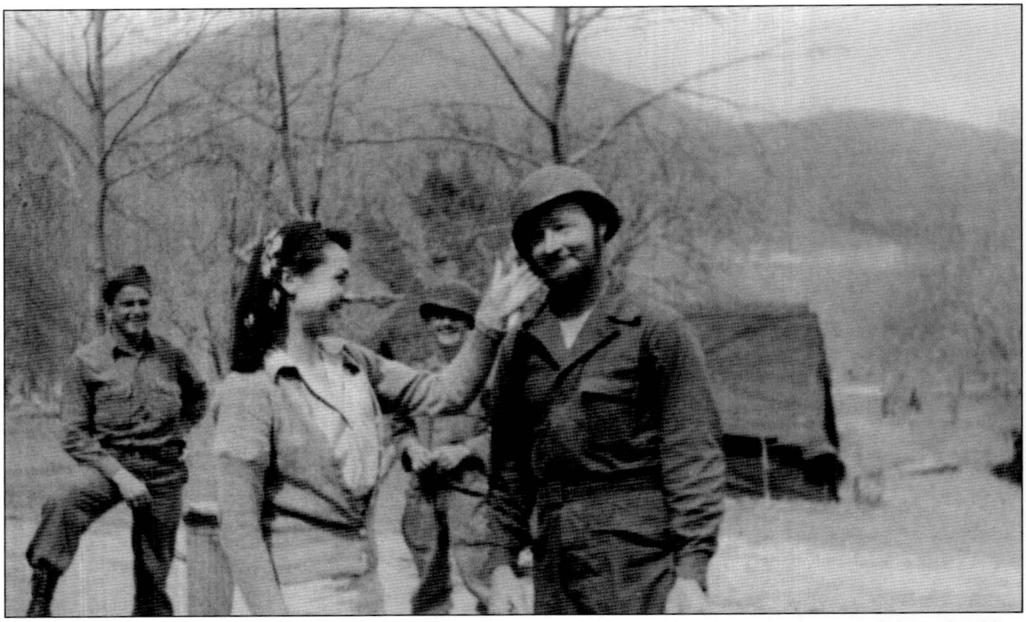

Lois Berney was the daughter of E.S. Berney, a local construction entrepreneur. Several of his descendants live in Fallon today. Lois, an adventurous traveler, worked for the State Department in Latvia, then as secretary to Franklin Delano Roosevelt's federal relief administrator, Harry Hopkins. After World War II began, she joined the Red Cross overseas. This photograph shows her cheering up troops on the front lines.

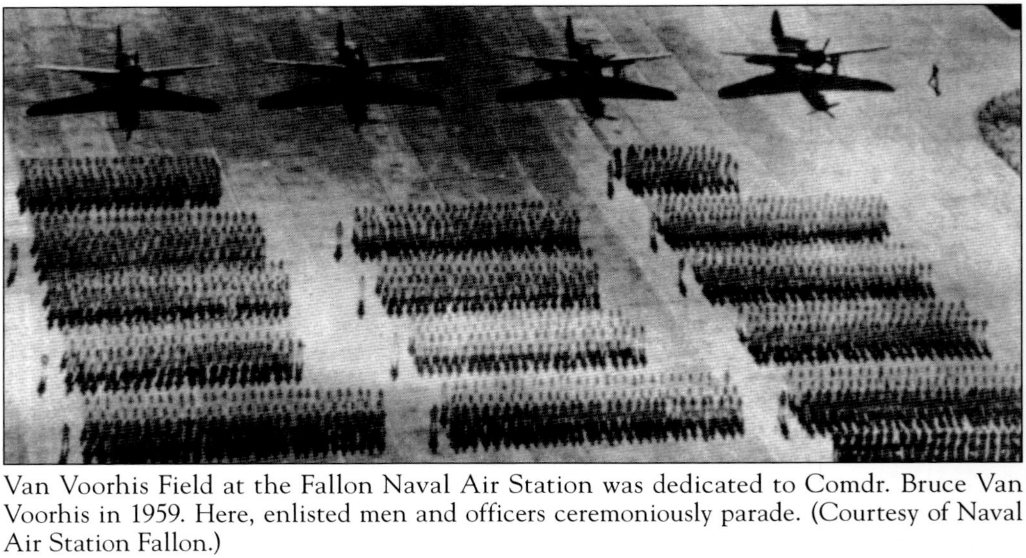

Van Voorhis Field at the Fallon Naval Air Station was dedicated to Comdr. Bruce Van Voorhis in 1959. Here, enlisted men and officers ceremoniously parade. (Courtesy of Naval Air Station Fallon.)

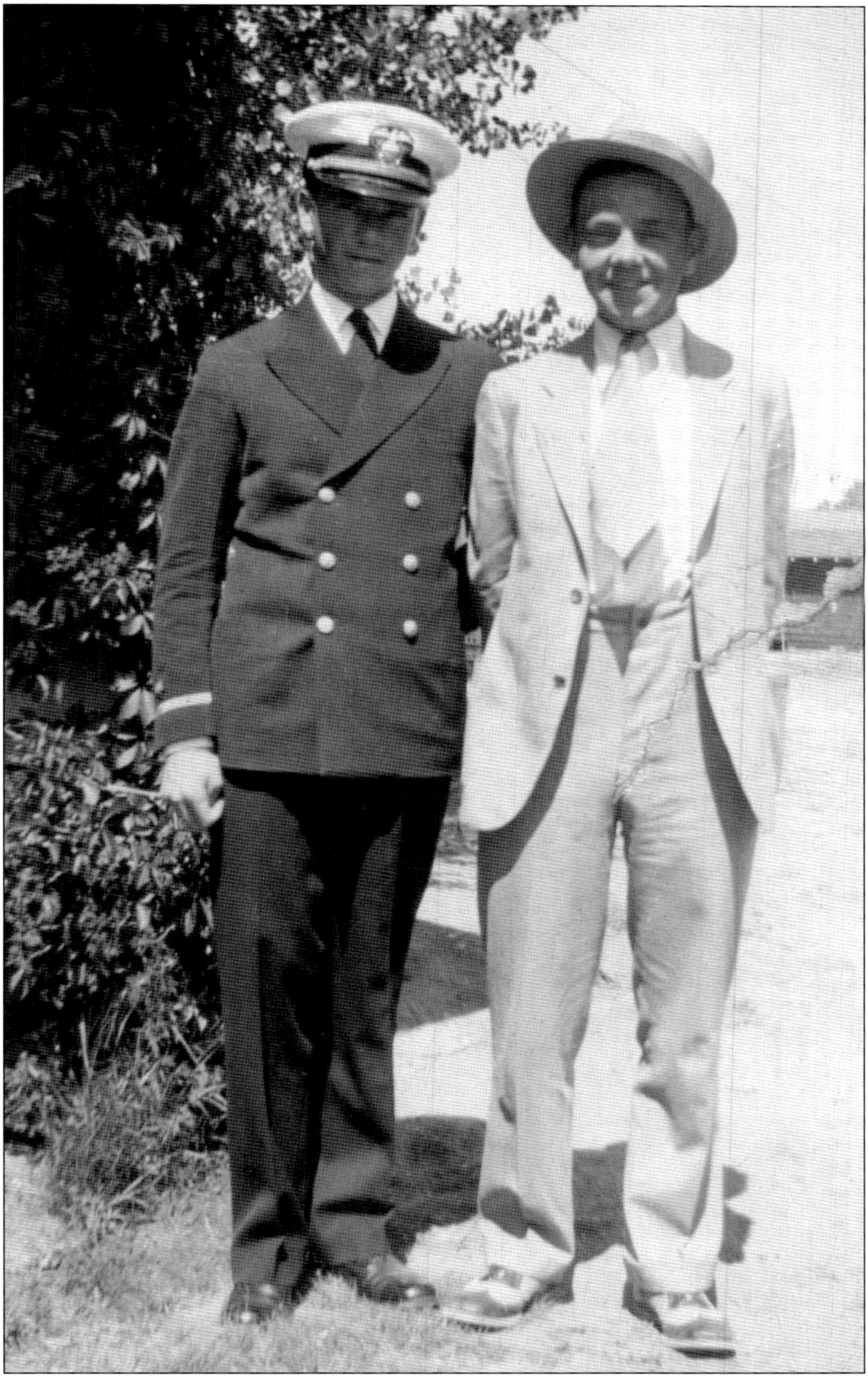

Shown here are brothers Bruce (left) and Wayne Van Voorhis. Both men died in World War II. Comdr. Bruce Avery Van Voorhis was the only Churchill County resident to be awarded a Congressional Medal of Honor in World War II after exhibiting heroism in the Middle Pacific. Wayne Van Voorhis died while on the Bataan Death March.

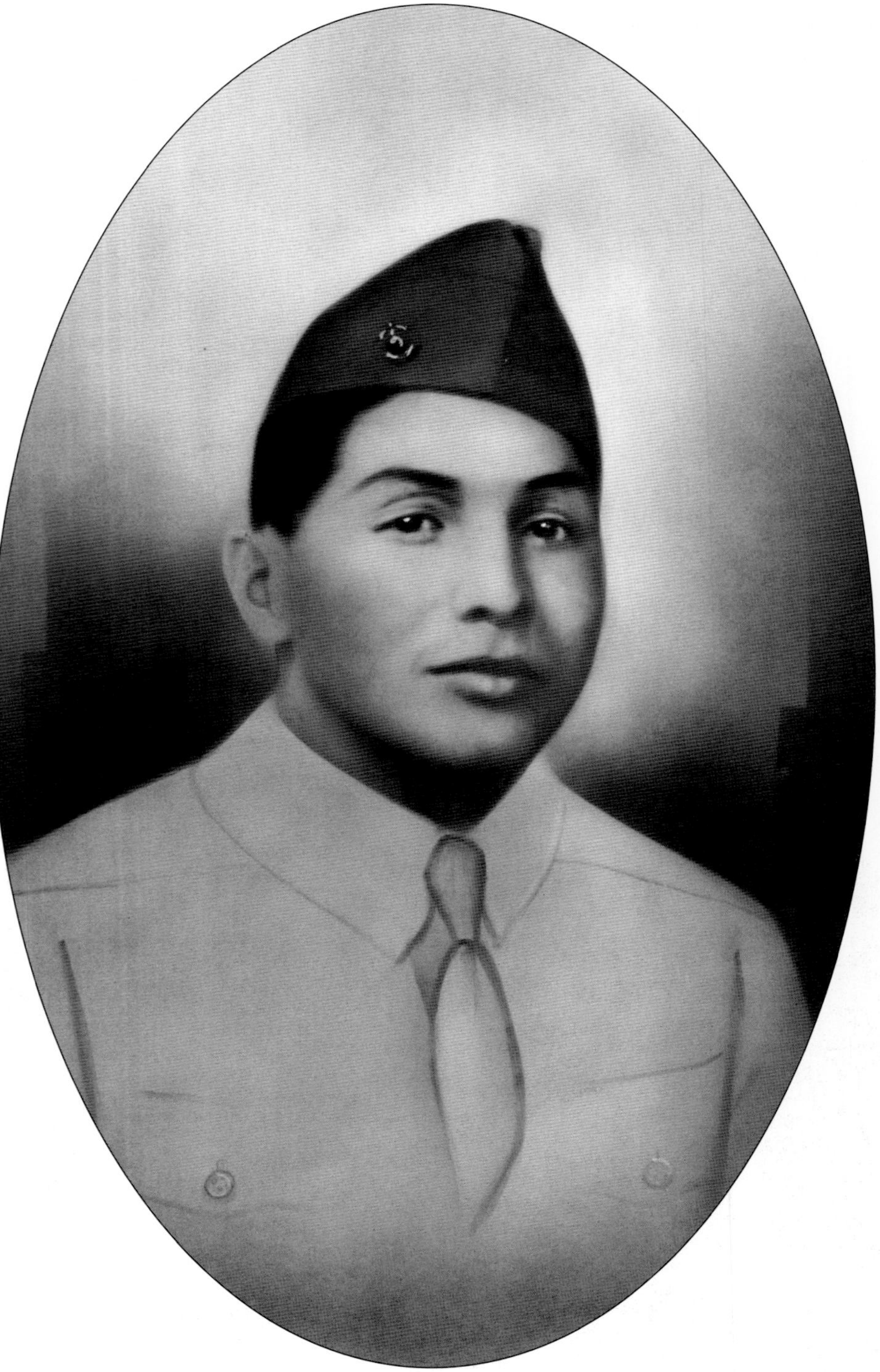

A Northern Paiute, Pvt. Donald Brown Sr. served in the US Marine Corps between May 8, 1942, and November 24, 1945, participating in operations against enemy forces the South Pacific. He later served as tribal chairman for the Fallon Paiute-Shoshone tribe.

This cover of the March 1945 edition of *Country Gentlewoman* features Fallon's Thais Ann Sherman, born and raised on a 400-acre ranch near Fallon. A senior at Barnard College and a volunteer nurse's aide who had accumulated 150 hours of service, she was honored as "proudly symbolizing a job which has a top priority on the time and energy of American girls and women."

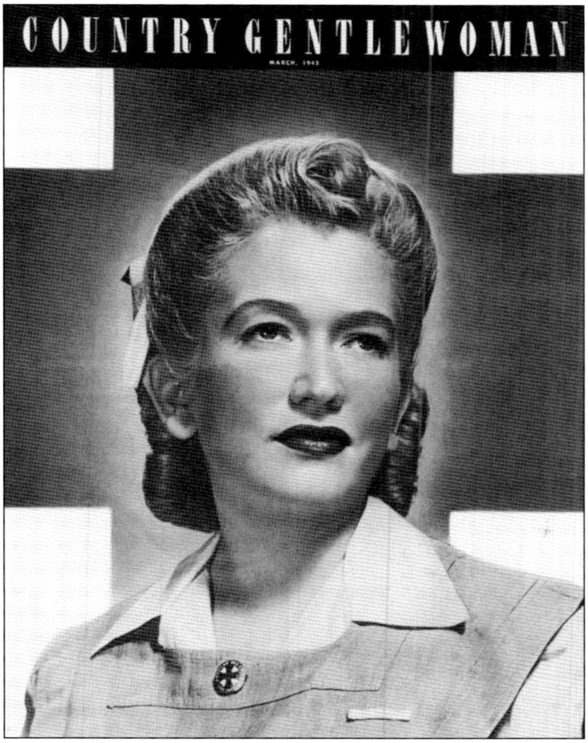

A group of Women's Army Corps (WAC) volunteers enjoys some time away from the pressures of the war. On the left is Mary Aldrich, who retired in Fallon.

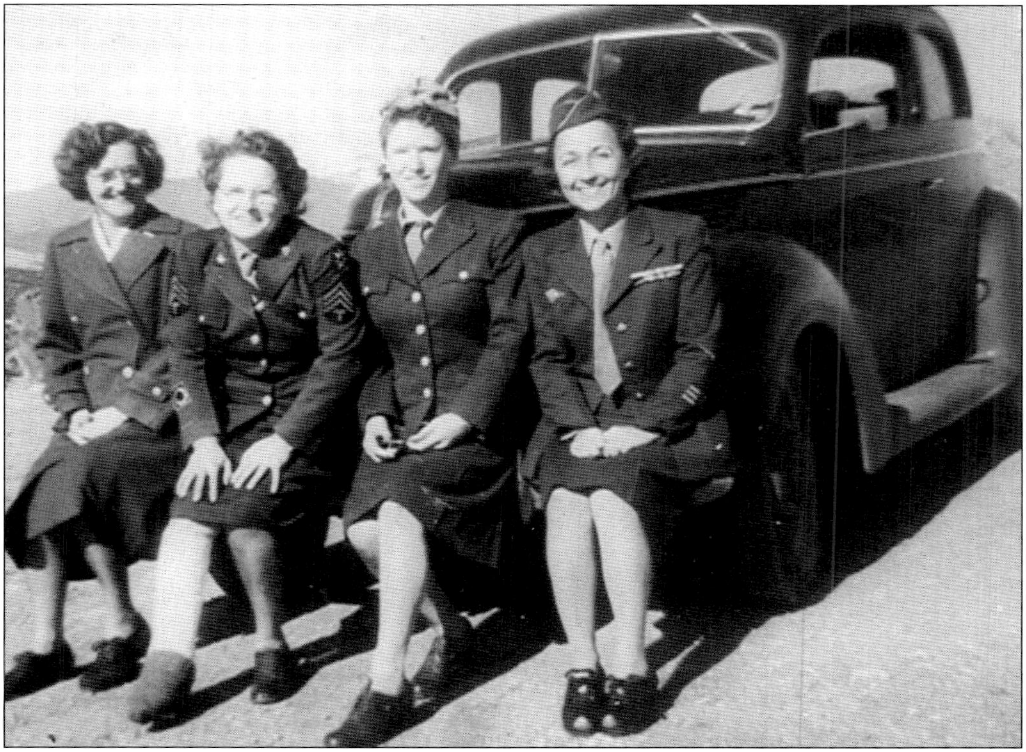

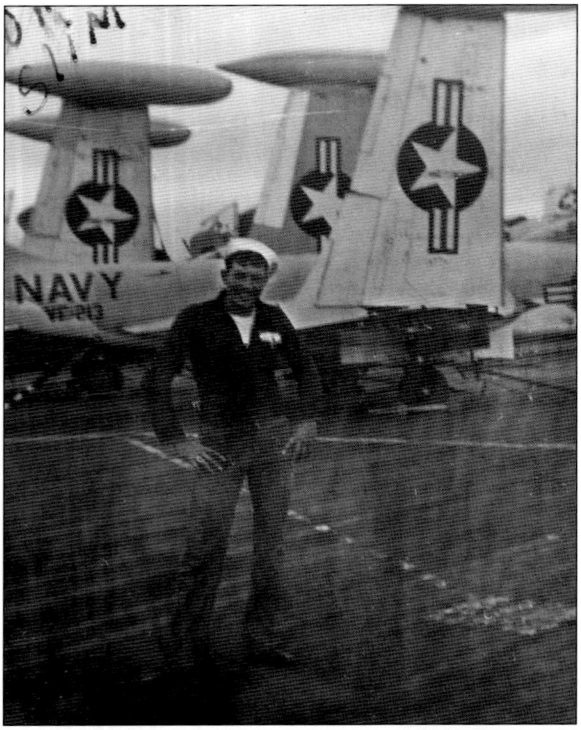

Eugene "Duff" Duffney, a native of a small town in Minnesota, was stationed at NAS/Fallon when he met Emma Peraldo Serpa. The daughter of Joe and Del Serpa, Emma was of Portuguese and Italian descent. They married, and, as many of those in the military, Duff stayed and called Fallon home.

Andrea Drumm, daughter of well-known Fallon road construction pioneer Andrew Drumm, proclaimed her patriotism in her own unique style. She is seated on the famous General Halsey saddle, ornamented with Nevada silver. (Courtesy of Naval Air Station Fallon.)

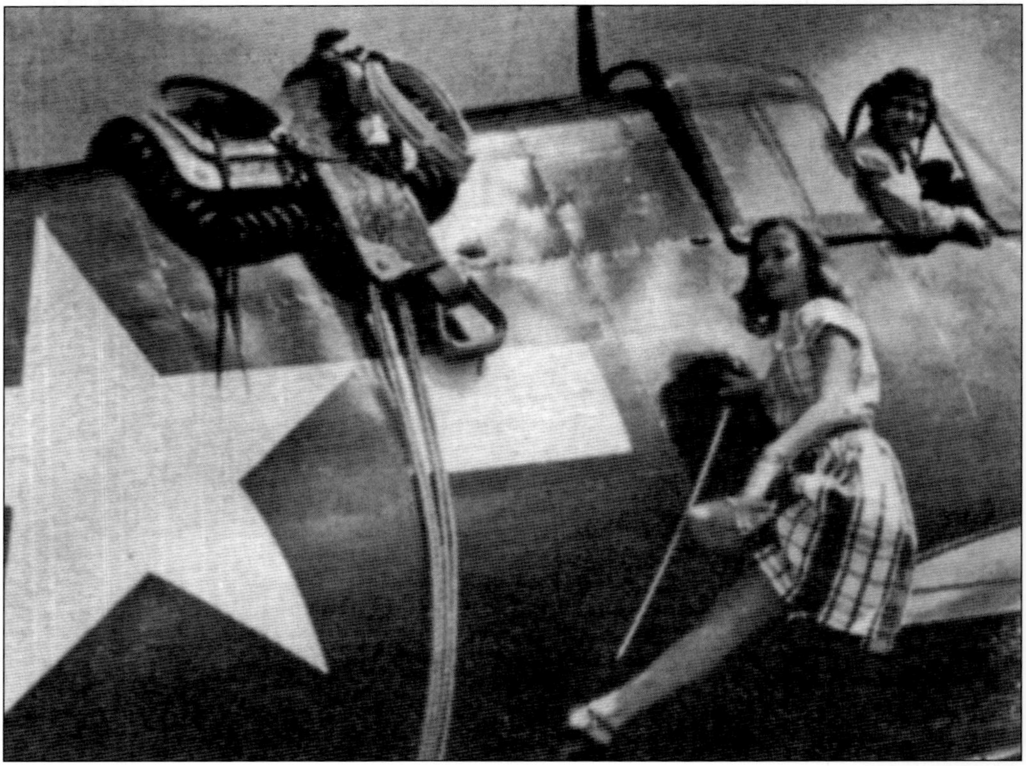

Six

Defining Home

It is much easier to analyze the past than to write about the present. In the words of cultural historian David Lowenthal, "The past is a foreign country." Like an anthropologist, one can sift through photographs, admire the vintage cars and clothes, marvel at what the community has been through, and muse about how it has changed or how it has remained the same. But, in defining the present, there is a risk or danger of missing elements that later historians will find significant.

That said, there are identifiable themes that stitch the past to the present. There is, and always has been, the influence of agriculture on almost every aspect of life in Fallon, from its historical celebrations of rodeos and state fairs and the fame of its cantaloupes and turkeys to the present and ongoing development of businesses and industries that capitalize on the valley's soil and water.

A lasting legacy can be found in the beautiful buildings that have housed Fallon's most important cultural and civic efforts. At the top of the list is the earliest government structure, the famous 1903 county courthouse on Maine Street, still functioning as a courthouse. What is now the Oats Park Arts Center was built in 1915 to house a grammar school. Today, it features art galleries, a theater, and a long list of local supporters. Churchill County High School was built in 1916. Although it is presently used for other educational purposes, it remains a useful and commanding landmark. Fallon City Hall, built in 1931, lost a brick tower to the major earthquake of 1954, but the city still goes about its business daily in the lovely tiled hallways and wood-paneled chambers. The Methodist church, the Episcopal church, and the Seventh-day Adventist church, all built in the first decades of the 20th century, still hold services.

The "Oasis Spirit," though, is not tangible like cantaloupes or courthouses. It was present in the 19th-century ranchers who believed in their risky desert enterprises. It persists in the Fallon business owners and farmers who weather recession and drought. The spirit informs the schools' sports competitions, parades, and performances of all kinds. We believe it will remain part of this community forever.

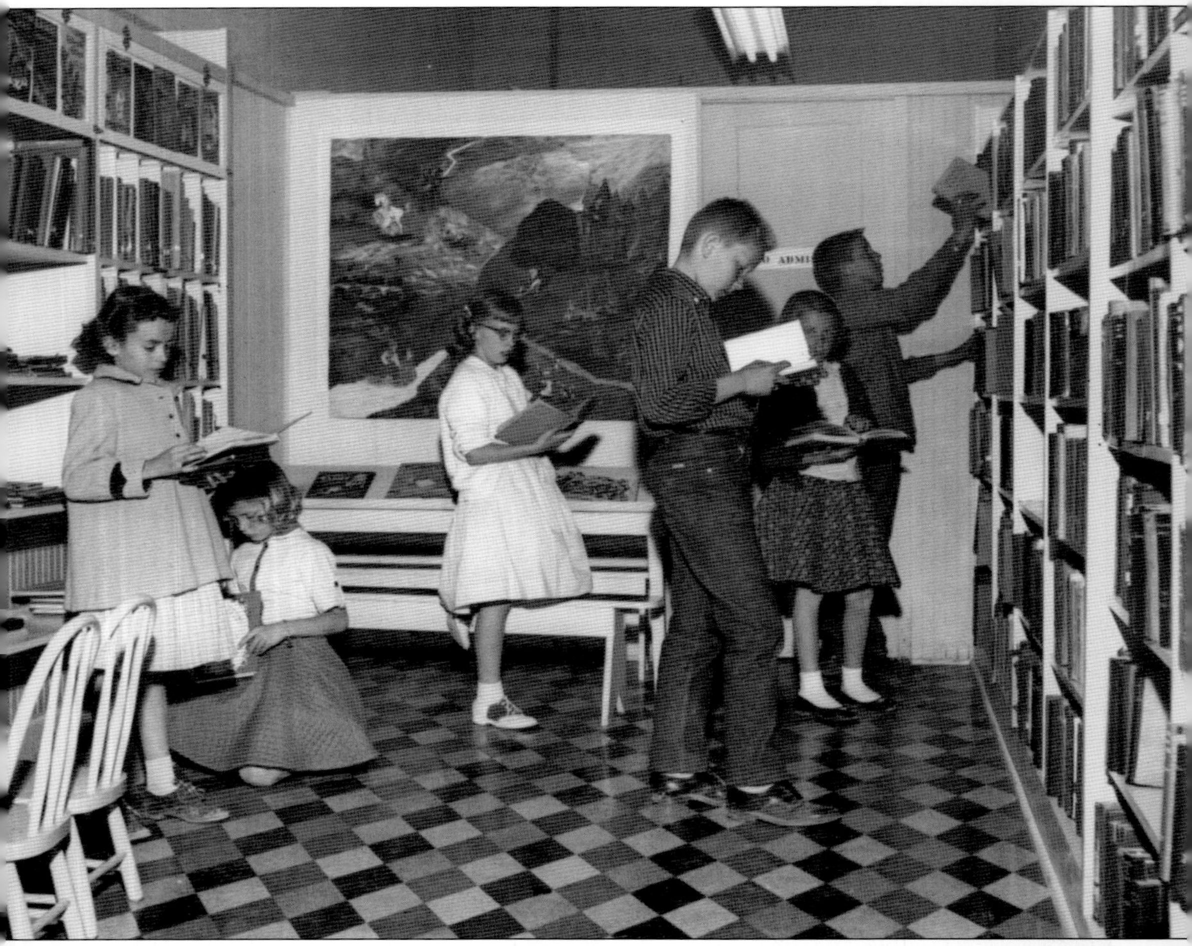

What parent or teacher would not love to see the eagerness on the faces of these children as they pull books from the library shelves?

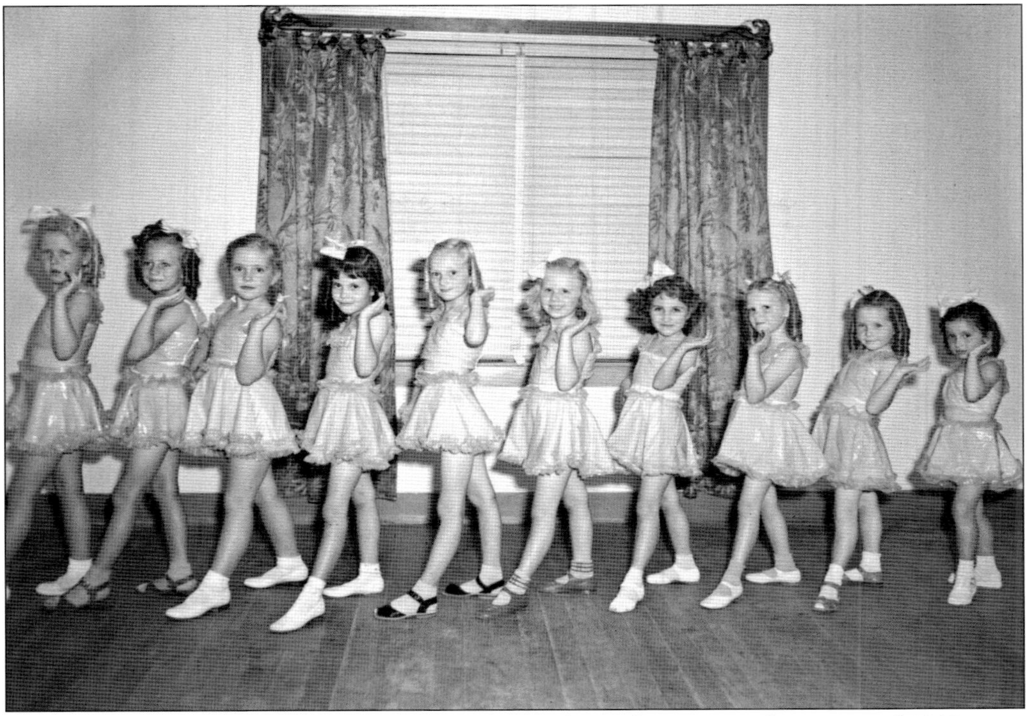

These aspiring young performers were taught dance by Wahneeta Matthews around 1948.

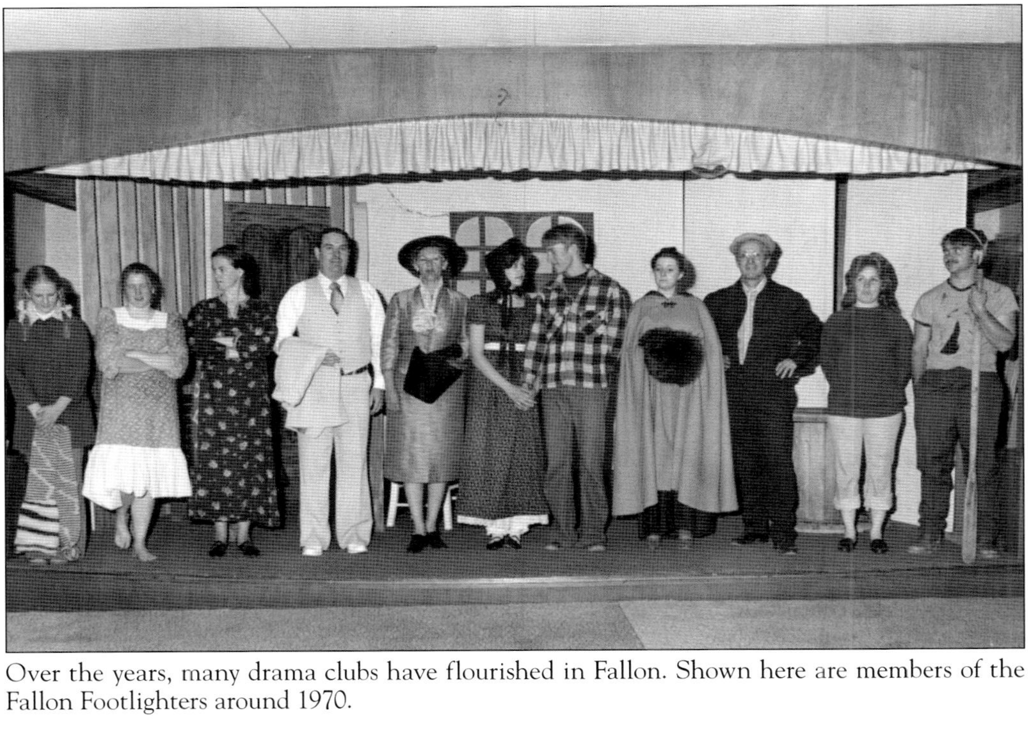

Over the years, many drama clubs have flourished in Fallon. Shown here are members of the Fallon Footlighters around 1970.

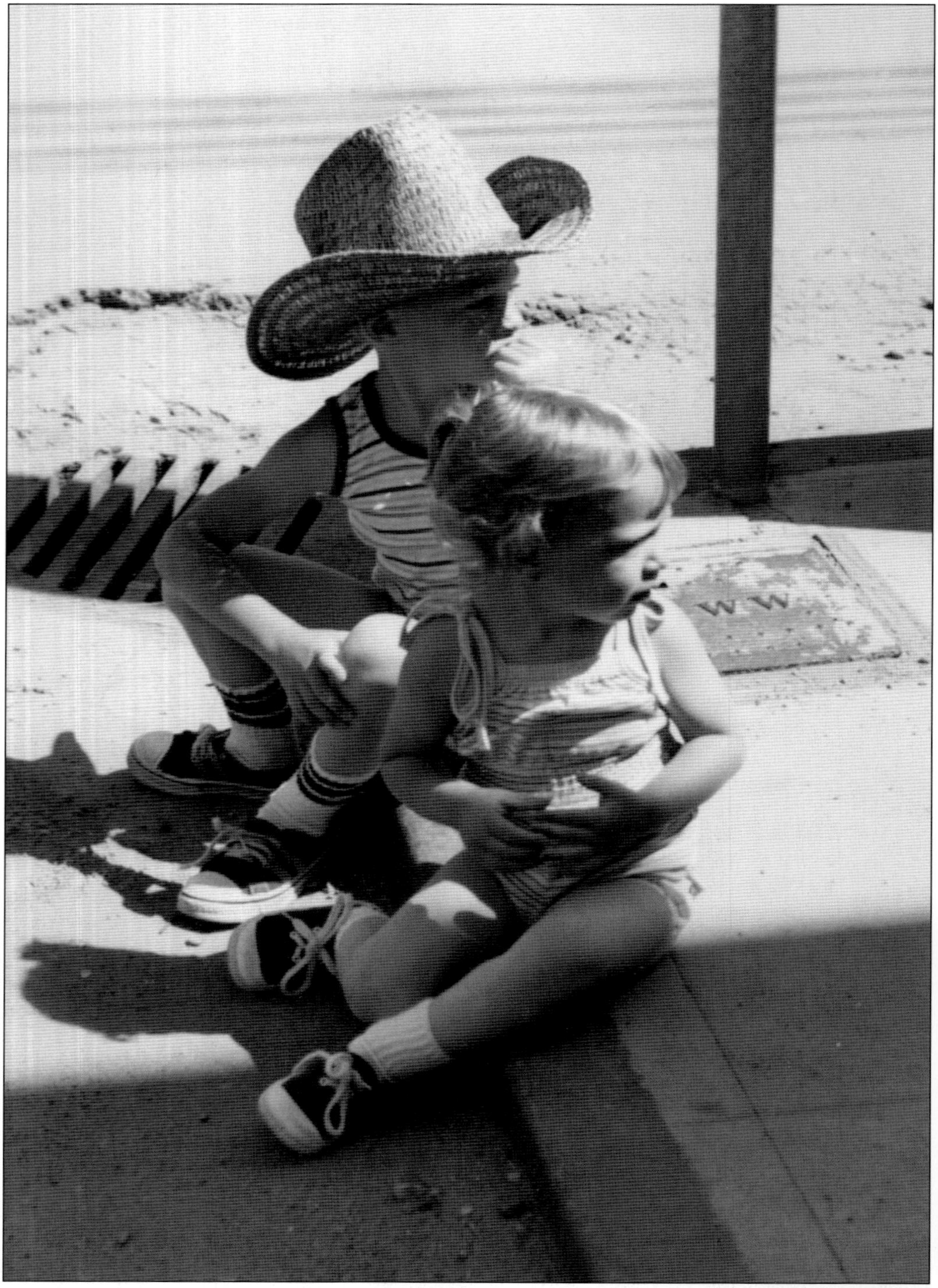

Two young children are ready for the parade to begin. Watch with them through the next six pages as the floats and marchers pass by.

Honoring Fallon's Hearts of Gold cantaloupe, a local beauty rides on a cardboard and crepe rendition of the famous melon. The float was entered in the Labor Day parade in 1967.

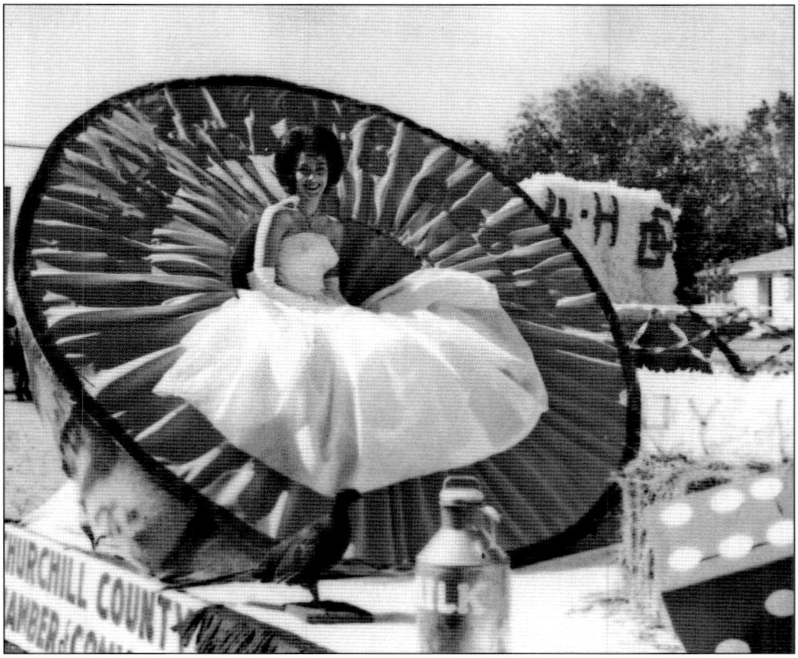

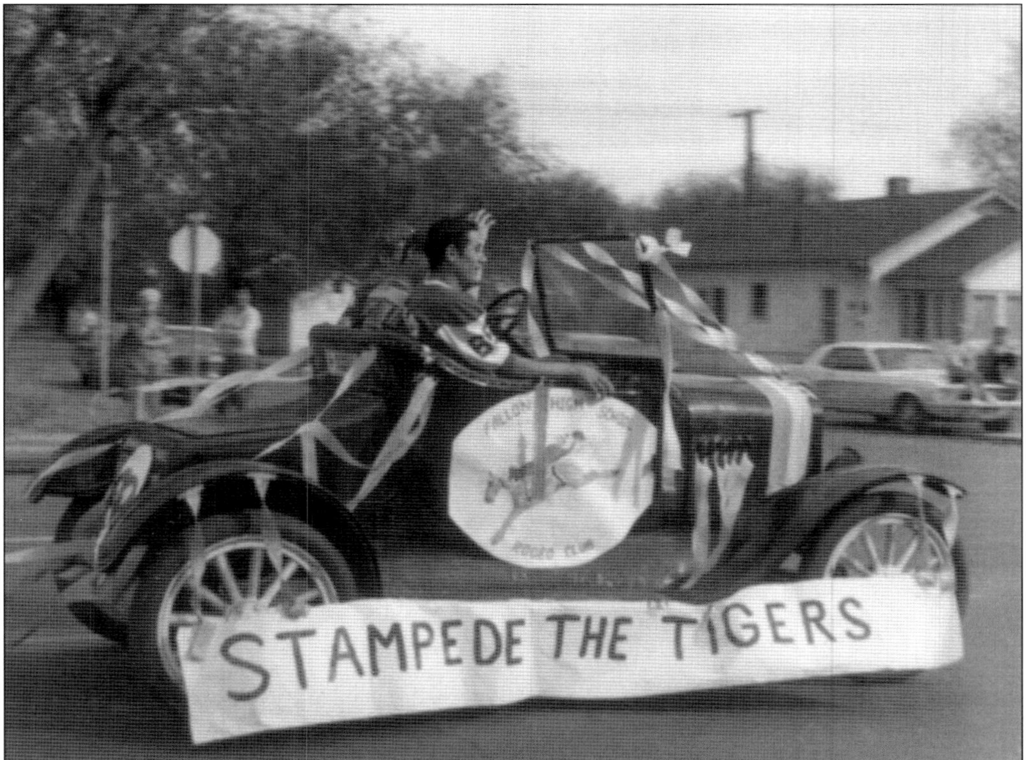

This decorated car was part of a high school homecoming parade, a tradition in Fallon. The sentiment is clear: the rival Tigers (Douglas County) are scheduled for a fall.

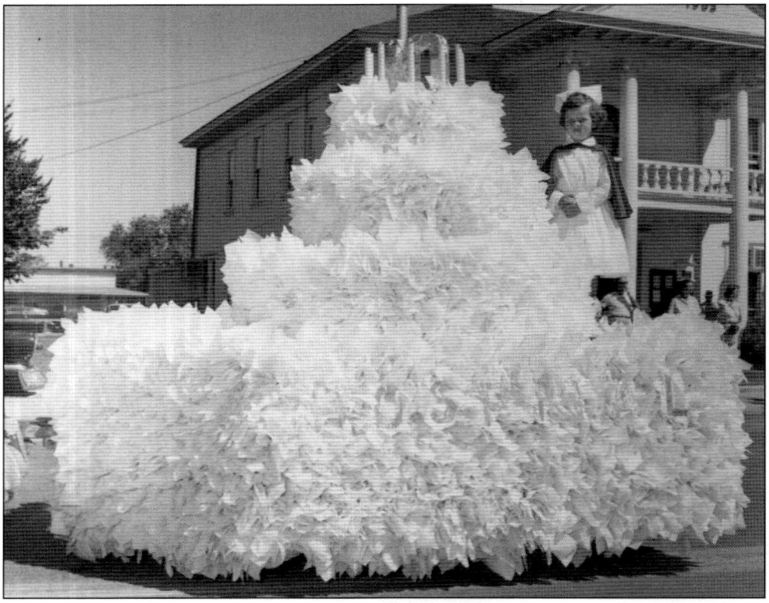

A four-layer crepe paper birthday cake is overseen by a future nurse on this float entered in a Labor Day parade. The Churchill County Hospital opened in 1949, and the cake holds six or seven birthday candles.

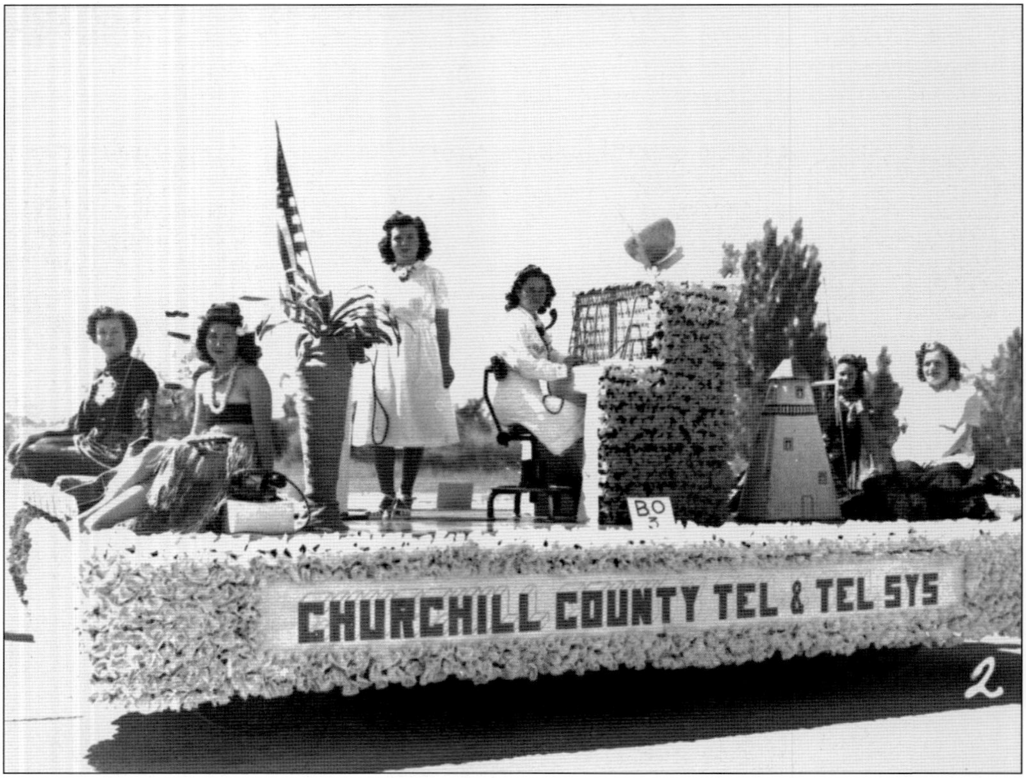

This float celebrates and commemorates Churchill Telephone and Telegraph, purported to be the only county-owned telephone company still functioning in the United States. In 1889, Churchill County took over telegraph lines built by Western Union, the first step in providing the valley over a century of telecommunications services.

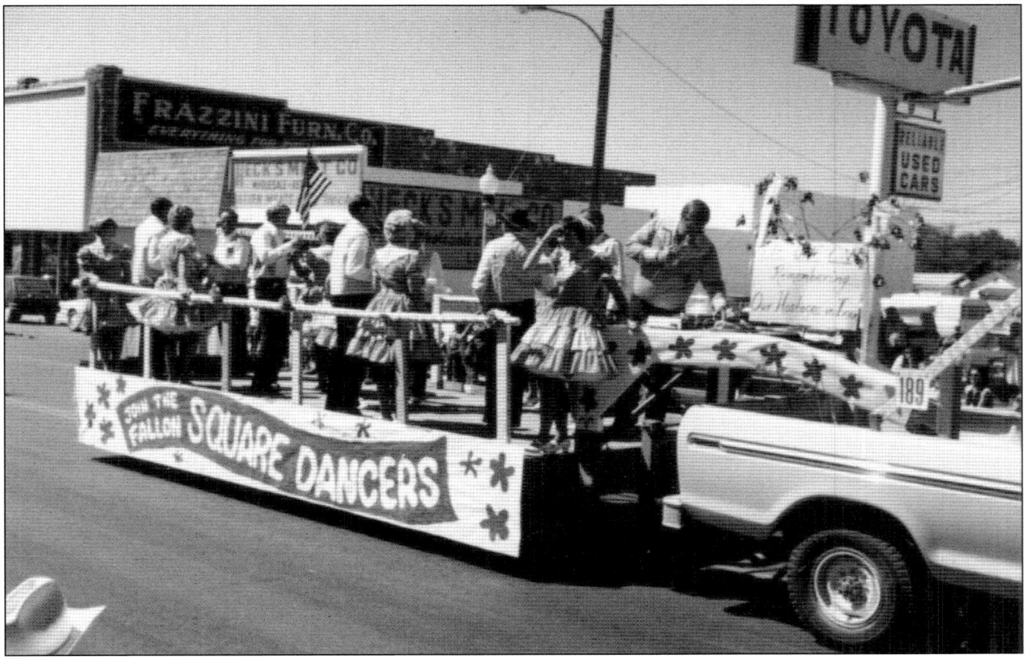

The area's rural traditions are kept alive by clubs like this square-dancing group. To entertain parade viewers and recruit membership, these dancers performed atop the float as it passed through the town.

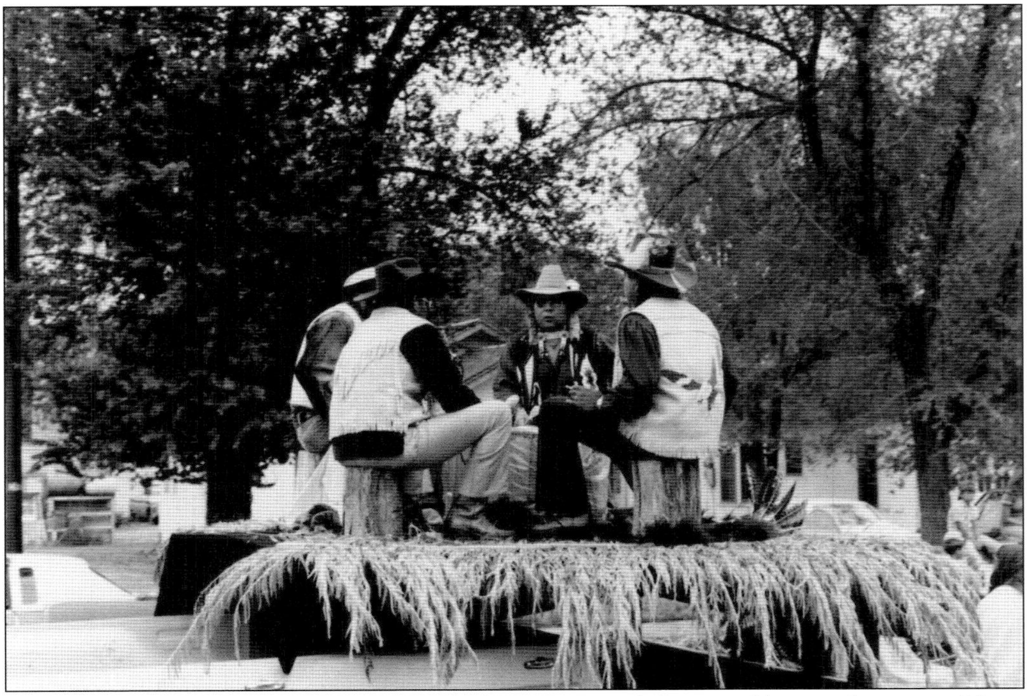

Members of the local Paiute Shoshone tribe have preserved their gambling traditions, and here they demonstrate the skills needed to understand and play the games.

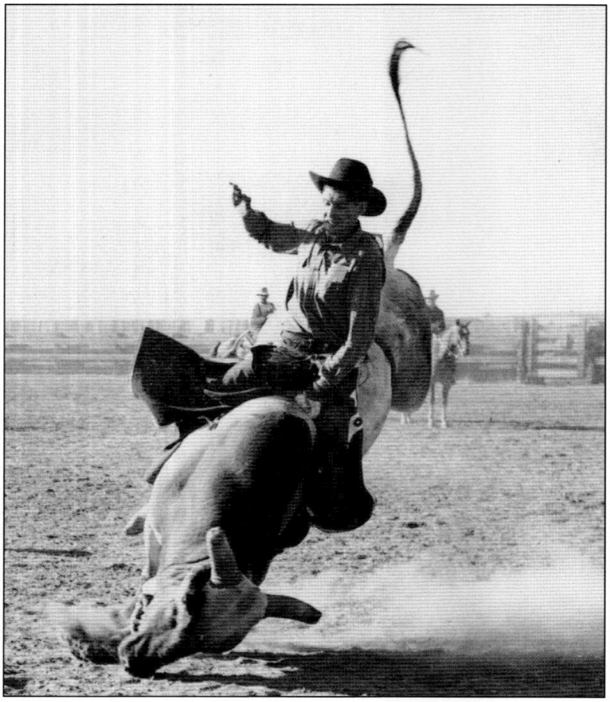

The Fallon Labor Day parade was until recently wrapped up with a rodeo, sponsored by the Fallon 20-30 Club or the local Lions Club. One of the most popular rodeo events has always been bull riding.

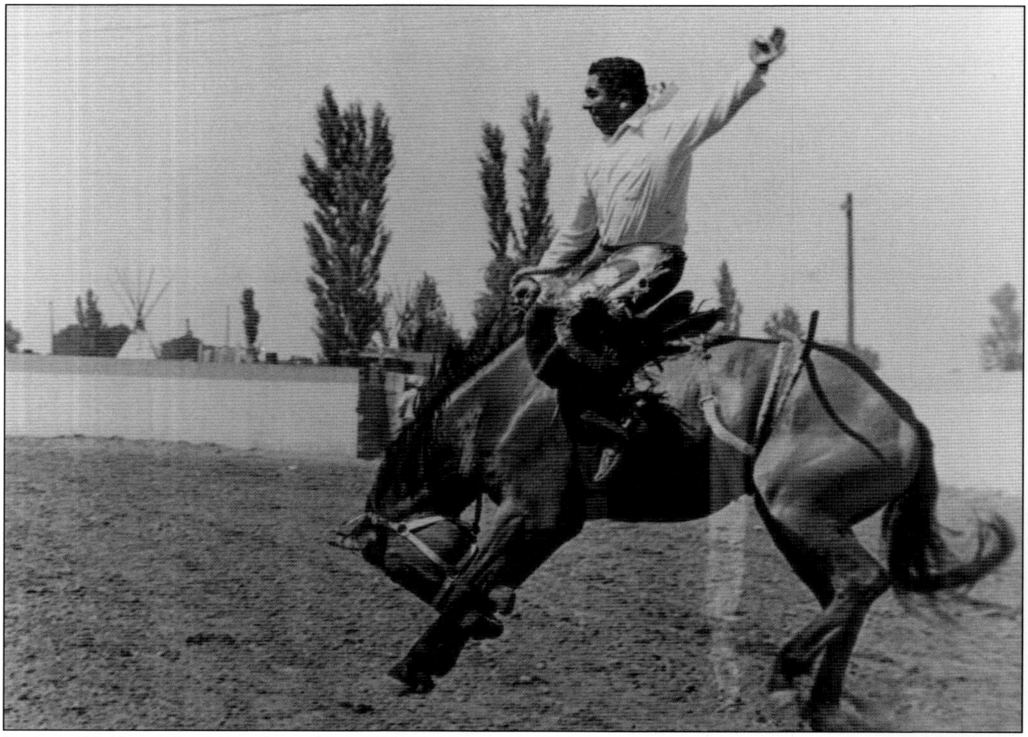

During Fallon's first few decades, saddle bronc riders performed on Maine Street for $5. Now, they are prized performers in Fallon's rodeos, including high school rodeos and senior rodeos.

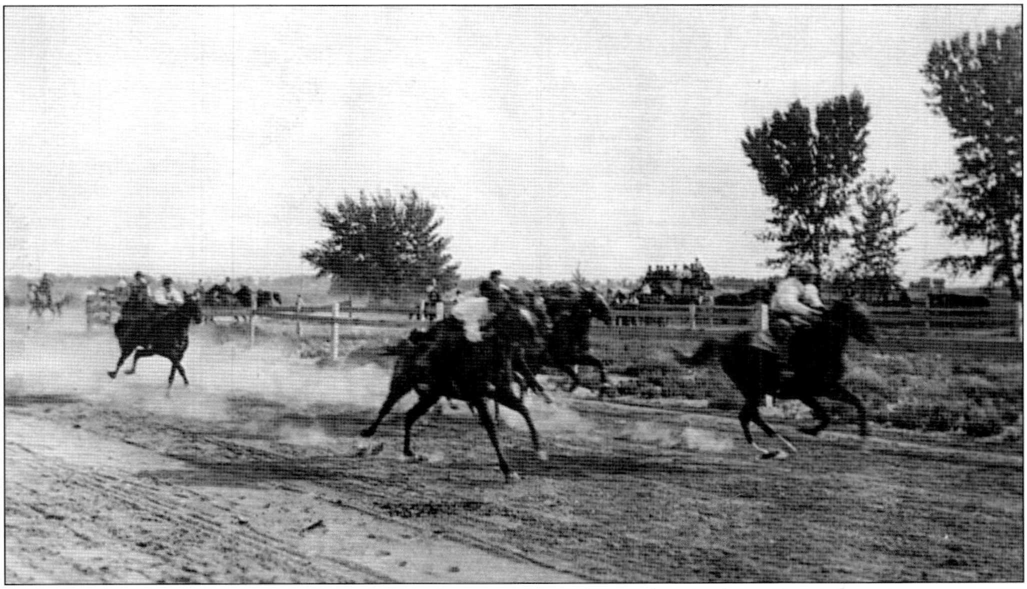

Horse racing is also traditional in the valley. This track was located on Gummow Drive.

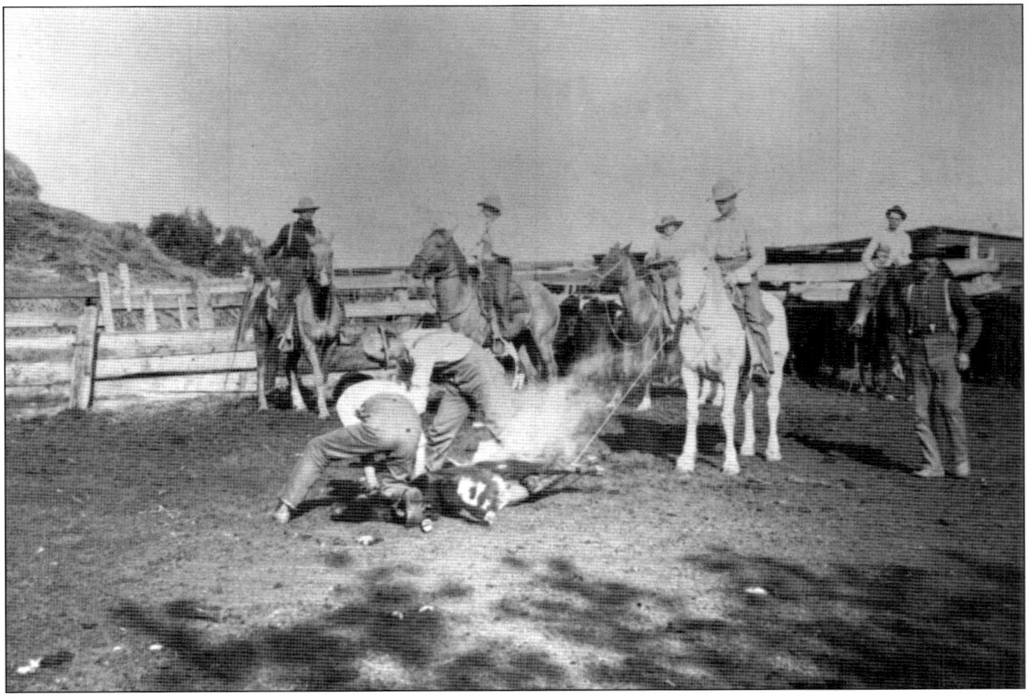

Almost all rodeo events originated on working ranches. Here, working cowboys rope and brand cattle. So-called "ranch rodeos," smaller and more practical than the ticketed events, are still common.

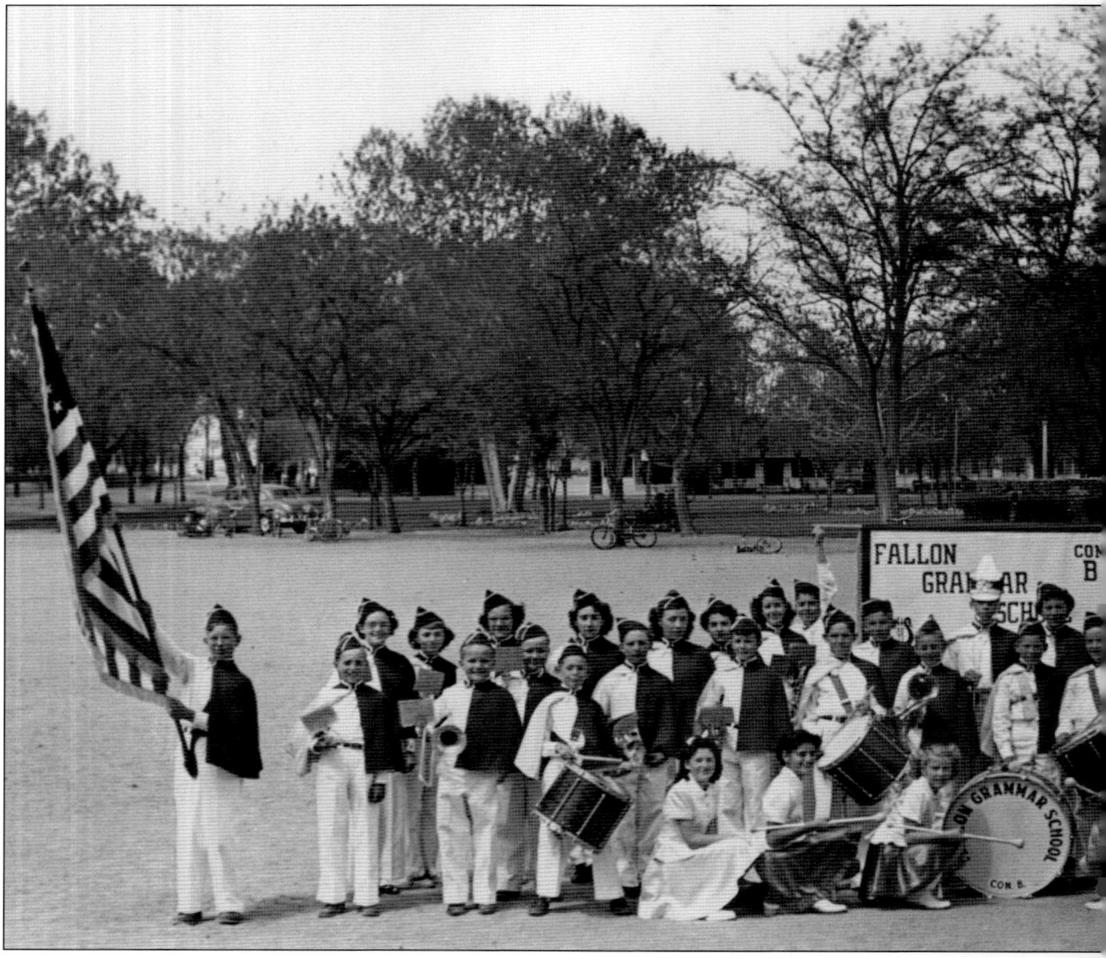

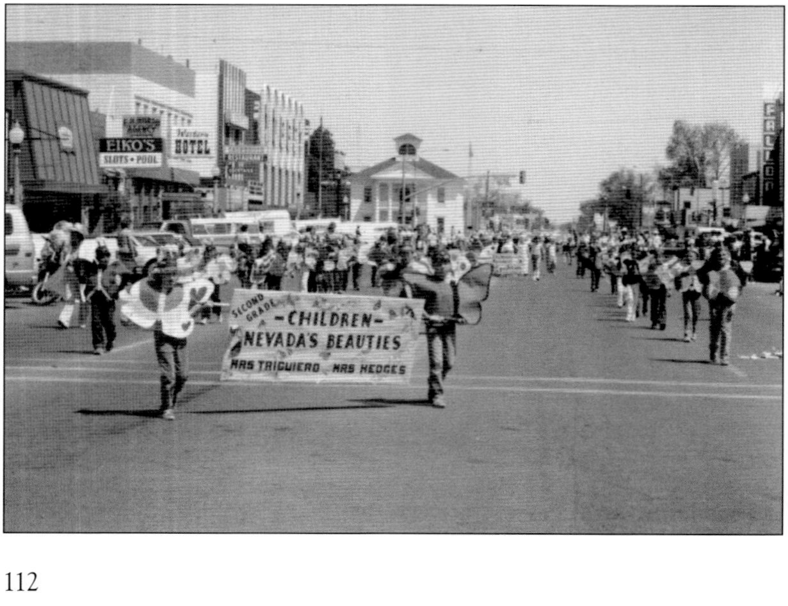

To prepare for the PTA parade, each elementary school class chose a theme, and students designed costumes and banners for the parade. The entire community turned out for the parade. The banner proclaims an entry titled "Children—Nevada's Beauties."

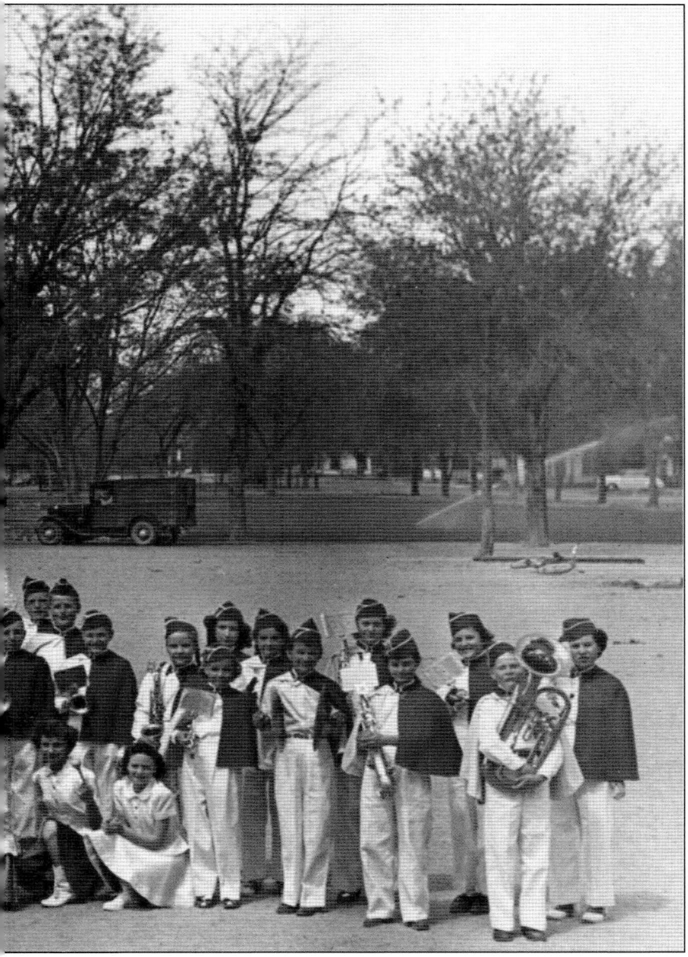

For about 30 years, from the mid-1950s until the mid-1980s, Fallon schools and the parent teachers association (PTA) put on a yearly parade and carnival to raise money. Here, members of the grammar school band line up in front of Oats Park School for the parade around 1956. What would a parade be without a band?

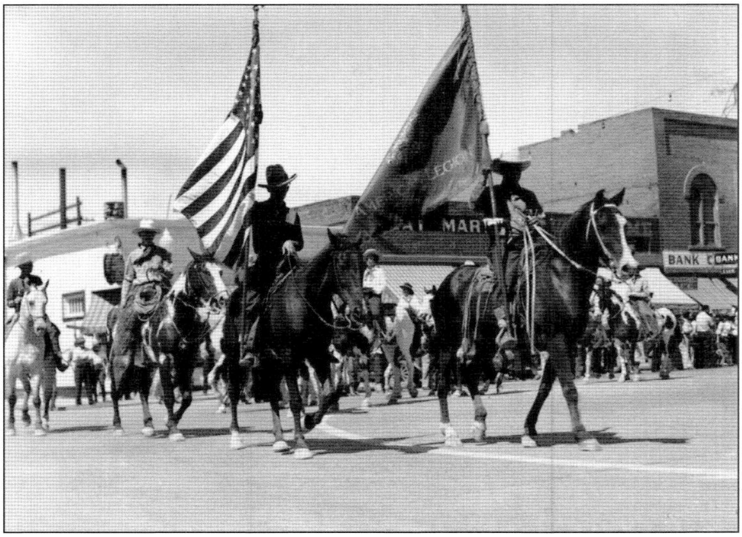

A good parade is led by good riders on good horses with flags flying.

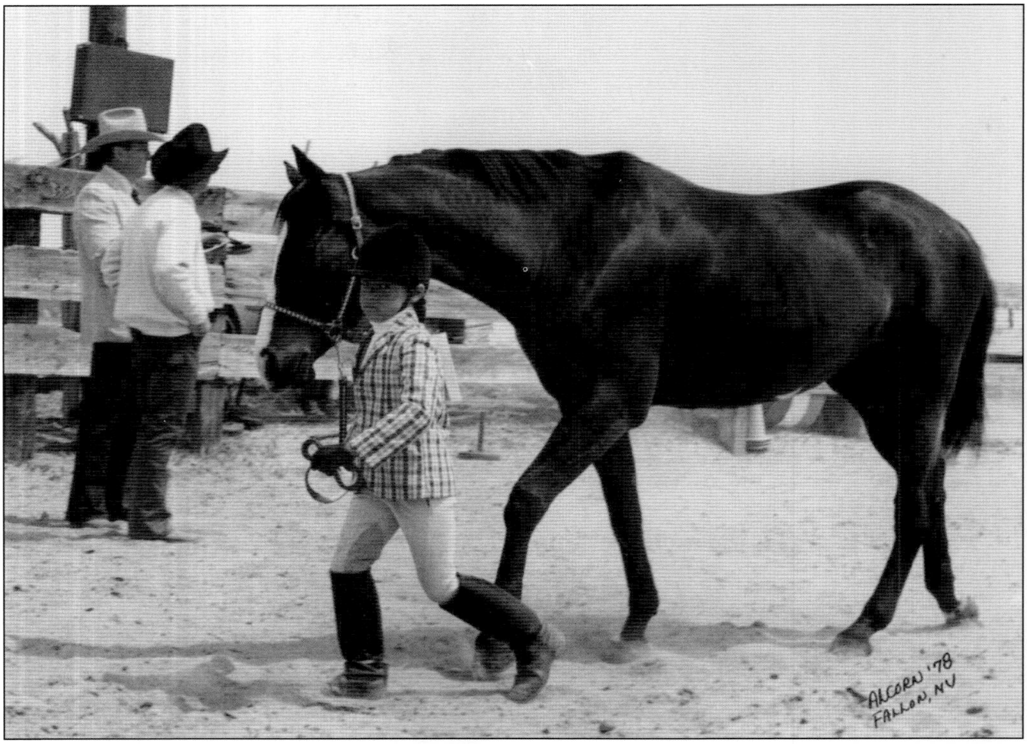

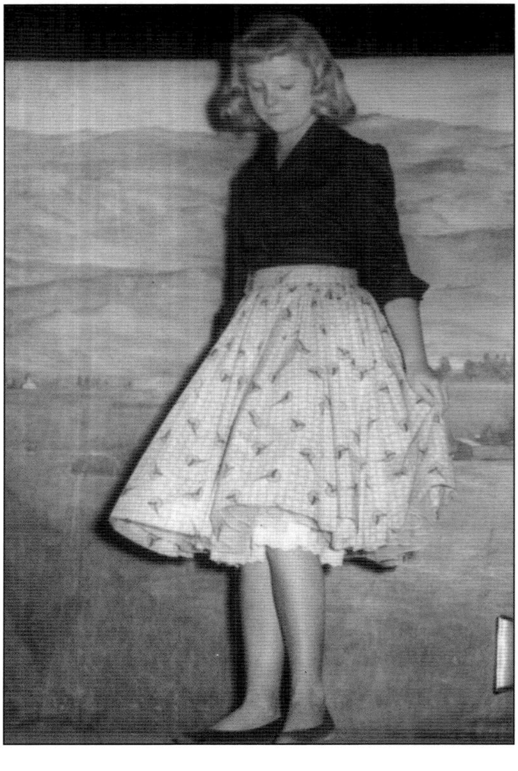

Although most local horsemen adopt the styles and traditions of the Wild West, this little girl seems taken with the English version.

Many 4-H clubs in the valley teach sewing skills. Finishing the garment construction process with a fashion show or dress review is part of the learning process.

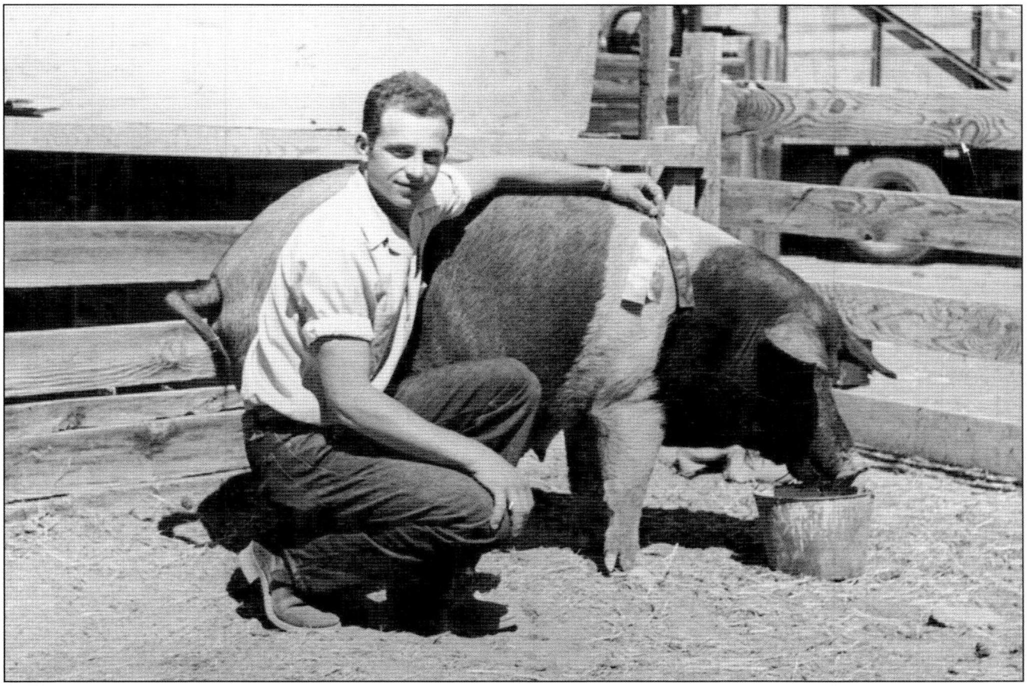

Virgil Getto shows his prize-winning 4-H pig. Getto was later elected to the local school board, then to the Nevada Assembly, and finally to the Nevada State Senate, always advocating agriculture.

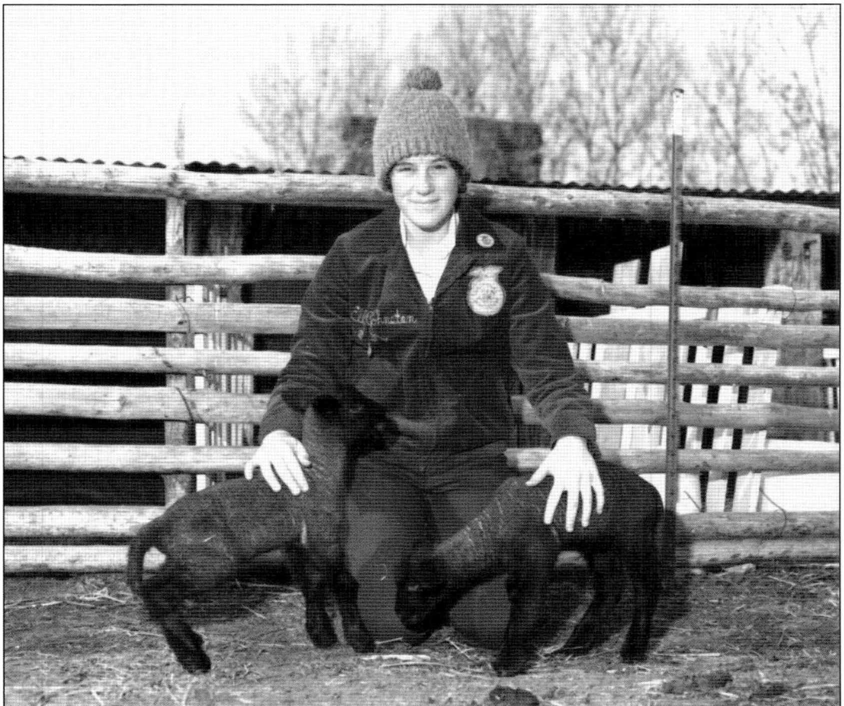

Ella Johnston shows her prize-winning lambs in the county fair around 1980.

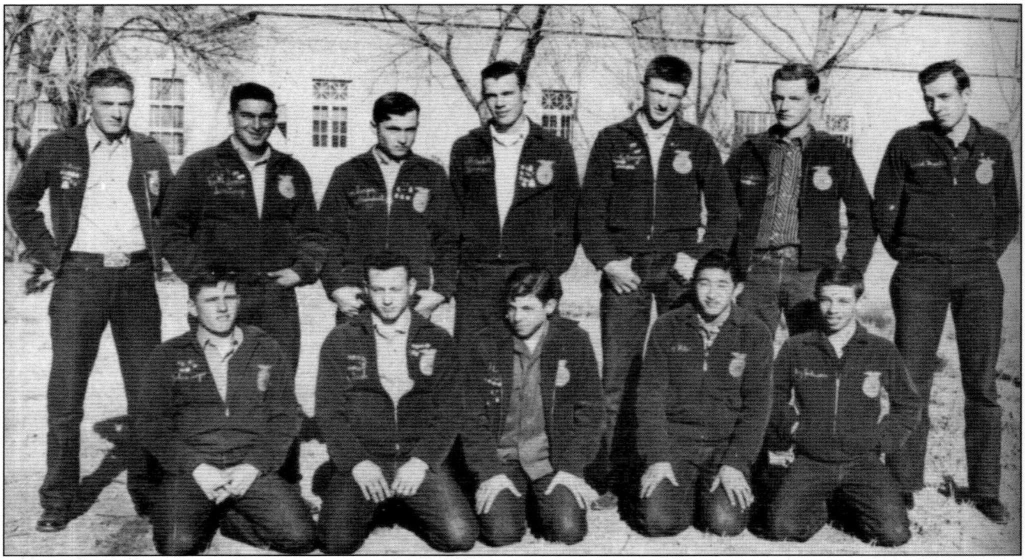

Churchill County High School has sponsored a chapter of the Future Farmers of America since the 1920s. Members wear their distinctive jackets with pride.

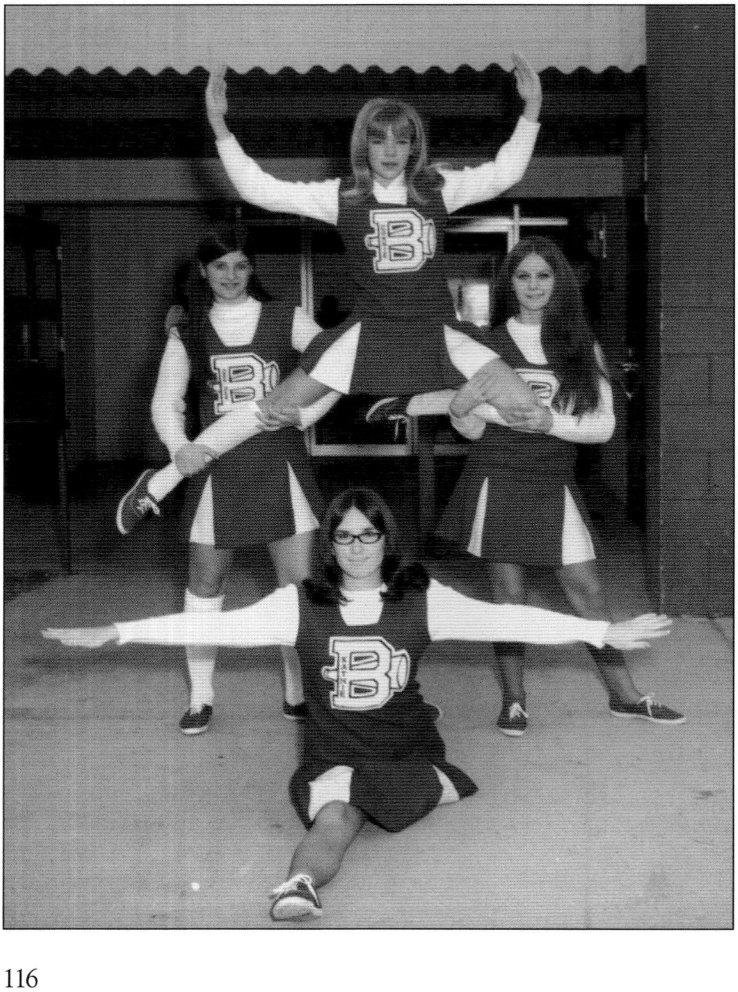

The Churchill County High School cheerleading squad is ready to root for the teams around 1971.

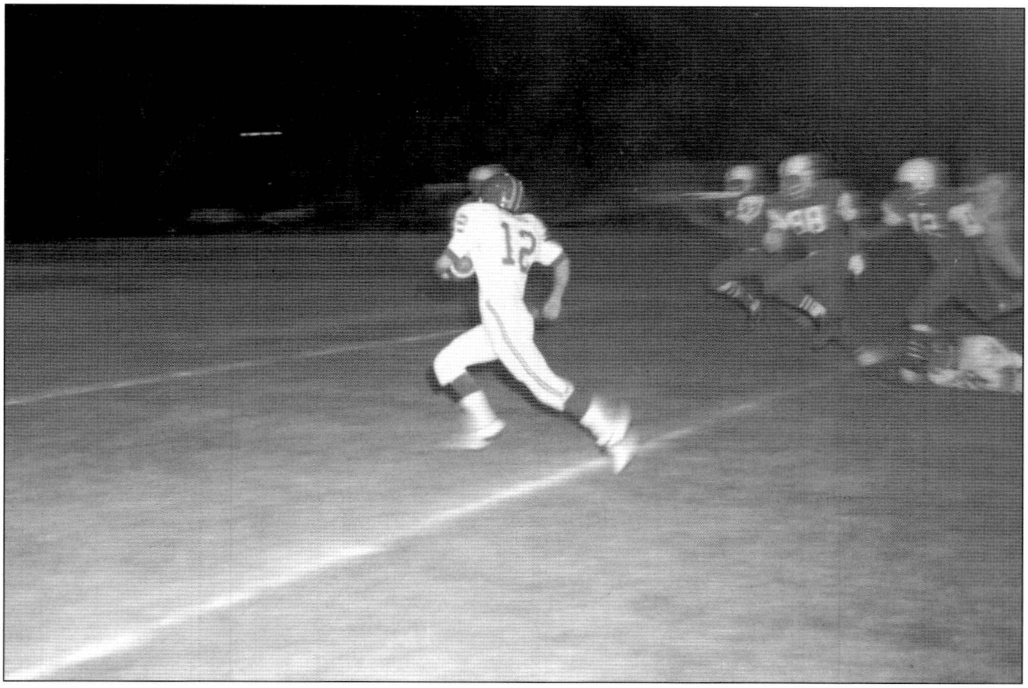

A Fallon Greenwave football player is caught by the camera in a moment of kinetic grace. Moves like this one have won the Fallon team many victories.

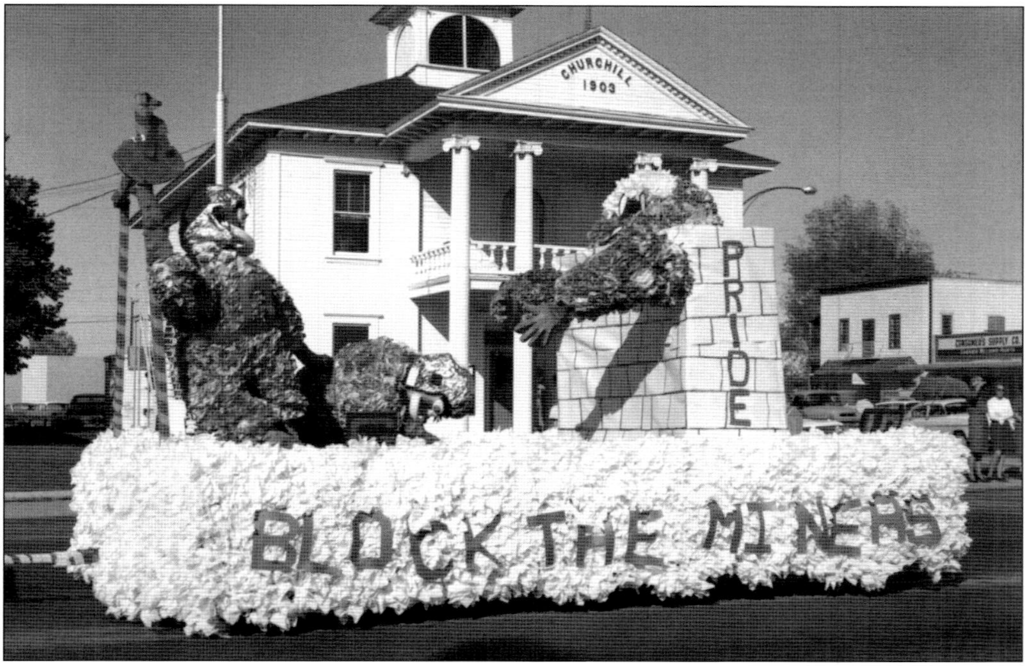

Fallon's school spirit runs high, especially at homecoming, when floats clearly exhibit tension and hope. The slogan "Block the Miners" targets Manogue High School in Reno. The courthouse forms a stately backdrop for the float.

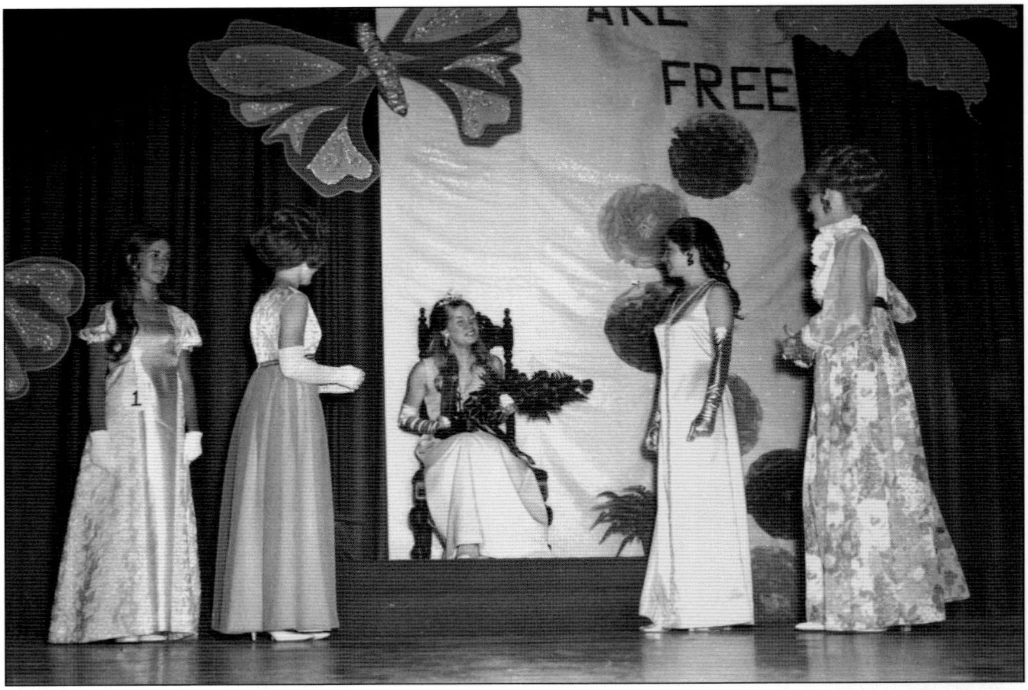

Miss Fallon is crowned on the Churchill County High School stage decorated with the motto, "Butterflies are Free," around 1975.

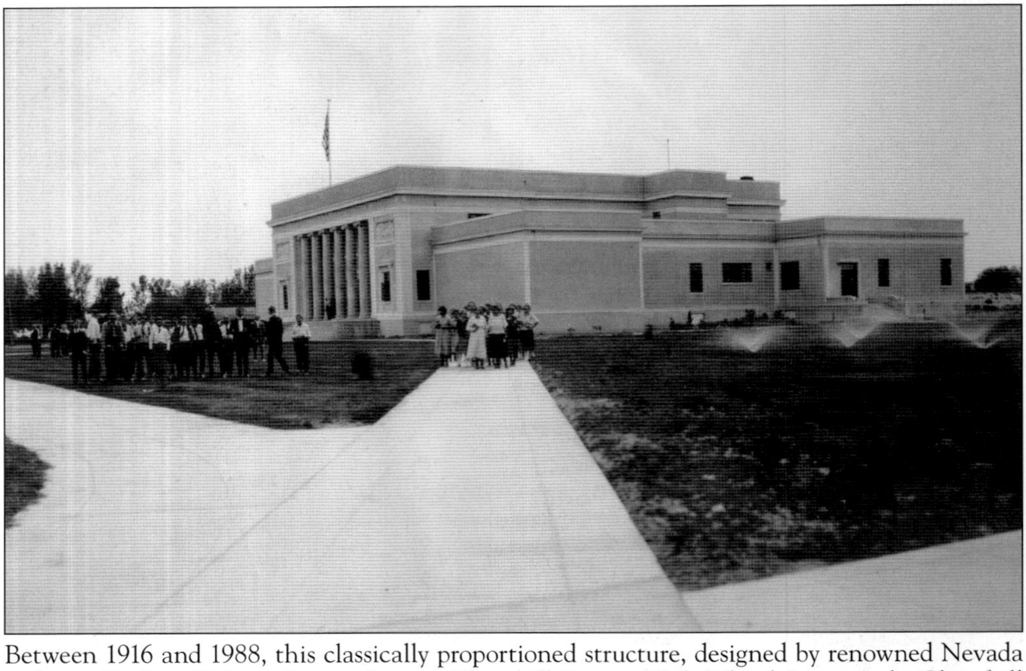

Between 1916 and 1988, this classically proportioned structure, designed by renowned Nevada architect Frederic DeLongchamps, housed Churchill County High School. It is now the Churchill County School District Administration complex. An addition was added to the north (right) of this historical photograph to house Churchill County Junior High School.

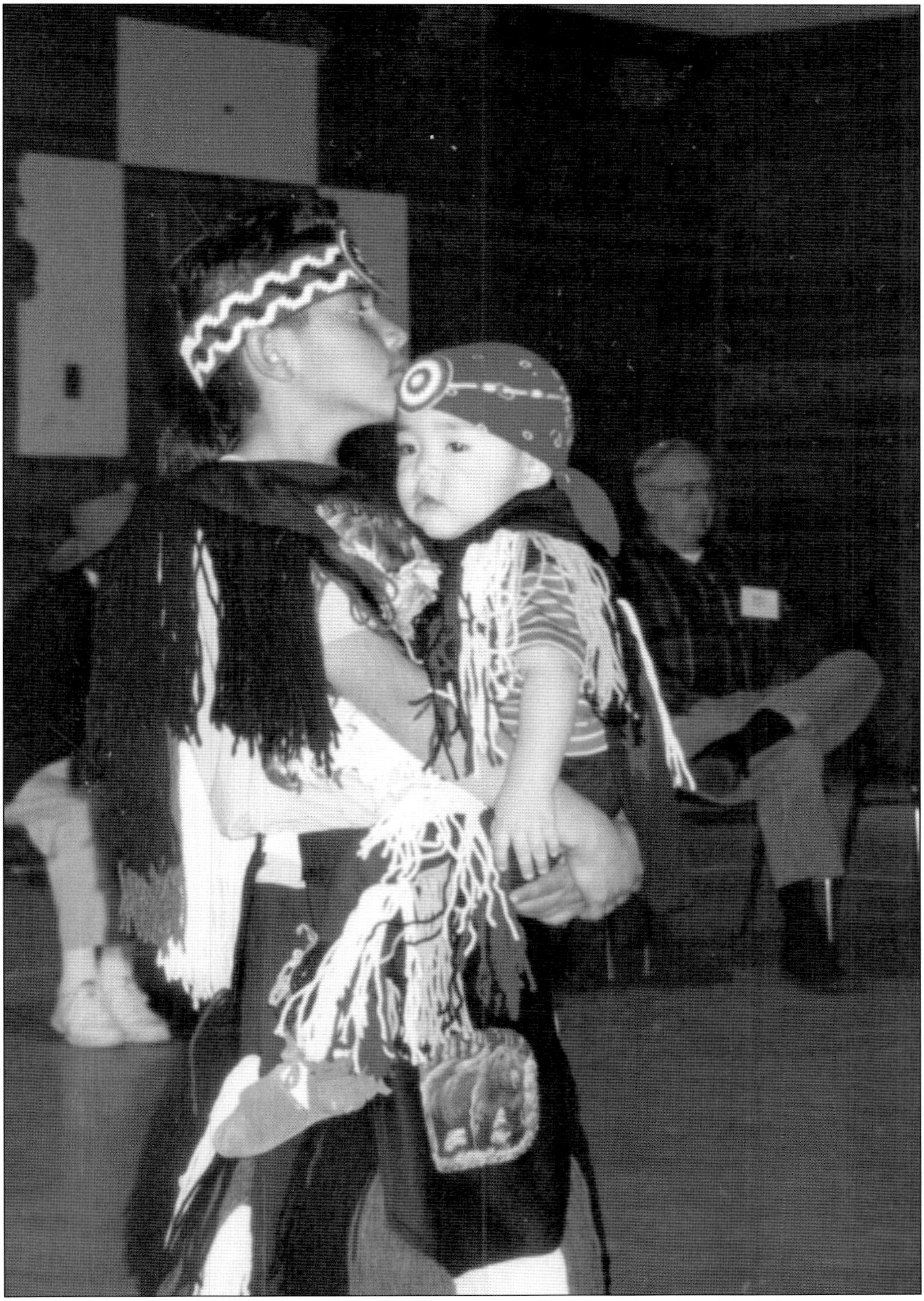
The Native American Spirit Sage dancers gather to perform in intricately beaded and feathered traditional costumes.

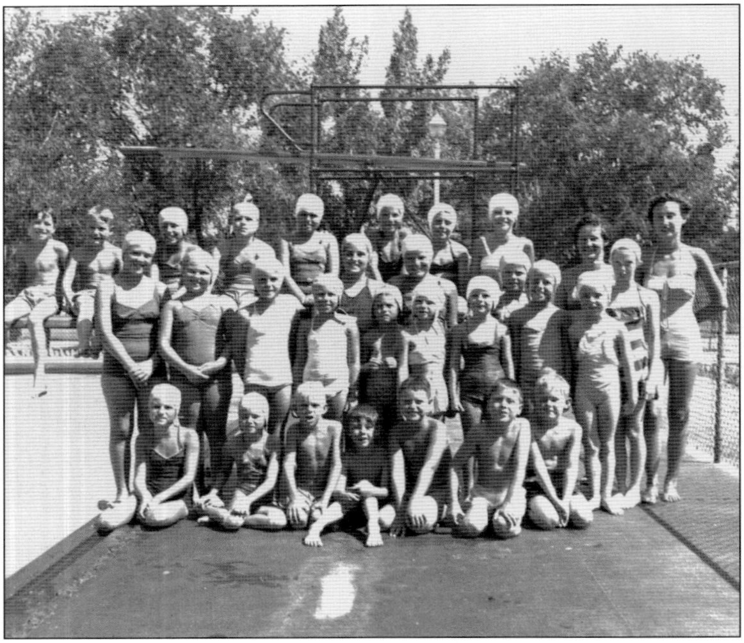

Shown here are members of one of the many swimming clubs formed at Oats Park swimming pool. The Works Progress Administration (WPA) granted monies to build the pool, which opened in 1939 and still operates. Fallon's 20-30 Club also played a major fundraising role, helping to install a modern chlorine treatment system, brightly painted stucco dressing rooms, and a colorful mural.

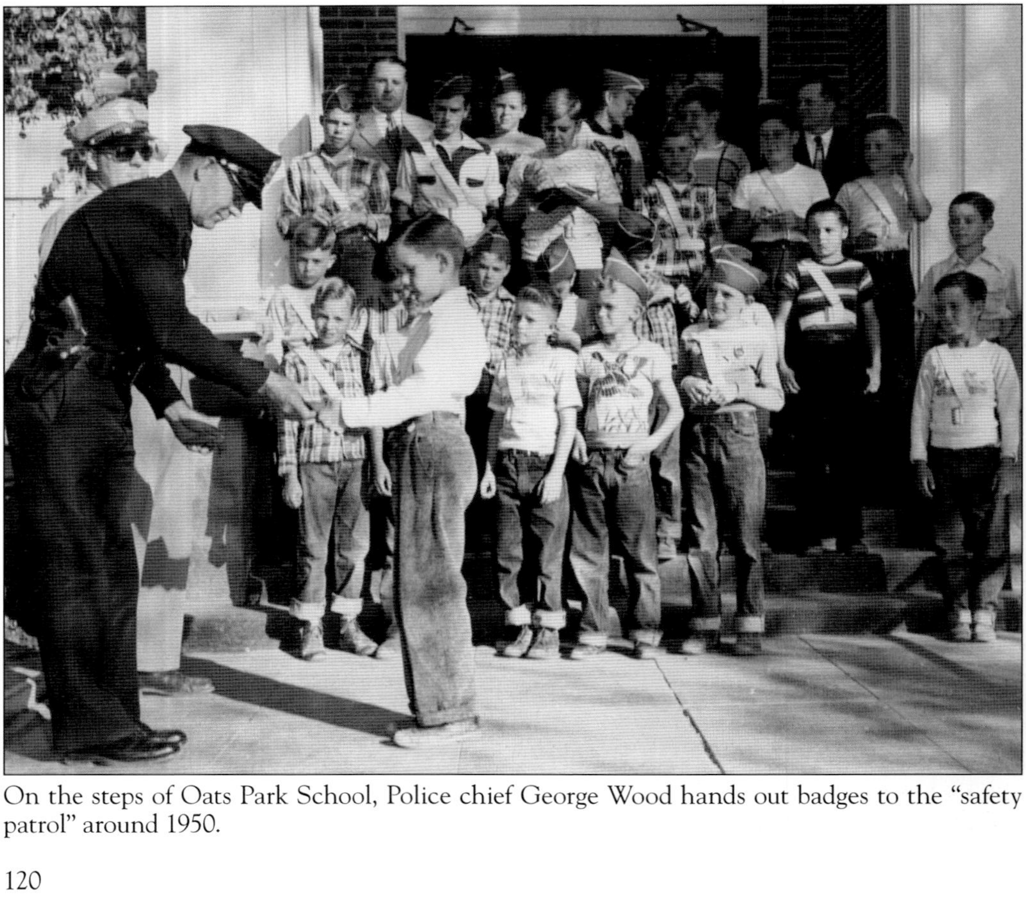

On the steps of Oats Park School, Police chief George Wood hands out badges to the "safety patrol" around 1950.

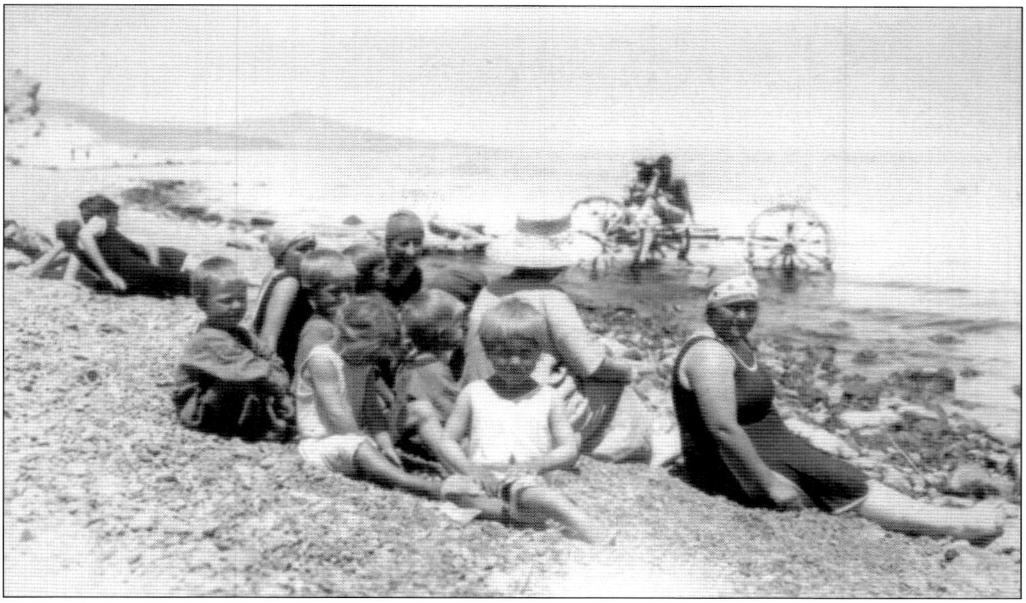

Since the completion of Lahontan Dam in 1915, the expansive beaches of Lahontan Reservoir have provided recreation and relaxation for countless folks.

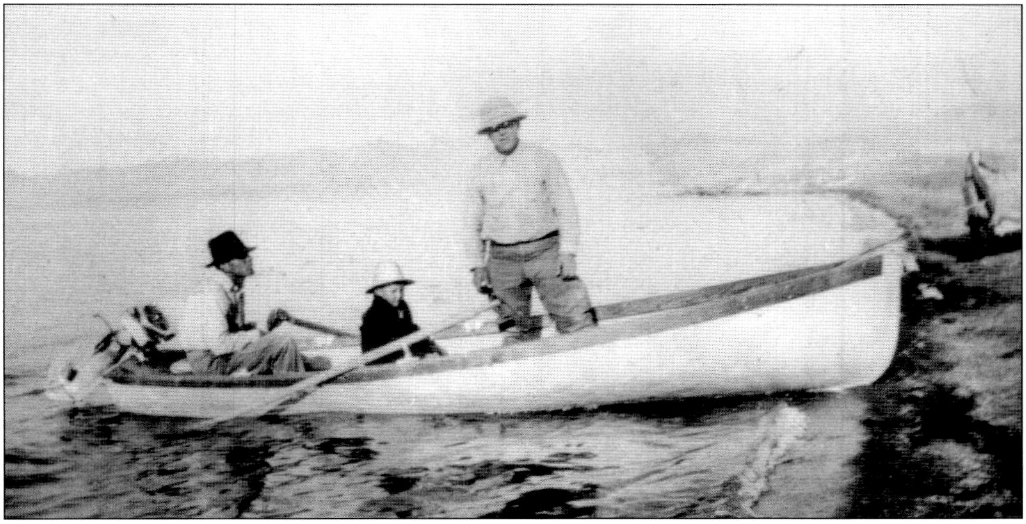

Like the beaches, the waters of the reservoir have always attracted recreation seekers, from fisherman and boaters to water-skiers, tubers, boarders, jet-skiers, and just plain swimmers.

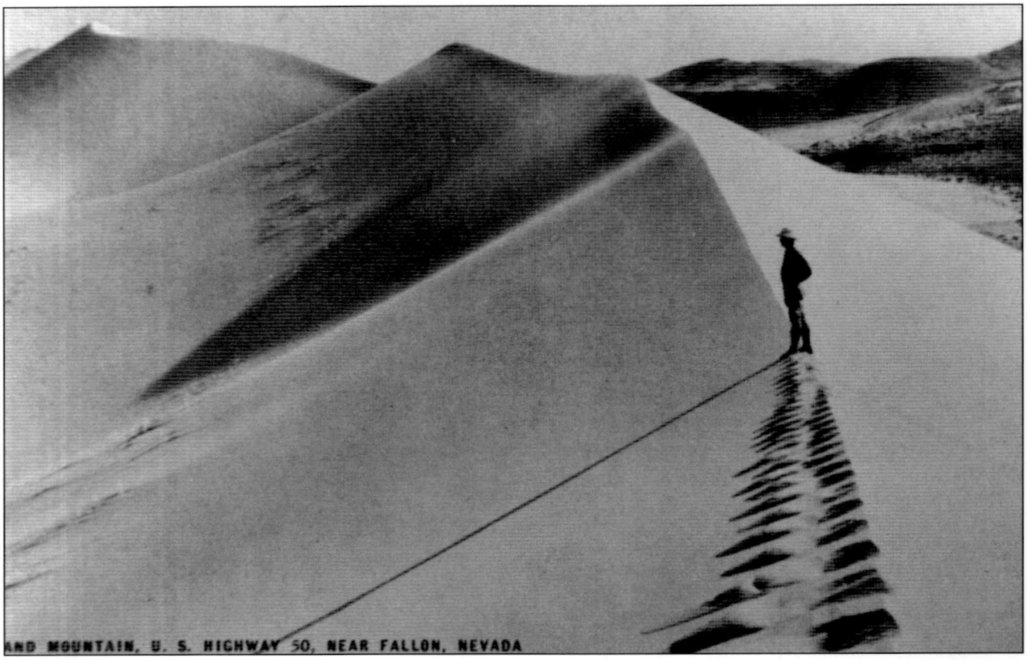

Sand Mountain is located about 25 miles east of Fallon alongside Highway 50. The mountain rises 500 to 600 feet out of a valley floor and measures about three miles in length, although its size, shape, and even its location shifts almost daily as the white sands are moved by prevailing southwest winds. The mountain is said to sing, and myths say that the Native Americans, feeling it was almost alive, gave it a wide berth. A 19th-century traveler reported that it sounded more like a Wagnerian opera than a lullaby. In any case, children and, more recently, dune-buggy enthusiasts love to climb it.

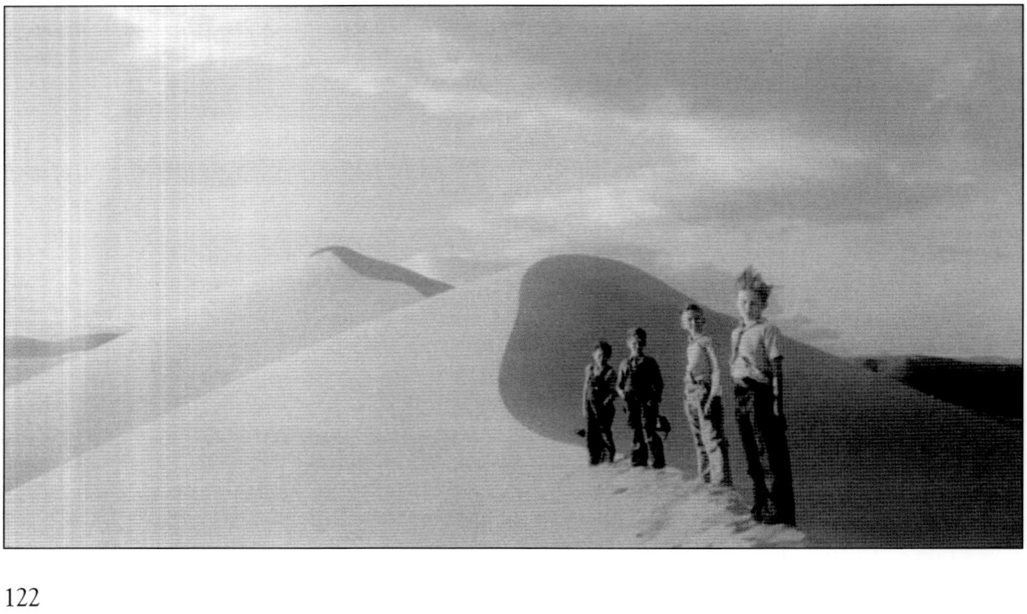

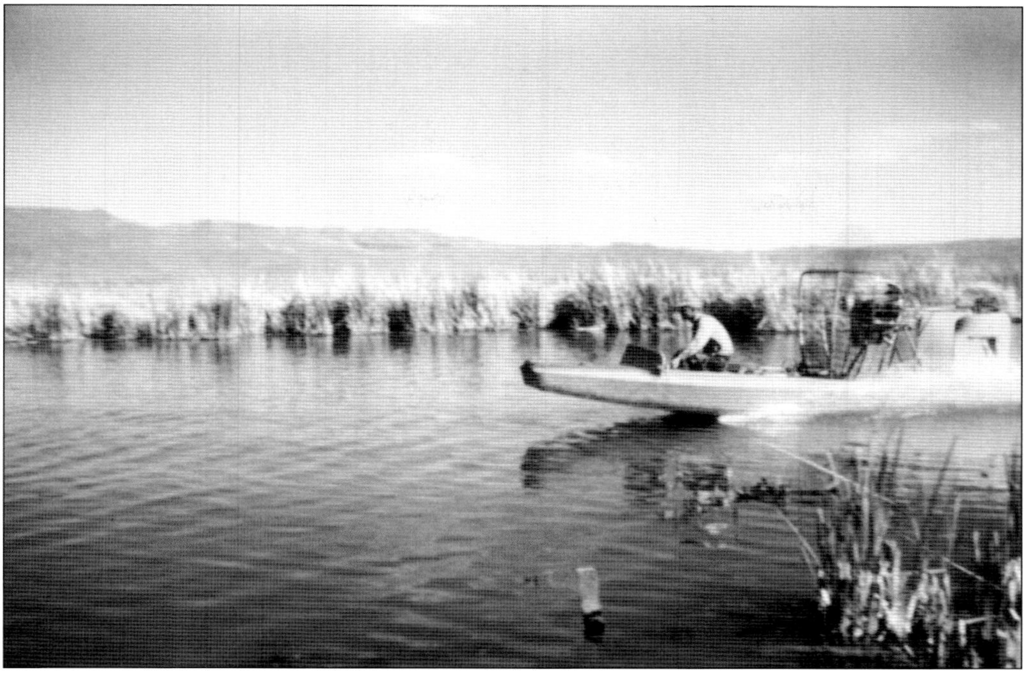

The Stillwater Wildlife Refuge and the Carson Lake Pasture, both in Churchill County, are known to provide some of the best migratory game-bird hunting in the state. Bird watchers also make pilgrimages to the sites. Here, an airboat easily navigates the shallow waters.

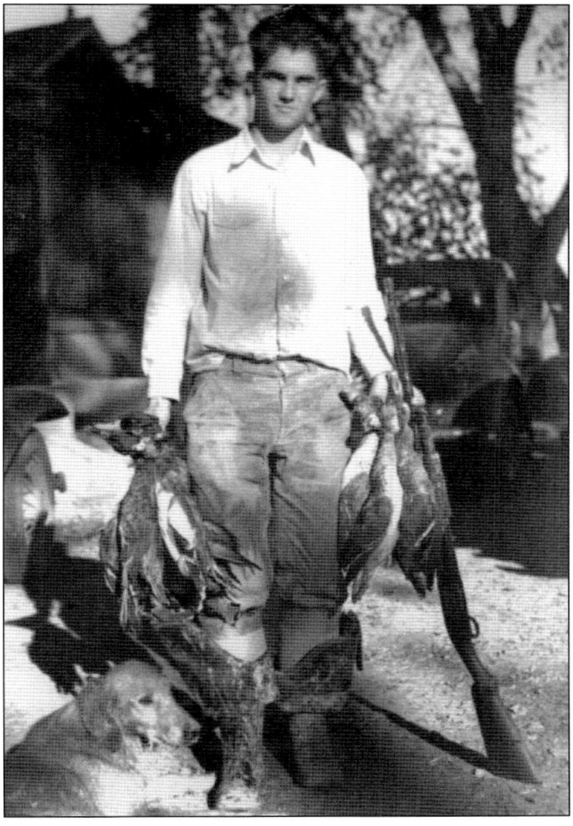

In this c. 1935 image, Fallon hunter Jim Gibbs shows off his limit of ducks, shotgun, and dog by his side.

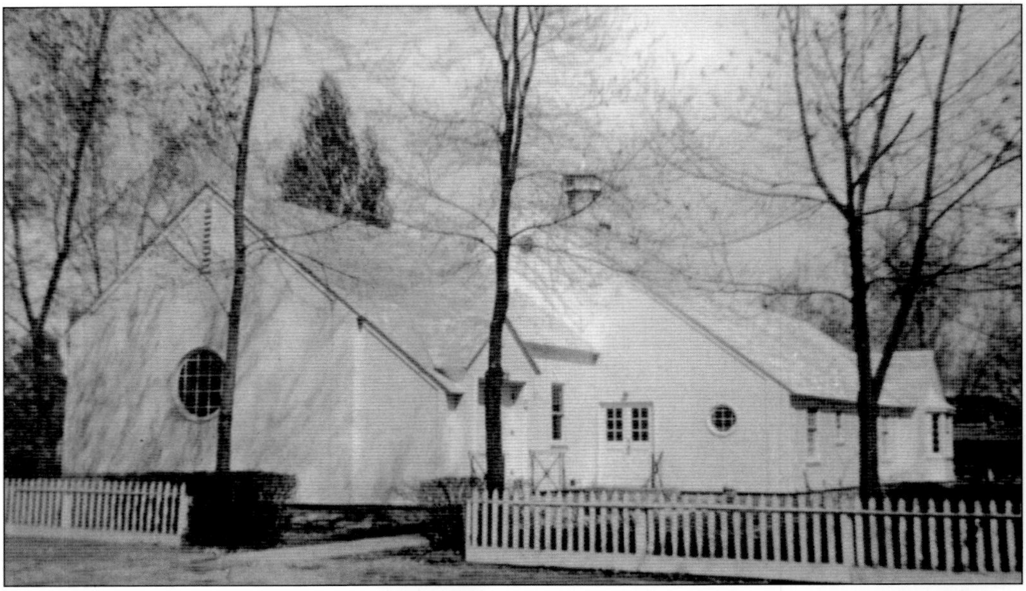

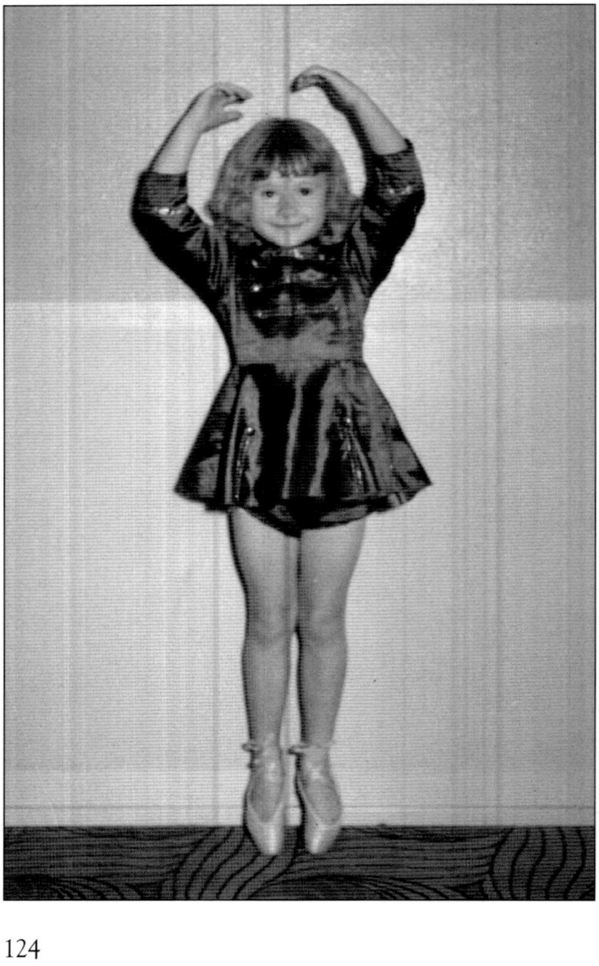

This structure served as the church for Fallon's LDS members until the 1970s, when new structures were built to meet the needs of a growing membership. For many years thereafter, it was a dance studio.

This little toe dancer symbolizes the popularity of dance and dance productions in the community. She might have practiced in the dance studio shown above.

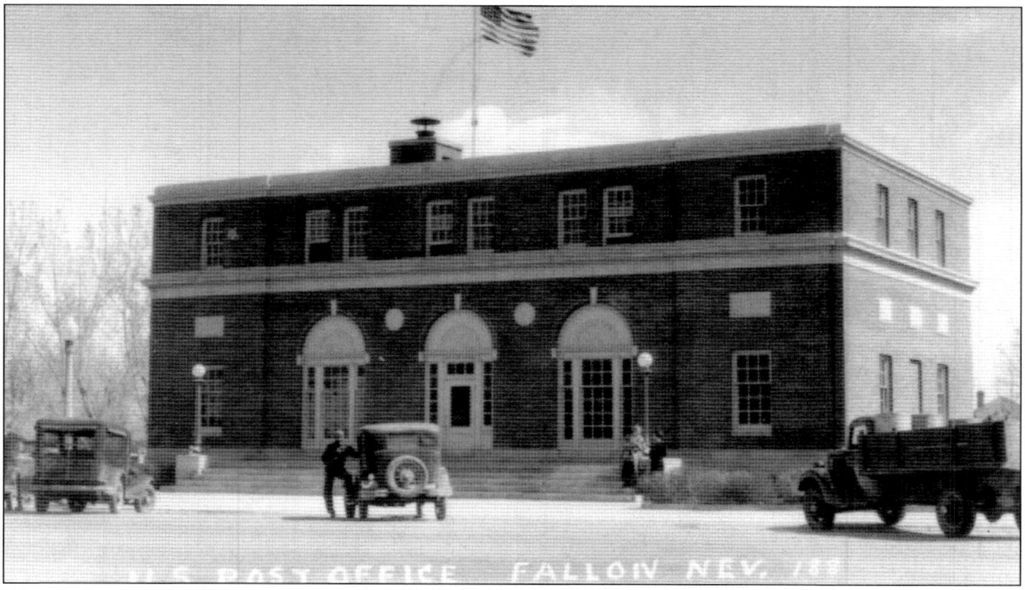

The Fallon Post Office opened on March 9, 1929, and served as a post office until 1978. Now, the City of Fallon hosts meetings and events in the spacious interior.

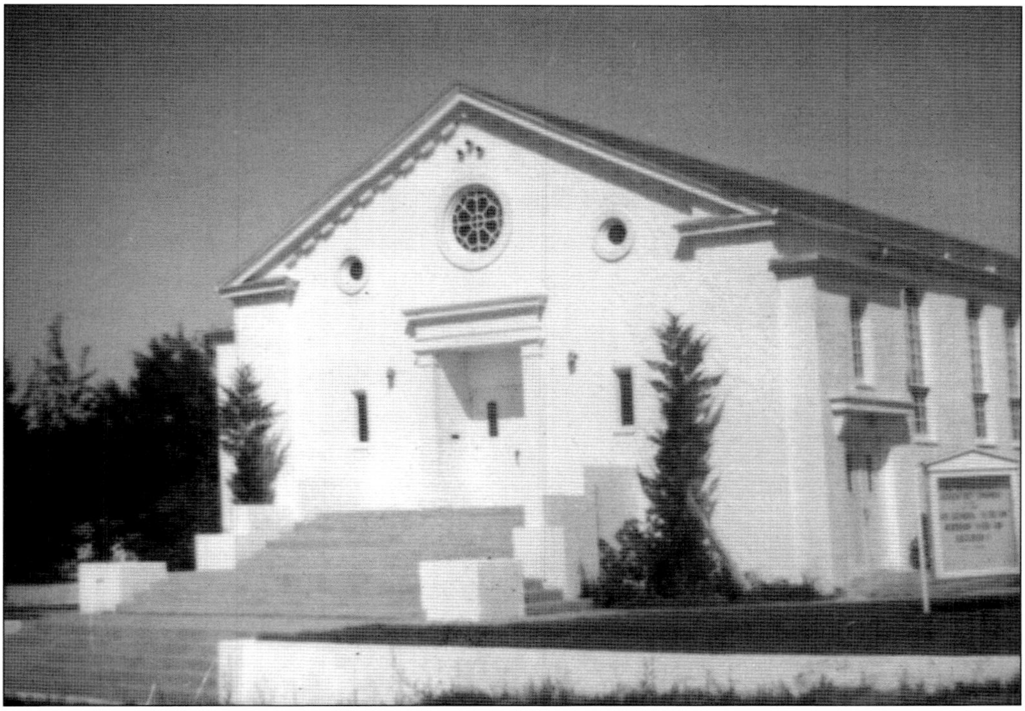
Jackson Ferguson was one of Stillwater's earliest settlers, establishing a community of Seventh-day Adventists. Today, members of the Seventh-day Adventist church worship in this stately structure located at 755 Esmeralda Street in Fallon.

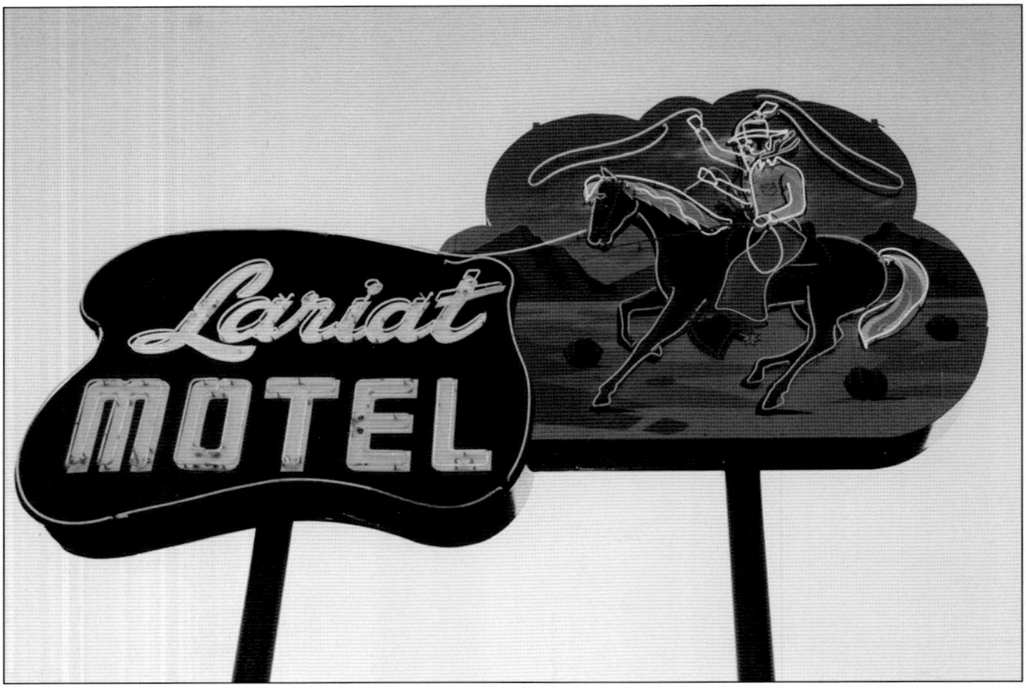

For decades, the neon sign above advertised the Lariat Motel on West Williams Avenue. When the motel was torn down, the sign was acquired and refurbished by the Churchill Arts Council. The restored sign was ceremoniously lit at the Oats Park Arts Center on October 31, 2013, launching Fallon's yearlong Nevada sesquicentennial celebration. Below, the Barkley Theater at the Oats Park Arts Center seats 350 people.

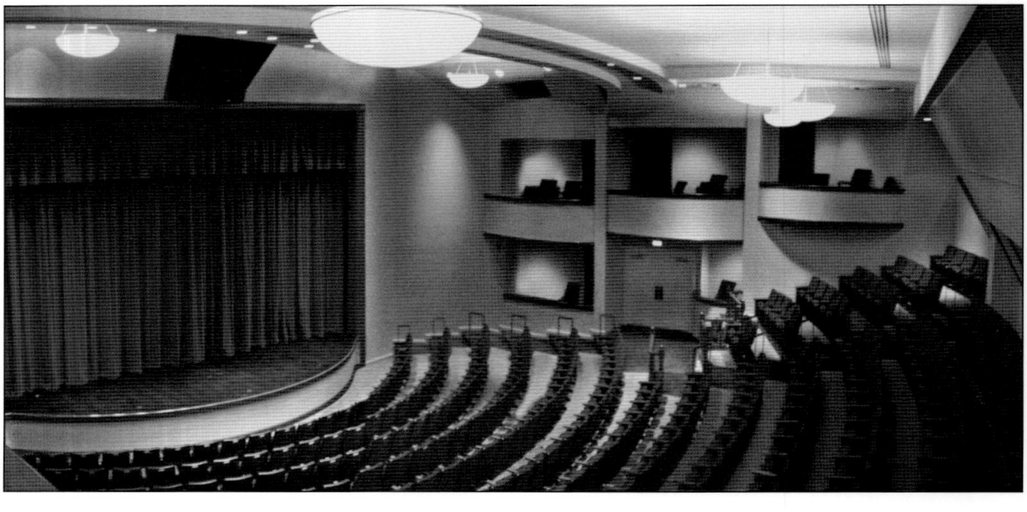

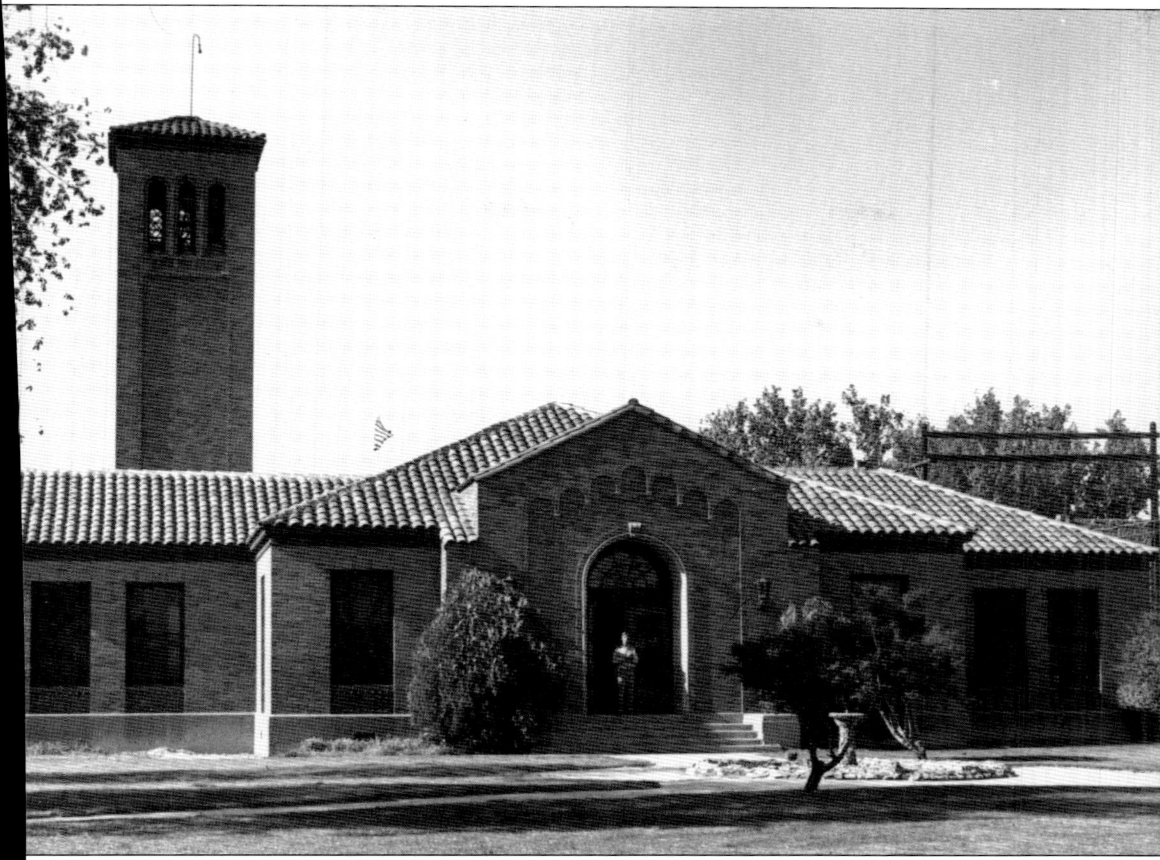

Fallon City Hall was built in 1931. The tower was damaged in the major 1954 earthquake and consequently repaired, albeit shortened in height. A fire whistle is mounted on top of the building, sounding not only the fire alarm but also the "noon whistle," a tradition harkening back to 1948.

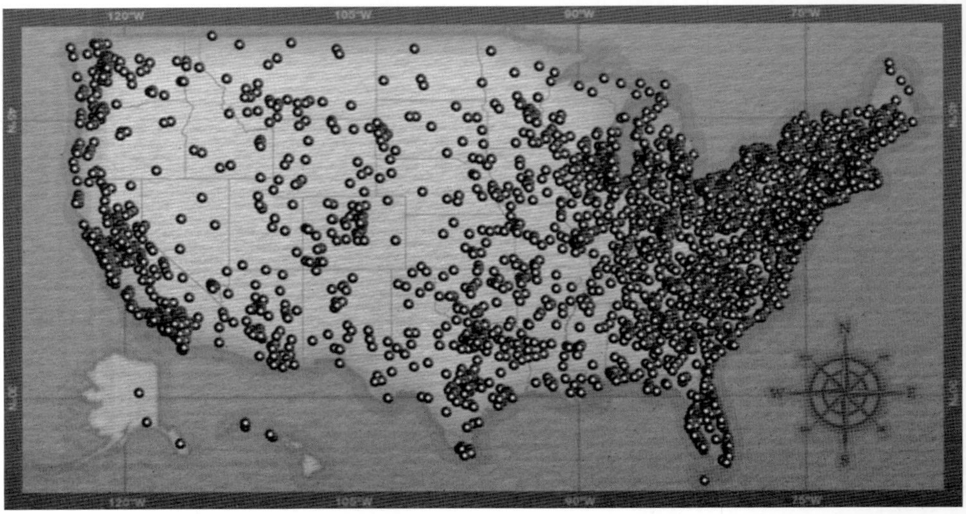